SO-BHG-716

THE INDEFINITE BOUNDARY

THE INDEFINITE BOUNDARY

An Investigation into the Relationship
between Matter and Spirit

GUY LYON PLAYFAIR

with an Appendix by Hernani Guimarāes Andrade

ST. MARTIN'S PRESS   NEW YORK

Library of Congress Cataloging in Publication Data

Playfair, Guy Lyon.
    The indefinite boundary.

    Includes bibliographical references and index.
    1. Psychical research. 2. Occult sciences. 3. Spirit writings.
    I. Title.
BF1031.P6   133.8   76.28051
ISBN 0-312-41195-2

Some reflections on medical research

Sing a song of particles
Infinitely small,
Tissue cultured specimens
From off your stomach wall.

Six and forty chromosomes
Dividing into two,
Hordes of hungry phagocytes
Like tigers in the zoo.

Endocrine secretion
From a ductless gland,
Amino nucleic acid chains
Dancing hand in hand.

Take mesons from a synchrotron
To fix the hellish brew,
For proton and electron,
That's me,—and you.

But tell me, dear Professor,
Explain it if you can
If microscopic entities
Are all that's left of man,

Yes, tell me, dear Professor,
Explain it if you please,
Why men, thro' countless ages
Have believed they're more than
these.

If our love is but a hormone,
And our sight an optic lens,
And beauty but an enzyme,
Why is homo sapiens?

If our mind is just a magnet,
And our will a chemist's shop
And if death of our life sentence
But just the last full stop,

Why then, my friend, is
consciousness
A thing you cannot hope
To see upon the slide of your
Electronmicroscope?

For if Descartes was a donkey—
And I'm sure you'd have him so,
You'll have to rub out not just
'sum',
But also 'cogito'.

QUINTIN HOGG

for
Allan Kardec
André Luiz
Hernani Guimarães Andrade
. . . that eternity promised . . .

CONTENTS

The Reincarnation Planners – Bioengineering – What the pineal gland is really for – Karma, action and reaction – The fish that got away – Intelligence and the bestial impulse – A religion of common sense

ACKNOWLEDGEMENTS

I am most grateful to Hernani Guimarães Andrade for permission to make use of his published and unpublished writings, and for access to his extensive library and files. It would have been impossible to write this book without his constant guidance and encouragement.

My thanks are also due, for help in various forms, to:

John Baines, Ted Bastin, Virginia Bressan, John Brunner, 'Celia', Michael Collins, Leonard Corte, John Cutten, Marjorie de la Warr, Dr E. J. Dingwall, Elsie Dubugras, Elizabeth Embacher, Luiz A. Gasparetto, Suzuko Hashizume, 'Marcia F.', Jarbas and Carmen Marinho, and Adam Polakiewicz. None of the above must be held responsible for any views expressed except where attributed.

I thank the Society for Psychical Research for permission to quote from its Journal and Proceedings, and for helping me in many other ways. For permission to use other copyright material, I thank the following:

W. H. Freeman and Co. for the extract from *Scientific American* in the Introduction; Lord Hailsham of St Marylebone and Hodder and Stoughton Ltd. for the poem by Quintin Hogg from *The Devil's Own Song and Other Verses*; the same publishers for extracts from *The Occult* by Colin Wilson; Francisco Candido Xavier and the Federação Espirita Brasileira for material used in Chapter 7; Harold Sherman for the Harry Loose material in Chapter 9; and the Edgar Cayce Foundation and the Association for Research and Enlightenment for extracts from Edgar Cayce reading transcripts.

G.L.P.

INTRODUCTION

Nothing is too amazing to be true. FARADAY

CRASH!!!
An upholstered footstool is flung downstairs from an empty bedroom, the door of which is closed.

A piece of furniture jumps over a seated woman and hits the table in front of her before falling to the floor, in front of four astonished witnesses.

A mattress catches fire while a woman is asleep on it, scorching her legs. The wing of a parrot is burned to a charred stump. A dog asleep under a table wakes up in terror as some unseen agent makes a large brand mark on his backside.

A jeep travels forty yards by itself, leaving no tyre marks on the ground. A baby, pram and all, disappears from inside a house and is found outside under a tree, safe and sound. Another baby, unable even to crawl, is discovered at the bottom of a basket of dirty clothes almost suffocated to death.

A young man closes his eyes and starts to draw in a dimly-lit room in front of a dozen witnesses. Taking a crayon in each hand, he draws two portraits at once, one with his right hand and the other, which is upside down, with his left. The double portrait is finished in three minutes, and he immediately starts another.

A half-blind man who left school at thirteen rests his pencil on a sheet of paper, puts his left hand over his eyes, and starts to write his 130th book. An uneducated woman screws her eyes tightly shut, points her face to the ceiling, and proceeds to extract a piece of tissue from a patient's neck with an unsterilised pair of pincers.

A three-year-old girl gives a vivid description of her previous life—and her previous death. A woman sees a road accident in detail four months before the event actually happens. She takes her husband on a guided tour of Pompeii, identifying every building, including her own former home.

A teenage ballet student impresses her teacher with her graceful movements during class. The teacher learns later that the girl committed suicide several months *previously*.

A man gives a fairly accurate description of two people he does not know who are going to sit in certain seats in a hall in three weeks' time the other side of the Atlantic.

A woman psychologist picks up a little plaster statue she finds on a beach. For the next few months her life is made hell as inexplicable accidents happen. Her troubles, which include the rare phenomenon of incubus, or rape by a spirit, only come to an end after she has been told to put the statue back where she found it, and does so.

All these things have happened. Some happened quite recently; some were described fully in my previous book,[1] and the rest, along with many other strange occurrences, will be described in this one. Whether sane and rational-minded readers wish to believe it or not, equally strange events are taking place all over the world, though you will never hear about most of them for the simple reason that the people they happen to do not want to be thought crazy. Either that or they are just plain terrified.

How are we supposed to react to reports of incidents like those mentioned above? First, we can assume that they are all untrue, along with thousands of others; the product of deliberate fraud, faulty reporting, excessive imagination, or a blend of all three. Secondly, we can assume that they are all literally true, along with flying saucers, fairies at the bottom of the garden, the man in the moon, and Uri Geller. (As some may be.)

Thirdly, we can study the original evidence ourselves and conclude that while there may have been a little trickery here and there, some inadequate testimony from bewildered witnesses, and some unjustified interpretation of presumed facts, some such phenomena really did happen more or less as described, although every one of them is quite obviously impossible.

When we say they are impossible, all we mean is that they appear to violate the laws on which our understanding of physical reality is based. Therefore, such laws as those of gravity, thermodynamics and cause-and-effect are either wrong or else they do not apply to such incidents as I have mentioned.

It is not likely that our physical laws are wrong, because they can be demonstrated over and over again until generally accepted as proven. If we pick up an apple and let go of it, it will fall to the floor (probably). If we go on doing this with a million apples, the chances are they will all do likewise.

We cannot be completely certain of this, however. There are no certainties nowadays, in science or anywhere else; only probabilities. One of the apples might rise to the ceiling and disappear altogether. Equally unlikely and inexplicable things do happen. Our laws are almost perfect, but not quite. Here are some words from a modern scientist who seems to be aware of this fact:

Men are apt to reject reports of very improbable occurrences. Persons of good judgment think it safer to distrust the alleged observer of such an event than to believe him. The result is that events which are merely very extraordinary acquire the reputation of never having occurred at all. Thus the highly improbable is made to appear impossible.

To give an example: Every physicist knows that there is a very small probability, which is easily computed, that the table upon which I am writing will suddenly and spontaneously rise into the air. The event requires no more than that the molecules of which the table is composed, ordinarily in random motion in all directions, should happen by chance to move in the same direction.

Every physicist concedes this possibility; but try telling one that you have seen it happen. Recently I asked a friend, a Nobel laureate in physics, what he would say if I told him that. He laughed and said that he would regard it as more probable that I was mistaken than that the event had actually occurred.

We see therefore that it does not mean very much to say that a very improbable event has never been observed. There is a conspiracy to suppress such observations, not among scientists alone, but among all judicious persons, who have learned to be sceptical even of what they see, let alone of what they are told.[2]

This was written by the American biologist and biochemist George Wald (b. 1906), himself a Nobel laureate. I often wonder whether his writing table really *did* rise into the air one day. I rather suspect that it did, for why else would he raise the subject with his colleague? If so, he was wise to keep quiet about it, for the sake of his reputation. But no matter; other tables have risen into the air in the presence of equally eminent scientists and honest laymen who have not kept quiet about it, regardless of their reputations. One of them, Charles Richet, even went on to win a Nobel Prize!

The Hon. Everard Feilding (1867–1936) saw a table rise into the air no less than *forty-five* times in the presence of the Italian medium Eusapia Palladino, at a series of sessions held in a fifth-floor room of the Hotel Victoria, Naples, in November and December 1908. (We shall hear more about them in Chapter 3.)

'One must regard them,' Feilding wrote, referring to the phenomena he witnessed with Eusapia, 'as the playthings of the agency which they reveal, and the more perfect revelation of that agency, whatever it may be, through the study of them, is surely a task as worthy of the most earnest consideration as any problem with which modern science is concerned.'[3]

Not only science, but also religion. Addressing an audience at the Newman Society in Oxford, which included a number of Jesuit priests, Feilding had this to say:

You are engaged in trying to teach an elaborate system of doctrinal theology based on a revelation of facts concerning a spiritual world to a material world which is in considerable doubt about whether there exists anything beyond itself. You seek to get men to pray, to receive sacraments, to prepare themselves for another life, when they hesitate to agree that there is any extra-mundane Inteliigence to listen to their prayers, or any other life for which they need trouble to make ready.

Supposing it were possible by experimental methods to establish at least some of the propositions on which you base your teaching;—by adducing irrefragable evidence of continued communication with an identified discarnate intelligence or by showing material consequences due to the action of such intelligence, to place on a basis of reasonable scientific certitude the fact that there *is* a spiritual existence parallel to ours, that there *is* another life to which man certainly will pass; to parallel, or at least supplement, belief by knowledge, faith by vision; would such an achievement be regarded by you as a gain or hindrance to your work, a stimulus or a clog to spiritual life?

Would you, in the construction of the Cathedral which you seek to erect, rejoice at finding that your toil might henceforth commence at a higher storey; that the foundation, which you had hitherto found the hardest portion of your labours, had already been laid?[4]

This is not the kind of talk Jesuits like to hear, even from a fellow Roman Catholic. The unanimous answer was—no, they wouldn't!

Today, many open-minded people probably feel otherwise. They would like to see the foundations of a cathedral laid—though not one to be built by Jesuits, or any other group of intolerant bigots. They would like to be given evidence—good evidence based on facts observed by responsible people—that there is indeed another world, and that we shall go there one day. Also that there is a theory, or the beginnings of a theory, that makes sense out of the arduous and bewildering ordeal of human life and death. It is for such people that I am writing this book.

I do not plan to build any cathedrals, or even design any. What I would like to see built is a House of Reason, and in the course of this book I shall try to round up a few of the building materials and leave them on the site, for qualified architects and engineers to use. Some of my materials may be defective, though if their defects encourage others to search for better ones they will have served their purpose.

Let us agree for a start, then, that improbable things do happen and that there is nothing seriously wrong with our basic laws of physics. Now, since these laws tend to state that improbable things do not happen, at least not as often as they apparently do, where does that leave our sense of reasoning? It leaves mine with the feeling that total reality consists of something more than the bits of matter to which our laws apply.

Such an idea is far from original. It is nothing new to Spiritualists, who have been describing the spirit world in great detail for well over a century, often at first hand and sometimes very convincingly. Nor is it new to a great many scientists, including a number of Nobel laureates. But neither scientist nor Spiritualist has yet managed to come up with a theory to tie together all these loose improbabilities that keep happening. Nobody has ever come up with a comprehensive hypothesis, backed by scientific reasoning and supported by observed fact, that offers an explanation for *all* supposedly paranormal phenomena.

In this book I shall introduce English-speaking readers to two such hypotheses, both by Brazilians, and both until now buried in the Portuguese language and largely ignored even in the country where they were written. One is by a scientist, and the other is apparently by a spirit. The former is summarised by its author in an Appendix specially written for this book; the other I have attempted to present (in drastically reduced and incomplete form) in Chapter 7.

I have no revelations to offer here, nor any dogmas to propound. If there are holes in the arguments to be presented, I hope they will be both picked and filled. If any of the ideas put forward are subsequently *proved* to be wrong, I shall welcome such proof as willingly as I welcome any new truth.

For the benefit of readers whose ignorance of any branch of science equals or exceeds mine, I have included a glossary at the end of the book, where such technical terms as I have been obliged to use are explained in words of one syllable wherever possible. I have had to keep such technical language as there is in this book simple in order to be able to understand it myself, and readers who cannot tell the difference between a proton and a photon have no need to worry; I am writing as a non-scientist for other non-scientists. (Real scientists are advised to read the Appendix at this stage, to satisfy themselves that some kind of scientific approach has been made before presenting the theories to be found later in the book).

Now, before we plunge into the spirit or psi world, let us take a brief look at physical matter.

Chapter 1

HAUNTED SPACE

The marvel is that we are associated with matter at all.   LODGE

The atom was always there, wasn't it?   SYBIL LEEK

D o you believe in atoms?
     Most people do, although nobody has ever really seen one or has much idea what they ultimately consist of. It may have been easy to disbelieve in such tiny things when their existence was first suggested as the basic component of matter by Demo-critus in the fifth century BC, or when John Dalton produced his table of atomic weights. It became very difficult to ignore them in 1945, especially for the people of Nagasaki and Hiroshima.

Visible or not, the atom, with its nucleus and attendant electrons, is a classic case of something that would have had to be invented if it did not exist already. Science simply could not get along without it. To the nuclear physicist, an atom is as real as a brick is to an architect, and the fact that he cannot see exactly what it looks like even under an electron microscope does not bother him too much. He can make it work for him, which is enough for the time being. Thanks to the atom, of which matter is made, a materialistic view of things becomes possible.

Science likes to think it has conquered medieval superstition, even if a few pockets of the latter remain to be wiped up. We no longer burn witches, though there are still plenty of them around, because they pose no immediate threat to our security, real or imagined. Some of us are still irritated, however, by the fact that the occult in general refuses to be conquered, even after two or three centuries of good solid scientific discovery. It even seems to be gaining ground, and some see this as a sign of a general decline in Western standards of living and thinking. But whatever ground it may have gained, the occult is not a serious threat. With moon rockets, colour TV, computers and bombs, who needs fear the witch in our midst? The ghost is welcome to haunt the machine, provided the machine keeps working.

Less than a hundred years ago, professors were telling students that there was really nothing left to be invented or discovered. Astrology had been refined into the science of astronomy, alchemy had grown into chemistry, while allopathic medicine and sterilised surgery could cure all diseases except a few not to be mentioned in polite society. Evolution had been shown to be merely a question of the survival of the fittest by a process of natural selection, and all was right with the world whether there was such a thing as God in heaven or not.

Then, in the twentieth century, everything fell apart. Astrology flourished as never before, chemistry became alchemy again —now known as nuclear physics—as it showed that one element *could* be transformed into another after all; while the sacred art of medicine became big business as doctors lost touch with the souls of their patients, who in turn sighed and went off in search of fringe healers to satisfy their inner needs.

Between 1928 and 1930, things became really complicated. Eminent scientists like Sir Arthur Eddington and Sir James Jeans brought out popular books that excited laymen's imaginations with scholarly speculations on the Great Architect and his Great Thought in a shadow world of symbols and abstractions. As for the poor atom, U.S. physicist Henry Margenau has wittily summed up what happened:

> The atom, which had been conceived as a solid pellet of stuff, turned out to be wholly empty, containing nothing that could be called 'matter' at all. It had degenerated into a series of singularities haunting space. This rather disposed of matter.[1]

It was exactly during this period of airy talk from scientists about Great Thoughts that two young biologists, Joseph B.

Rhine and his wife Louisa, embarked on what was to be a life-long effort to establish the reality of improbable or paranormal phenomena by scientific methods, at the newly formed Department of Psychology of Duke University. While the heads of men like Jeans, Eddington and Sir Oliver Lodge were somewhere up in the Milky Way, the Rhines began to fill the air with terms like *psychokinesis, decline effect, psi missing, target variables* and *terminal salience*. The spirits became *psi entities*, and the dear old poltergeist was eventually renamed a *Recurrent Spontaneous Psychokinetic Phenomenon*. (I prefer Everard Feilding's definition: 'A geist which poltered'.)

Science and the occult have always had a certain amount in common. Each has tended in the past to assume that things exist because they must, and not because anybody has actually proved they do. Scientists have been lucky in that their dreams often come true: Rutherford, for instance, postulated the existence of the neutron in 1920, but it was not until 1933 that anybody managed to discover it. Pauli dreamed up the neutrino in 1931, but it was only directly observed (if that is the word) in 1955. The neutrino is a subatomic particle that, as one scientist has said, 'zips through the earth as if it wasn't there'. Can anything be more occult?

Certainly. How about the tachyon? This is no less than a particle that is said to travel faster than light, which Einstein said was impossible, and accelerate itself out of existence. It has been described as 'more like something out of a physicist's nightmare than part of the real world'.

The idea that anything can travel faster than light opens up possibilities of which even science fiction writers may not have dreamed. But since I am trying to avoid anything resembling an occult way of thinking, I had better leave neutrinos and tachyons (along with anti-matter, gravity waves, black holes and quarks) to their own devices, whatever they are, and turn to something that seems far more real and credible—the non-material, spiritual, or *psi* world.

The existence of such a world has often been postulated by philosophers, mathematicians and physicists as well as Spiritualists and occultists. But its existence has not yet been proved, or even made to look overwhelmingly probable in the eyes of the majority.

I doubt if any of the world's post offices made plans to issue a special stamp in 1976 to celebrate a hundred years of telepathy. As far as we know at present, this is not a physical phenomenon, so we call it a *psi effect*; the Greek letter *psi* being used for convenience to denote anything that does not seem to fit into any established category.

For it was in 1876 that a scientist and pioneer of psychical research first publicly presented the idea that nervous energy could act by influence, or induction, across space. The word *telepathy* was not invented until 1882, and its inventor, Frederic Myers, later defined it as 'the transference of ideas and sensations from one mind to another without the agency of the recognised organs of sense'. Professor (later Sir William) Barrett, who unsuccessfully tried to interest the British Association in 'thought-transference' in 1876, had to wait a long time before it became accepted.

Telepathy did become accepted, with little help from the establishment, simply because it kept on happening to so many people. It happened in its own time and without warning, like an earthquake. Yet gradually people came to realise that it did happen often enough to be regarded as a real, if still inexplicable, phenomenon. It has happened to me more than once in front of witnesess, as I will describe later, and when something happens to you, you tend to start believing in it.

Telepathy is an example of something that obviously exists, but cannot be fully explained in terms of physical laws or principles. (Nor can electricity, for that matter, which can also act by induction across space.) So for the time being we regard it as an effect from the psi world. It may come as a shock to many to be told that there is just as much evidence for (but not proof of) the existence of the psi world as there is for the physical one, with its atoms in which we all believe without ever having seen one. Some will deny this, but to do so they must ignore the evidence rather than disprove it. Few psi effects have yet been proved, but *none* has ever been disproved.

A competition was once held in the U.S. to summarise Einstein's theory of relativity in 3,000 words. Einstein himself, it is said, thought of having a go, but decided that it was just not possible. The main theory I am putting forward in this book, which will be just as revolutionary as Einstein's if proved correct, has been distilled from a total of fourteen books by the two Brazilians I have already referred to. A drastically simplified summary of it would go something like this:

We live in two worlds. One is the familiar physical world of matter, which consists of atoms, molecules, elements, and in the case of what we call living matter, cells. All of these arrange themselves, or are arranged, in a wide variety of combinations, and obey strict laws which we do not yet fully understand, although we know enough about them to make life fairly comfortable. The other world is the psi world, a real non-physical world of psi matter, which has its own structure of psi atoms, psi molecules, psi elements, and so on. The physical world appears to have three dimensions of space and one of time, whereas the psi world must have at least four of space and two of time. The two worlds can and do interact; indeed, in the case of living matter they have to. Life is not possible without such an interaction. Psi matter, however, can exist solely in its own world, and is not subject to our laws of physical matter. Genuine direct communication between members of each world is possible, if rare and often very confusing.

Now, before we disappear into a four-dimensional world of psi atoms, biomagnetic fields, biological organising models and all sorts of other interesting things, we must first make sure that psi phenomena that provide the evidence we need for the reality of the psi world do indeed happen. So in the next two chapters we take a look at the psi world as understood, or more often misunderstood, at three stages of our history: the

Stone Age or thereabouts, the period of Ancient Greece and Rome, and the past two centuries.

First, meet Uglug, a character I have borrowed from Ogden Nash in order to tell the allegorical story of the world's first medium—or go-between: the first man to provide a link between the two worlds.

Chapter 2

THEN AS NOW

Out of the long Stone Age our race is awakening into consciousness of itself. We stand in the dawn of history. Behind us lies a vast and unrecorded waste . . . Since the times of that ignorance we have not gone far; a few thousand years, a few hundred thinkers, have barely started the human mind upon the great aeons of its onward way. MYERS

ONCE upon a time there was a Paleolithic man called Uglug. His father, the local chief, had just died, and there was a lot of argument as to who was to succeed him. Uglug was rather weak and a poor hunter, and he had little control over the masses, who were demanding a tough leader. So one day we find Uglug sitting alone in his favourite cave; cold, hungry and altogether miserable.

Although he did not know it at the time, Uglug was what we nowadays call a medium. Suddenly, to his surprise, there was his father in front of him in the dark cave, looking much as he had when alive, but sort of glowing all over.

'Greetings, son,' said the apparition. 'I am thy father's spirit, and I'm not happy at the way things are going. Do something about it. Good-bye.'

Uglug was terrified. He rushed out to tell the rest of the tribe what he had seen and heard. They decided he was not only a useless hunter, but also crazy, so they pushed him over a cliff.

Some time later, Uglug's teenage daughter ran into the same cave to escape from a club-wielding boy friend. Just as she thought she was safe behind a pile of stones, in he rushed and was just about to grab her when one of the stones picked itself up and bashed his head in. The girl duly gave her account of what had happened, and was judged to be a menace to society. She followed her father over the cliff.

Before long, however, even the most sceptical members of the tribe had to admit that strange things were going on in Cave Uglug. Lights would be seen, stones would bump around by themselves, and people who slept there would have night-mares. Finally, one of the wiser elders decided it was no use just killing everybody who showed signs of madness. He went into the cave himself, peered into the gloom, and called out: 'All right, whoever you are, come here and tell me what you want!'

Uglug duly appeared, looking pale and cold, and told the old man not to get excited. He was just an ordinary man, like his father and all the others, and he could not understand what all the fuss was about. Instead of killing everybody who spoke to him, why could the tribe not show a little respect? He only wanted to help. Did they know, for instance, that right now there was a juicy reindeer stuck in a bush behind the cave?

The elder listened with interest, and as soon as Uglug had faded away (muttering something about 'losing the power') he rounded up the hunters and led them to where there was indeed a reindeer stuck in a bush. No animal had ever been found in the area before, and the wise elder was the hero of the ensuing feast.

'Listen,' he began his after-dinner speech, 'there is something after all in this extra-sensory perception business. Uglug isn't dead, although we threw him over the cliff. Don't ask me what happens, but it would appear that human personality does somehow survive bodily death. It's a question of higher vibra-tory states of matter, or something. The point is, I say we should be nice to our brothers when they stop breathing from now on. Then maybe they'll find us more reindeers.'

And so the tribe began to be nice to their dead. They cleaned up the bodies, painted them red (they always looked so cold in apparitions) and buried them neatly with a good supply of food and weapons for their journey—nobody knew exactly where to, but it was obvious they were going somewhere, since they kept coming back. Before long, they noticed that dead people seemed to favour certain places for apparitions, so they marked these spots with special stones.

In due course, the world's first religion was born—Uglugism. Like most later religions, it was based initially on direct personal experience of the spirit world. It was a simple affair at first, with gatherings at the sacred cave where the tribe would jump around and shout until Uglug appeared and said a few words before vanishing again. After a good apparition there would invariably be another reindeer caught in a nearby thicket.

For a long time, Uglugism was a huge success. It united the tribe, kept everybody well fed, and stopped people killing each other on the slightest pretext. But as the generations passed, Uglug's apparitions became less and less frequent, until the time came when even the oldest elder had to admit that although his father often used to tell him about such things, he had never actually seen one himself. Which, of course, was not to say they never happened.

A crafty old man called Po-face happened to be listening to this confession, and a few days later he called a general pow-wow and held forth as follows:

'Friends, I have good news, for once. I was in the sacred cave the other day when Uglug appeared to me and said that from now on he is only going to appear to a select few, like for instance myself. It's too much of a strain for him to materialise for any of the *hoi polloi* who need a trifling problem solved. Uglug says he wants me to move into the outer cave—that means you will all have to move out, of course—and hold regular meetings every Sunday. He also wants each of you to leave all the food and money you can spare with me. I'll see that he gets it. This tradition starts as of next Sunday.'

And so the world's first religion produced its first priest, while Uglug moved sadly elsewhere, looking for a tribe that might prove easier to enlighten . . .

The few traces of Uglugism (or similar early religions) that still survive today suggest that this fable may be based on actual fact. Numerous carved human figures, made from the metacarpuses of mammoths, have been unearthed at such sites as Predmost and Gagarino, showing clear signs of having been placed near a fire. Why would Paleolithic man have bothered to do such a thing? Could it be that he was trying to keep his ancestors warm in their new abode? Art was a ritual operation in those days, and it must have had a specific purpose.

Paleolithic man was not a great thinker. Life was hard, what with the cold, the terrifying darkness of the caves, the constant attacks by wild animals, and the perpetual problem of finding enough to eat. Even if his mind had been sufficiently developed, he would have had little to think about other than the barest essentials: where his next meal was coming from and how to stay alive.

The one thing that must, however, have provoked the stirrings of intellectual reasoning inside his misshapen skull was—death. Even a Paleolithic man must have been attached to members of his family, and felt a sense of loss when they fell over cliffs or got mauled to death by wild beasts. Now, since the business of staying alive was so important and so difficult, why should he have bothered to pay any attention to the dead? He must have had very good reasons. To him, it was a necessity to bury them in the foetal position, with a supply of food and weapons, to paint the body with ochre and to place stones on certain parts of the ground. We know this was done, but why?

All modern authorities on Spiritism agree that some spirits of the departed remain what they term earthbound, unaware that they are dead, especially when they have met a sudden or violent end. In 1961, the spirit of a young soldier killed during the 1932 Brazilian revolution apparently manifested itself at a Spiritist meeting being held in São Paulo. The entity identified himself correctly, as was later checked in official records, and gave information unknown to any of those present and unavailable from any single source. He expressed great surprise on being told that almost thirty years had elapsed since the battle in which he had been, as he thought, merely wounded. This case has been published in full,[1] and was summarised in my previous book.

If modern spirits are confused after violent death, those of ancient man must have been even more so, especially since they were barely able to think even when incarnate. Spirit manifestations like that of the young Brazilian soldier must have begun to take place as soon as man began to live in organised societies. For all his simpleness of mind, Paleolithic man could not fail to have understood the obvious fact that his 'dead' father was not really dead after all, just invisible most of the time. When he was visible, he looked cold and hungry. He must have asked for food and weapons, and if he had any awareness of the process of reincarnation he might even have suggested that bodies be buried in the foetal position, or inside a foetus-shaped urn, in order to make it easier for a soul to come back to earth.

Primitive man must have realised that when somebody clouted him on the head, which happened fairly often, he lost what we now call consciousness. Therefore, the skull must be the place where the spirit-thing was kept. It would seem quite logical to cut off the heads of enemies to make sure their spirits could not escape and cause more trouble. Skull cults are known to have existed since earliest Stone Age times; the human head was the object of religious belief and skulls were preserved because they were thought to contain the seat of the body's vital force. The fact that skull cults have been observed in many different parts of the world suggests that there was a widespread early awareness of a non-physical element in man. Modern aborigines may mistake aeroplanes for birds, but what could Stone Age man have mistaken the spirit for?

Po-face, our primitive and wily priest, was the man who unwittingly divided religion into its exoteric and esoteric (or public and private) aspects. He was the first of the shamans, and the first professional medium. It was his job to act as go-between, to keep the incarnate in touch with the discarnate, and to summon such spirits as were required for a specific function, whether good or evil. Skilled shamans today can make use of suggestion or skill at conjuring to reinforce the phenomena their religion is supposed to produce. Many Spiritist mediums are certainly guilty of this. But Po-face had no imagination at all. All he could deal with was fact, and to him the reality of spirit survival must have been a fact, not mere superstition. He could hardly have invented it.

Eventually, shamans must have noticed that their own power and influence would increase or decline in direct proportion to the number of phenomena they were able to produce. As long as the paranormal information kept on coming, their position was secure. But what happened when the source dried up, as such sources all too frequently do today? Obviously, a smart shaman would step in and do some phenomenon-producing himself. Modern mediums do just the same thing; the Italian medium Eusapia Palladino is a good example of somebody who certainly produced paranormal effects, and equally certainly helped them out with tricks of her own whenever she thought she could get away with it. (More about this remarkable lady in a later chapter.)

Magic, the art of performing the apparently impossible, has become a respectable part of the entertainment industry. If a successful magician decided to found a new religion today he would probably do very well. It can be no coincidence that most major religions have their roots in a magical setting, and that the more primitive the religion the closer it is to those roots.

Magic was probably no more, originally, than a pact between shaman and spirit. Certain symbols, formulas, written and spoken words, served to recall and identify the pact. These became more complicated with time, increasing in splendour in strict proportion to the distance of the religion from its original source of inspiration. The little scorched figures from Predmost and Gagarino have evolved into sacred images, relics and statues, while the piles of stones have grown into cathedrals, where some suppose God is more likely to be available than anywhere else.

A visit to an Afro-Brazilian *umbanda* or *candomblé* meeting today shows how inseparable ritual and religious practice can still be. Elaborate meals are prepared and laid out for the spirits to enjoy. Traditional and very beautiful chants are sung in

African dialects nobody present can understand, including the singers, while the insistent beat of drums brings an exotic touch to modern metropolises like São Paulo or Rio de Janeiro. It is common to find regularly practising Roman Catholics at such meetings, who come for the direct personal touch they find lacking in their own church. They go to Mass to keep up outward appearances, and they go on to the cult to satisfy their innermost needs. The personal touch is provided by the cult priest or priestess (*pai de santo*—father-in-sainthood)—or *mãe de santo*, mother-in-sainthood), through whom it is supposed that the spirits communicate. It is a hot line to the other world, and more personally satisfying than watching an elaborate and distant ritual in a church. A recent survey in a leading Brazilian magazine has revealed that while 87 per cent of the country is supposed to be Roman Catholic, only two per cent are able to say what the basic beliefs of this church are! (Sixty-eight per cent admitted the validity of Spiritism.)[2]

At Kardecist Spiritist meetings (based on the writings of the nineteenth-century Frenchman Allan Kardec, of whom more anon) ritual and pomp are reduced to the barest minimum. There are no Spiritist priests or churches, and meetings are usually held in somebody's living room, or perhaps in an ordinary house rented specially to serve as a meeting-place for larger groups, with no special décor. Meetings usually take place around a big table covered with a plain white cloth, consisting of readings from the works of Kardec, discussions of the ideas they contain, and finally a period when the lights are turned off and the spirits are invited to join in and say a few words. Somebody then stands up, takes a deep breath, and begins to speak as if inspired by a discarnate entity. Some Spiritists are convinced that all such utterances come directly from the spirit guide of their group, while others see the practice as a symbolic contact with the spirit world, just as the wine and wafers at Holy Communion are symbols of the blood and body of Christ rather than the real thing.

The important feature of Kardecist Spiritist meetings is that there is nobody between you and your personal source of inspiration. Po-face has been banished from his cave or altar, and you are in direct contact with your personal Uglug. Allan Kardec always used to insist that Spiritism (the word he gave to his modified version of Spiritualism) was no more than Christianity restored to its original simplicity, purity and accessibility —with no intermediaries allowed.

It is possible, to judge from past experience with other religions, that Spiritism may eventually acquire cathedrals, popes, priests, inquisitions and other trappings of decadent religions. If this happens, somebody will go back to square one and start all over again. Despite the efforts of churches, man never seems to lose his simple individual desire for direct religious experience, with nobody standing between him and his ideal. For surely all religions came into being as a result of man's personal experience of the psi world, and the sense of mystery and wonder such a contact awakened in him?

Now we turn to a recent civilisation, that of what is misleadingly known as Ancient Greece, which flourished a mere two to three millenia ago, not long when you think that our globe may be anything up to fifteen billion years old.

The Greco-Roman period is useful to us because it has been well studied, much of its culture has survived, and above all it is a period we still find relevant to our everyday life and thoughts in the twentieth century. It is often said that all Western philosophy has been no more than a series of footnotes to Plato, though this may be simply because insufficient records of any earlier philosophers survive. Had the Egyptians, Babylonians, Sumerians, Celts or American Indians left writings easily available today in paperback editions, we might all be in a very different state of civilisation. The great thing is not so much that the Greeks had a word for it, but that they wrote it down. And with regard to psi phenomena, it is remarkable what a great deal the Greeks and Romans did write down. For instance:

The tenth book of Plato's *Republic* contains a detailed account of the experiences of Er, the son of Armenius, who was apparently slain in battle but suddenly came back to life after

lying ten days on a funeral pyre. (Fortunately, this had not
been lit.) Er describes how his soul left the body and came to a
sort of high court, where judges decided whether new arrivals
should return to earth or move on to a higher plane. For every
wrong they had committed on earth, they were made to suffer
tenfold, while tyrants and criminals were bundled up in thorns
to be shipped off to hell. Souls of the good were allowed to
choose their next lives, provided these were different to their
past ones. Er's adventures are presented as fact, not fantasy,
and the moral of the story, with which the *Republic* ends, is
that 'we hold fast ever to the heavenly way and follow after
justice and virtue always, considering that the soul is immortal
and able to endure every sort of good and every sort of evil'.
This is pure nineteenth-century Spiritualism, written four
centuries before Christ.

The Greeks must have had a large amount of evidence for
psi phenomena. On the baffling subject of precognition, for
example, Aristotle observed that it was difficult either to ignore
the evidence or to believe it. (Darwin was to say the same thing
about William Crookes' experiments with mediums in the
nineteenth century.) Aristotle would not have made such a
remark unless there was plenty of evidence of a type a mind
like his would take seriously. Pity he did not quote more of it.

From Professor E. R. Dodds' study of psi phenomena in
classical antiquity,[3] it seems clear that many such phenomena
known to us today were perfectly familiar to the Greeks. An
interesting exception is the poltergeist (the ghost that flings
things around) of which Dodds says he can find no 'recognisable pre-Christian tale', although Suetonius mentions a man
who went to sleep in a holy place and found himself ejected,
bed and all, 'by a sudden occult force'. Andocides tells a story
about a banker called Hipponicus keeping an evil spirit (*alit-
erion*) in his house, which upset his table (*trapeza*). Nothing
supernormal was intended here, Dodds points out, since the
spirit in question was Hipponicus's spendthrift son, and the
word *trapeza* was a pun, since it also meant a bank. But, Dodds
says, the joke would have additional point if the speaker's audi-

ence were familiar with stories of real poltergeists. Spirits, in fact, might have been *thought* capable of upsetting tables. As for Suetonius, why would he refer to an 'occult force' unless he accepted the fact that such things existed?

Plotinus had no doubts whatsoever as to the reality of the psi world. Part of our soul is never embodied, he said, but maintained an immaterial existence 'yonder'. 'There are not a few souls, once among men, who have continued to serve them after quitting the body, and by revelations, practically helpful, make clear as well that other souls, too, have not ceased to be.' Such were the basic beliefs of the theurgists, a group of which Plotinus and his fellow Neo-Platonists Proclus, Porphyry and Iamblichus are the best known. Some of the finest evidence we have for psi phenomena during the early Christian period (apart from the New Testament, of course) comes from this group, who seem to have had a surprising amount in common with the Spiritualists of the mid-nineteenth century.

Professor Dodds (who incidentally does not believe in human survival) defines theurgy as 'magic applied to a religious purpose and resting on supposed revelations of a religious character', a definition he regards as also fitting to modern Spiritualism. The theurgists had their mediums, which they called *docheus* (the recipient) or *katochos*—the one who is held down! Iamblichus even mentions the word medium (*meson*) itself, saying that the best ones were 'young and rather simple persons'.

Unlike modern Spiritualists, the theurgists did not communicate with familiar spirits by name, but with anonymous gods and benevolent entities whose help they sought in matters of both everyday life and the future salvation of their souls. Their mediums would go into trance and speak in strange voices, and if the medium was not too well developed, inferior earthbound spirits would come through and cause general confusion, just as they still do today. According to the eleventh-century Byzantine scholar Psellus, who had access to books now lost, theurgist mediums would often be 'moved and guided by another spirit, which utters things outside the subject's knowledge and sometimes predicts future events'. Inferior spirits would barge in and push higher ones out of the way, while occasionally there would be physical phenomena produced in order to reassure sitters of the reality of communicators.

Many of Iamblichus's descriptions are familiar stuff to modern Spiritualists. He mentions the appearance of lights as the medium enters or leaves the trance state, levitation of the medium's body, and even visible spirit forms entering it. The latter sounds rather like ectoplasm, the substance that mediums are supposed to emit for spirits to use at materialisation sessions, and reabsorb when the spirits are through for the day.

There is an account by at least four different writers of séances being held around what is unmistakably an early form of the ouija board in the year AD 371. This consisted of an olive-wood tripod supporting a round metal dish with the twenty-four letters of the Greek alphabet engraved on its rim. The operator held a ring suspended on a thread above it, in the way modern radiesthesists use pendulums. After prolonged incantations the device would begin to work, the ring swaying from letter to letter as it spelled out hexameter verses in reply to questions put to it. Spirits seem to have been more elegant in those days.

At one theurgist ouija session, a sitter asked who was to be the next emperor after Valens, to which question the ring began to spell out *theta . . . epsilon . . . omikron . . .* , or THEO . . . It was assumed that this meant Theodorus, and the session was broken off. Seven years later, Valens was killed and his successor was—not Theodorus, but a chap called *Theodosius*. Then as now, psi researchers did not always pay enough attention to their source material.

The Greco-Romans were definitely stronger on mental phenomena than physical ones. Reports of psychokinesis (PK), the moving of objects by forces other than physical, are hard to come by in the literature, though there are one or two. A Jewish exorcist called Eleazar is supposed to have placed a cup of water near his patients for the exorcised spirit to kick over on leaving the body, while another story actually has a spirit overturning a statue !

The theurgists presumably thought such trivial antics to be beneath the dignity of their gods, who were accustomed to give orders rather than take them. They were not concerned with demonstrating the survival of the spirit, which they took for granted, just as modern Spiritualists do, and their main purpose was to improve their own souls through communication with superior discarnate entities.

A devout Brazilian Spiritist has assured me that she once saw a gramophone record float off the turntable and up to the ceiling (which I seem to remember seeing in an old Olsen and Johnson movie), telling me that the spirits didn't do much of that sort of thing nowadays because they had no further need to prove their existence. The same lady gave me good evidence to suggest that her own life had been greatly enhanced by help from the spirit world; even if spirits do not exist, whatever people mistake for them can obviously be very useful and helpful. This point might be borne in mind by people who dismiss Spiritualism as trivial nonsense. Trivial and nonsensical it can sometimes be, for sure, but no more so than life itself.

There are too many similarities between theurgy and modern Spiritualism to be dismissed as coincidence. 'We seem driven to recognise a case of like causes independently producing like effects.' Dodds says. We could also be driven to conclude that both groups based their beliefs on personally witnessed fact. The most striking similarity of all has to do with the earthbound spirit of someone killed violently. Theurgists used to think that these were in fact the only spirits readily available, but since they were probably angry and dangerous they were better left alone. A great many modern cases of convincing communication from the psi world involve people who claim to have died prematurely, violently, or by suicide.

Another point to bear in mind about the similarities between theurgy and Spiritualism is that when the latter began to appear, around the middle of the nineteenth century, theurgy was almost unknown even to classical scholars; and the early Spiritualists were not even classical scholars but ordinary men and women from every walk of life. Like causes can always be expected to produce like effects, and it is theoretically possible that all theurgists and all Spiritualists have suffered mass delusion, but if the causes concerned were not genuine personal experiences of the psi world, then what could they have been?

This seems to be the right moment to deal with the subject of fraud, which has been connected with psi phenomena throughout recorded history and remains very much so today.

The Greeks knew about fake mediums. There are many stories in the classics about people trying to take advantage of their status as mediums for their personal gain, usually by claiming to extract information from spirits of the departed. These individuals were known as necromancers, and they were strongly disapproved of by the Greeks and actively persecuted by the Romans. Plato recommended solitary confinement for life for those who 'fool many of the living by pretending to raise the dead', while by the fourth century AD anybody who even visited a graveyard in the evening was liable to be hauled off and charged with necromancy.

The Greek word *nekromanteia* simply meant 'divination by corpses', though eventually the word became corrupted to *nigromantia* in Medieval Latin and *nigromancie* in Middle English. Hence the term Black Magic. Here we have a case of what might originally have been a respectable art, founded on direct experience, becoming corrupted as its practitioners forgot their desire to help others in their greed for status, adulation and money. Then as now.

'If we look at imposture as a historic phenomenon,' wrote William James, 'we find it always imitative. One swindler imitates a previous swindler, but the first swindler of that kind imitated someone who was honest. You can no more create an absolutely new trick than you can create a new word without any previous basis. You do not know how to go about it.'[4]

Allan Kardec goes into the question of fraud in great detail in his *The Mediums' Book* (1861), where sceptics may learn a few tricks even they had never thought of. Kardec points out that while it is obviously possible for a skilled conjuror to imitate *some* Spiritist phenomena, there simply were not that many skilled conjurors around when these phenomena began to appear, regularly, in many countries from about 1848 onwards. Even if all Spiritist phenomena were tricks, it would be no less surprising that so many brilliant conjurors suddenly emerged from nowhere, with no professional training, than it would be if the phenomena were mostly genuine.

James's theory seems to apply to the relatively recent phenomenon of psychic surgery—the apparent paranormal opening of human bodies by medically unqualified people, without the use of such refinements as anaesthetics, antiseptics, or indeed anything except rusty penknives or bare and often rather dirty hands.

The first psychic surgeon to become widely known was a Brazilian, the late José Pedro de Freitas ('Zé Arigó'), who died in 1971 at the age of 49. Arigó began his extraordinary work in the mid-1950's, several years before writers Ron Ormond and O. McGill introduced the similar work of the Philippine psychic surgeon Eleuterio Terte to English-speaking publics. I cannot find any reliable accounts of anything similar to the work of Terte or Arigó before this period. The only exception is a single and intriguing mention by the early twentieth-century Polish explorer Ferdynand Ossiendowski of a Tibetan mystic opening up a man's thorax with an ordinary knife and immediately reclosing the wound, apparently just to show he could do it.

It is not likely that Arigó or Terte had ever heard of each other (or of Ossiendowski's Tibetan pal) when they began their psychic surgery. Brazil and the Philippines are as far apart as any two countries can be, and I can find nothing in common between them except a certain similarity of some of their landscapes, and—which may be more significant—large and well-entrenched Christian Spiritist movements. They are, in fact, the strongest such movements in the world.

Arigó was scarcely laid to rest in his grave before 'mediums' began popping up all over Brazil and claiming to receive the spirit of his faithful guides Dr Fritz and Dr Pierre. Operations were performed for the faithful, usually in the dark and with a good deal of general mystification involved, and occasionally somebody would claim to be cured. In October 1974, I was interested to hear that Dr Pierre was alive and well and carving people up in the city of Campinas.

There is good reason to suppose that Arigó was that 'some-one who was honest' of James's theory. He worked in public under bright lights for about fifteen years, seldom objected to examination by all and sundry, and was never caught using trickery. He undoubtedly had some paranormal abilities. True, he has been accused of fraud, though not to my knowledge by anybody who actually saw him at work. His chief attacker today is a turbulent Jesuit priest named Oscar G. Quevedo, who runs a phoney parapsychology institute in São Paulo. His im-possible mission in life is to abolish Spiritism before it drives Brazilian Catholicism altogether into the sea, and his objections to Arigó, which are too ridiculous to repeat here, have been firmly denied by several qualified doctors, two of whom have personally assured me that what they saw Arigó doing was paranormal beyond any shadow of doubt. (Quevedo's attacks are based on the assumption that if a skilled stage conjuror like himself can occasionally appear to repeat some of Arigó's feats, under conditions established by the conjuror, then it follows that Arigó, who had no training in conjuring or indeed in anything else, must have been using trickery all the time.)

With such a precedent as Arigó, opportunities for imitation by outright swindlers were unlimited. I do not regard all Brazilian psychic surgeons as swindlers, though I must men-tion here that early in 1975 I was given very strong evidence to suggest that the man I called Zeca in my previous book has been caught in deliberate and premeditated fraud at least once. I must also report the sad news that Edivaldo Oliveira Silva was killed in a road accident in March 1974, aged 43. I am still searching for evidence to suggest that he ever resorted to trickery, and have found none.

However, in August 1974, I managed with some difficulty to get hold of a piece of tissue allegedly extracted from the brain of a girl known to me by a man who still enjoys a wide reputation as a paranormal healer in Brazil. The tissue was analysed in a São Paulo laboratory and found to be probably a piece of animal muscle, and certainly not human. An independent analysis of a second piece of tissue from a different patient of the same 'surgeon' gave a similar result. I will not name the man concerned (who was not mentioned in my previous book, though I knew of him) until I can be sure he is personally responsible for this apparent fraud. It is possible that his own assistants are deceiving him.

An honest medium who does his thing in a state of trance will be the last person to know whether what he is doing is genuine or not. He must rely on what his friends or helpers tell him. I remember how surprised Edivaldo seemed when I told him he had operated on me. How would an arch-sceptic react if he spent an evening snoozing on a friend's sofa and woke up to be greeted excitedly: 'Wow! You just materialised Katie King!'? He would find himself in the same quandary as Aristotle and Darwin before him; he could neither accept the evidence nor reject it, if he trusted his friend.

Some mediums, like Eusapia Palladino, could be fraudulent or genuine as the mood took them, as we shall see in the next chapter. Others, like Stanislawa Tomczyk, claimed *themselves* to be fraudulent while convincing others they were genuine. (I have this on good authority, but cannot yet reveal my source.) It is all very confusing. Miss Tomczyk, by the way, eventually married one of her investigators, Everard Feilding, and I cannot see a man of his reputation for integrity marrying a phoney medium.

Mediums are funny people. However honest they may be in their normal state, when they go into trance they lose control of themselves, literally, at least in part. Frank Podmore, an experienced and hyper-sceptical researcher of the early SPR days, once pointed out that mediums in trance suffered from 'impaired moral control'. In using the word 'fraud' in this connection, he said, 'we do not necessarily imply a higher

THEN AS NOW 45

degree of moral responsibility than when we pass judgment on the play-acting of a child.'⁵

Andrew Lang put it even more plainly. 'The punctual paid medium, being human, and earning a livelihood by his or her alleged faculty for making tables float in the air, or jump about the room, is tempted to cheat, and gets caught by the ankle, like Eusapia, where her ankle should not be.'⁶

It is not surprising that many people are put off the whole idea of the psi world because of all the fraud associated with it, often quite rightly. Some feel that the whole field is the invention of delirious Spiritualists and dishonest writers. They also feel that if somebody has been caught cheating once, nothing they ever do or say subsequently should be taken seriously.

William James tells an amusing story to show that this attitude can be mistaken. As a medical student, he was once in charge of projecting the heart of a live turtle onto a screen during a physiology lecture. The professor was telling the class how the heart would beat when stimulated in a certain way. Unfortunately, when the professor did his stimulating, the turtle's heart stopped beating altogether. Acting, as he thought, like a military genius converting disaster into victory, James promptly stuck his finger under the heart and made its shadow beat realistically on the screen, to the satisfaction of all, especially the lecturer.

James considered he was 'acting for the larger truth' and admits that according to the rules of the SPR, 'my conduct on that one occasion ought to discredit everything I ever do'. Yet history has not chastised America's greatest philosopher because of that one instance of deliberate fraud. Likewise, I think it is unreasonable to dismiss a medium simply because on occasions his or her ankle turns up in the wrong place. Fraud is an effect for which there may be many causes.

Not only mediums have been caught cheating. In 1974 Dr Walter J. Levy resigned from his post as research director of the Foundation for Research on the Nature of Man after being caught fiddling with a computer in order to produce false data on an animal psi test. *The New York Times, Time* and *Scien-*

tific *American,* none of which is noted for its readiness to report positive results of psi research, immediately found ample
space in their columns to report this incident, *Time* even managing to imply that the whole field of parapsychology was
suspect.*

(In the same year, a researcher in immunology at the famous
Sloan-Kettering institute was caught marking skin grafts on
mice to make it appear that they were taking. 'There was no
talk, of course,' comments Alan Vaughan in *Psychic* (December 1974, p. 8) 'about the general field of immunology being
suspect.')

In the following chapter, I shall give some examples of what
I mean by psi phenomena, mental and physical, that have taken
place under conditions that seem to rule out fraud altogether
as a likely explanation for them. Two from my own recent experience are included, for when something very strange happens to *you,* it becomes very difficult to ignore the feeling that
our solid and familiar world may not be quite what we always
thought it was . . .

---

* *Scientific American* has some excuse for acting suspicious of psi. In
1922, it offered $2,500 for the production of a real psi phenomenon be-
fore its own committee. It almost had to pay up, to the Boston medium
Margery Crandon, but the five voting members of the committee were
unable to agree on their findings. This was due to the outrageous behaviour of the magician Harry Houdini, which surpassed that of any
fraudulent medium or psi researcher in history. Now that more than
fifty years have elapsed since this lamentable episode, perhaps this fine
magazine would like to try again?

Chapter 3

FACTS IN SEARCH OF A THEORY

The improbabilities of today are the elementary truths of tomorrow. RICHET

SATURDAY, June 8th 1974. It is 6 p.m., and I am sitting at a large table with six other people in a São Paulo Spiritist centre. The young man directly opposite me is Luiz Antonio Gasparetto, aged twenty-four, a social worker and psychology student who for the past ten years or so has produced a steady stream of work in what appears to be a relatively rare field nowadays—that of psychic art. Luiz has never sold a picture, or even tried to, and he has never learned to draw. Those are just two of the unusual things about him.

Artists have often been known to go into trance and produce work unlike what they can do in their normal state—if any artist worth the name can ever be said to be in a normal state. William Blake, for instance, seems to have been in trance much of his life. Trance painting by untrained mediums was a popular and often fraudulent phenomenon in the nineteenth century, though the work of Victorien Sardou and the remarkable Scotsman David Duguid attracted much attention. In this century, we have had interesting trance art from Augustin Lesage, a French miner, and from professionals like Austin Spare and Ingo Swann, while in England a lady named Coral Polge does fine pencil drawings of spirits she claims to see around her sitters.

My friends, who have heard of most of these people, assure me that Luiz has some surprises in store for me. He has indeed.

We sit in silence for a few minutes. On the table between Luiz and myself is a pile of fourteen pieces of thick drawing paper, measuring 28 by 20 inches, and a new box of sixty artist's crayons of all colours. I have already taken elementary precautions against possible fraud, holding each sheet of paper up to the light, making sure it was blank and that there were no concealed finished drawings in the pile. I do not feel it necessary to search the medium, since you cannot very well hide a 28- by 20-inch drawing up your sleeve.

The session begins. It is, they have told me, a regular Saturday evening session held whether there are visitors like myself present or not. The purpose of the sessions is to enable Luiz to develop his abilities under the orientation of his spirit guides. These, I am assured, include a host of discarnate artists such as Manet, Renoir, Modigliani, the Brazilian Tarsila do Amaral and many others.

The bright lights are switched off, leaving the room lit only by two weak red bulbs on the side walls some twelve feet from where Luiz and I are sitting. I notice that in the red light you cannot tell one crayon from another, though it is light enough to see what is going on and also to write on my notepad.

At 6.13, Luiz goes suddenly into action. Leaning his head on his left hand and turning slightly to the left, he runs the fingers of his right hand over the crayons in the box, without looking at what he is doing. With his face still covered, he attacks the paper with his right hand with such energy that the paper starts to slide around on top of the pile. I hold down the corners nearest me with two fingers. In just under three minutes, Luiz has completed a vivid portrait of a girl, his hand flying over the paper at astonishing speed. As soon as he has finished and signed it (from where I am it looks like 'Renoir'), the lady beside him lifts it off the pile and he starts another drawing without a moment's pause.

Very interesting, I say to myself. It cannot be easy to draw in semi-darkness even without a hand in front of your face. But it is hardly paranormal. What else can he do, I wonder?

As if reading my thoughts, Luiz embarks upon his next drawing. Taking a new chalk, he makes the outline of a face at great speed, still without looking at what he is doing, and immediately sketches in a pair of eyes at the *bottom* of the face. For a moment I decide he has missed out on this one, but as his hand continues to fly around the paper, jabbing at it like a high-speed boxer in a hurry to finish off his opponent, it gradually dawns on me that he is doing a portrait upside down, or the right way up as seen from my position. I begin to feel quite impressed.

He draws upside down as quickly and assuredly as he does the right way up, and the new portrait is finished in a little over three minutes. Next, he takes the pile of paper and turns it sideways, picking up a chalk in each hand, and proceeds to draw two heads at once, one beside the other.

This is not at all easy. Just try it yourself—your left hand can copy what your right is doing, mirror-fashion, but try drawing a circle with one hand and a triangle with the other. Luiz's two heads are quite different, and his two hands seem totally independent of each other, though I notice that occasionally one hand will jump across the paper to help the other's portrait. While one hand dots in an eye, right on the spot, the other shades in a background of the other head. I would have said this performance was almost impossible, but one never really finds out what human beings can be capable of.

Luiz seems to pick up that thought as well, because for his next picture he repeats the phenomenon of drawing two heads at once. This time, however, he introduces yet another refinement: one of the heads is the right way up and the other is *upside down*! I feel distinctly impressed.

As he starts his next picture, I fear Luiz has gone mad. He picks up a light-coloured crayon (it is difficult to tell what colour in the dim red light, though one can tell light from dark shades) and using the side of it he makes a huge oval blob in the middle of the paper, like a furious child just making a mess. When he is satisfied with his blob, which has used up almost the whole of the crayon, he picks up a darker one, makes a few lightning strokes on the paper, and in a matter of seconds there is an unmistakably Modigliani face in front of me.

To imitate a Modigliani portrait cannot be too difficult, with those oval faces and exaggeratedly long necks. Luiz promptly does it again, only this time he starts with the outline of the face and fills in the blank spaces later, using several different crayons. At this stage it occurs to me that every drawing so far has been made in a different way. We have had linear portraits drawn with great precision, another in a more impressionistic style with great economy of line, and another with the strong colour areas and bold strokes of an expressionist. It seems I am being given a demonstration of every possible way of reproducing the human face on paper.

The only feature I can detect that is common to nearly all of them is a kind of aura effect around the faces. It is not an exaggerated aura, such as you find in paintings of saints, but just a faint line following the contour of the cheek. On more than one occasion I notice that Luiz draws the outline of a face in thick strokes, then throws the chalk aside and immediately picks up another lighter one and follows the outline of the face exactly with the second chalk. The chalks, incidentally, may have begun the evening in a neat row in their box, but before long Luiz has used more than half of the sixty, and their stumps are lying all over the place. And more than once I note that he locates a colour he has already used and discarded in order to complete a certain line or shaded area.

The session ends at 7.05, by which time Luiz has produced a total of fourteen drawings, averaging just under four minutes each. Throughout the session neither he nor I have spoken a word until the start of the last picture, another of his double-portrait feats. At this point, Luiz starts to speak in a voice they told me later was that of the centre's spirit guide-in-chief, a certain Father Zabeu, who is well known in local Spiritist circles. Luiz certainly gives a fair impression of speaking in the voice of an elderly priest, and for three or four minutes there he is, drawing two portraits at once and delivering a homely little sermon at the same time. This may be possible, but normal it is not.

After the session, the lights are turned on again and Luiz looks at his evening's output, like a photographer eager to see how his film has come out. He gives no sign of having any recollection of what he had been up to for the past hour. I am impressed by the quality of the drawings. They might not pass for original Renoirs or Modiglianis, but they would decorate any home wall. They are all full-face portraits, none of them of anybody present, and each face has a lively expression and an air of serenity about it. Although done at frantic speed, they bear no resemblance to the lightning cartoons people often do in cafés and bars for tourists. They are pleasing pictures skilfully drawn in the styles of the artists whose names were signed on them.

I decide without much hesitation that Luiz should be investigated more thoroughly, and promptly make arrangements to return the following Saturday with the full IBPP research team, to which Luiz agrees at once.

The following week, Ney Prieto Peres of the IBPP shot about twenty minutes of colour film of Luiz at work, while Suzuko Hashizume tape-recorded the sound of his hand flying over the paper, and Hernani Guimarães Andrade and I took nearly 200 colour slides of the session. When we showed the film later, nobody could believe it. It looked as though it had been speeded up, like an old Keystone Cops comedy. We checked the projector and found it in perfect order. We showed other films, which appeared to be running at the right speed. I went over my original notes and found the time of each drawing matched with the film.

This was quite an interesting situation. You might suppose that if you film something apparently paranormal, you will satisfy yourself that it really happened when you see the film afterwards. But the opposite seemed to be the case here. I had watched two of Luiz's hour-long sessions and seen him produce thirty drawings and two oil paintings within a few feet of where I sat. I had ruled out all the obvious possibilities for fraud or hallucination. I had been present when the film was shot, and yet—seeing it all on film was far less convincing than seeing the real thing had been.

'There must be something wrong with your projector,' our friends who had not been present at the original session insisted.

We talked to a number of professional artists and showed them a selection of Luiz's work. All agreed that for a man with no art training to produce pictures of such quality in a weak red light, without looking at what he was doing, drawing upside down, doing two heads at once, and firing off portraits of unseen sitters one after the other sometimes in as little as thirty seconds simply could not be done. We also agreed that it had been done. A leading Brazilian artist, teacher and critic, after studying thirty of Luiz's drawings, pointed out a few minor anatomical errors here and there, but stated very firmly that he did not think even a trained artist could produce work of such variety and skill under the conditions we described—which he later saw for himself.

There remained one other doubt to clear up. Luiz had been producing drawings for about ten years, and somebody suggested that he might have simply memorised a set of portraits to the point where he could reproduce the same ones on demand. Accordingly, we asked to look at all the drawings he had preserved, and Luiz obligingly produced a number of thick folders containing over a thousand examples of his work. Many more had been given away, but none had ever been sold. No two pictures were identical, though many could be grouped into categories that strongly recalled the work of a dozen masters from Rembrandt and Hals to Manet, Degas, Renoir and Modigliani. There were ornately dressed laughing cavaliers, more sombre faces of elderly Jews, elegant Parisiennes, shapely ballerinas, voluptuous-looking models and a host of others, many unsigned.

Here indeed was the Rosemary Brown of the art world. London housewife Rosemary Brown has baffled critics for several years by producing a stream of piano pieces in the style of several dead composers, especially Liszt. She has had little musical training, yet she has somehow written down music that is recognisably in the style of the composer who purports to have dictated it from the spirit world. British (living) composer Humphrey Searle, a recognised authority on Liszt, has said that one of her pieces, *Grübelei*, is the kind of music Liszt might have written had he lived a few years longer, and that it is not a paraphrase of anything he is known to have written while alive. Mrs Brown's pieces contain faults, according to Vernon Harrison, a founder member of the Liszt Society, but they are 'too good to dismiss lightly'.[1]

So it is with Luiz Gasparetto. His drawings are there for all to see, and he is convinced that they are the work of the spirits of the artists concerned. Luiz is an intelligent, well-educated young man from a comfortable middle-class family. He has never sought publicity, nor objected to being studied by researchers. He spends much of his time working without pay at a school for retarded children, and he does intend eventually to sell his drawings—to raise money for a new Spiritist centre. I am sure we shall hear more of him.

Next, let me introduce you to a lady from Pompeii.

Celia, as I shall call her here, is an attractive and vivacious lady of about fifty, though she looks fifteen years younger. Her husband, Leo, is a very successful construction engineer, and their daughter has married into one of Brazil's grand old families. I have known them well for more than three years, and have spent many hours listening to Celia's accounts of her extraordinary life. These would fill a book, and will one day, hopefully written by Celia herself . . .

From a very early age, it was clear that she was not like the other little girls in the small town where she was born into a wealthy and traditional Catholic family of pure Brazilian lineage. As her mother and family servant (both still living) and Celia herself readily agree, she was a little terror.

By the time she was six years old, she had developed two great passions; dancing and boys. Rather than play with her many expensive toys, she would be out in the streets with the gang, inventing contests in which the winner had to kiss her on the mouth. She would go out of her way to play off one little boy friend against another, and one of her early triumphs was a knife fight provoked in her honour. She loved every minute of it.

At the age of eight, she saw a man shot dead in front of her. She calmly gave her parents the details over dinner, putting them off their appetites while she munched a bloody underdone steak without a qualm. On another occasion, she watched impassively as a man was lynched to death with iron crowbars. Such callousness in the face of death is most untypical in Brazilian women; once, Celia was driving me across São Paulo when we passed the scene of a rather gruesome road accident in which a motor-cycle had been flattened by a large truck. Celia drove by without a single comment; the incident meant no more to her than a hole in the road.

Almost as soon as she was able to walk, she began to dance. Most little girls like dancing, but Celia really took it seriously. When her parents went out for the evening, she would make up her pugnacious little face at her mother's dressing table, drape any piece of cloth available around her skinny body, put a record on the gramophone and simply take over the whole house, dancing wildly all over the place. One night her parents brought some friends home, to find Celia swirling sensuously around the living room stark naked. Her father's colleagues watched in amazement. 'Who taught you to move your body like that?' one asked. But nobody had taught her anything; behaving like a Spanish gypsy seemed to come naturally to her.

After lunch, she would reluctantly have to lie down in her room and rest. But instead of sleeping, she would often lie and stare at the white ceiling, where she would see scenes of startling eroticism. Men and women were taking part in Roman-style orgies, drinking, lying around and making love to each other, and Celia felt she was part of the action as well. One of her older boy friends had told her, when she was six, all the details of how men and women made love, and she had listened without interest. She already knew.

She had her first clear memory of another lifetime at the age of five, as she sat on the steps of the house one day and gazed into the blue sky above. Suddenly she seemed to be somewhere else, under another blue sky, and the thought of it gave her a sudden feeling of melancholy and nostalgia. Nostalgia for what, she could not say.

From then on, throughout her life, Celia has had a series of recurrent dreams, some of which still come two or three times a year. Three of them are especially vivid, and it has often taken her all day to recover from the effects of them.

In the first, she is in a boat approaching an island—not a typical Brazilian one with sandy beaches and palm trees, but a bare slab of rock lashed by violent seas. She feels she is being taken there for some specific reason, and can see flaming torches dotted around the island.

The second recurrent dream takes place in a dark room that seems like a sort of corridor made of blocks of stone. Various men are lounging about on benches, flirting with a young girl whom Celia knows to be herself. Through a window she can see people walking about with baskets on their heads, coming back from market. Everybody is wearing tunics. At the end of the dream, she walks down a passage on the way out of what seems to be a bath house, and meets a sallow-faced old man who blocks her way. She feels a great desire to excite him sexually, and kisses him on the mouth, but is horrified to find his lips are stone cold. 'You can't do me any more harm,' the man says, 'because I have been dead for two thousand years.'

The third dream is by far the most vivid and frightening. Celia is at the window of her house, looking over the rooftops at a distant mountain. Suddenly she gets a feeling of terror, runs out of the house, along a street, through an archway and on to a beach. Then she rushes headlong into the sea and is drowned.

In addition to these three recurrent dreams, Celia has had a number of once-only ones that she has remembered in great detail. In one, she is dancing around a camp fire and doing her best to provoke a man who eventually takes her by the waist, forces her to the ground and kills her. In another, somebody is singing a Spanish gypsy song to guitar accompaniment, while she plays a game where she has to eat a whole plate of grapes before the music stops. In another, she is simply eating a meal in a poor-looking brick house, picking up pieces of sausage with her fingers and dipping them in salt. In all these dreams, she is aware that she is a member of a tribe of Spanish gypsies, and one of its star dancers.

When Celia heard the sound of castanets for the first time, she became so excited that she followed the sound to a ballet school near her house, where she marched in and immediately started to learn Spanish dancing. Or, more accurately, she just started to do it, for she seemed to know it all and there was little her teacher could tell her. She took to the castanets like a duck to water and became the best dancer in the school.

Spanish dancing is not widely popular in Brazil, where the majority of the people are of Portuguese stock and Spanish immigrants have tended to abandon their native customs. Even traditional Portuguese folk music is rarely heard, and Spanish music almost never. Yet to Celia, flamenco dancing was the most natural thing in the world, and soon she was to become quite well known for a time as a Spanish dancer on television, convincing many of her partners that she came from Spain, although she had never been there. At least, not in this lifetime.

Girls tend to be strictly brought up in Brazil, especially in Catholic families from small towns in the interior. But Celia refused to conform to any conventions. As a child, she would peel off her clothes and jump naked into the swimming pool regardless of who might be watching. She would drink wine and beer without feeling this was in any way unusual. Early in her teens, she would go all out not only to attract men but to sleep with them, and by the time she was an adult, she was something of a nymphomaniac.

Moving to the city of São Paulo, she soon met her future husband and married him when she was twenty-four. Leo was engaged already, but Celia simply set out to push the other girl out of the way and get her man. They became a couple of young swingers, living it up all night in bars and clubs and making love to each other (which they still do at least twice a week) on all possible occasions. Eventually they had to reinforce their sex lives with pornographic films and books, of which Celia bought and read large quantities although she has scarcely ever read any other kind of book. They even indulged in sex à trois, with the help of a lady friend brought in to liven up their night life.

After some years of this sort of behaviour, odd things began to happen. Doors would slam loudly in the night, lights would turn on and off, and inexplicable noises of all kinds would be heard when there was nobody else in the house. On the advice of a close friend familiar with poltergeist phenomena, who told them that such things often happened to people who led sexually depraved lives, they decided to change their way of living and behave more normally.

Both Leo and Celia learned to their surprise that they were what are known as mediums. They went along to the São Paulo Spiritist Federation to study this strange phenomenon, and Leo soon found he had an unusual ability to transfer energy to other people through what are called mediumistic passes. Neither of them was ever what could be called the religious type, as they are not today, but in retrospect both feel that they were literally saved by their Spiritist friends from a life of total depravity and uselessness.

In 1970, Celia went abroad for the first time in her life, on a grand tour of Europe with her daughter and three close friends. They saw all the usual tourist sights, none of which made much impression on Celia. But when they took a boat to the island of Ischia, off the Italian coast, she had one of the most profound shocks of her life. There was 'her' rock, the one she had been dreaming about for forty years. It was exactly the shape it had been in her dreams, although it was now dotted with luxury villas instead of flaming torches. She had unquestionably been there before.

Then the party went to visit the ruined Roman city of Pompeii, near the volcanic Mount Vesuvius that had showered it with flaming lava in the year AD 69. As soon as she set foot in the place, Celia led her friends on a guided tour of the well preserved ruins, pointing out *her* bath house, *her* amphitheatre, and finally *her* house. To everybody's alarm (except Celia's), they learned from the real tourist guide that this had been the local brothel and was not open to visitors.

The following year, Celia came back to Pompeii with Leo and they spent more time there. She was furious to find that *her* house was still locked up, and only after much persuasion and bribery were they able to get inside. Celia had already described the place in detail to her husband. Upstairs there were a number of small rooms, each decorated with friezes of pornographic scenes, showing naked men and women doing things that may be new even to students of the Kama Sutra of Vatsyayana. And from the small window in her room, there was a perfectly framed view of Mount Vesuvius.

They went into the building, and there it all was, exactly as Celia had so often seen and described it. The friezes were still there, and Vesuvius was still where it always had been—neatly framed in the window of her room. In great excitement, Celia led her husband out of the whorehouse and showed him the route she had taken on the day the mountain had erupted. She led him along *her* street, the Via dell'Abbondanza, under the arch and outside the city limits.

Here, something was wrong. There was no sea in sight. The coastline was more than a mile away, and a group of archaeologists was digging in the ground near the spot where Celia recalled making her fatal dash into the waves. They went over to talk to the archaeologists, asking if they knew by any chance where the shoreline had been at the time of the destruction of Pompeii.

'Right here, *Signora*,' they replied.

Celia had hardly heard of Pompeii in her present life. As a child she had scarcely read anything, and her filmgoing had been restricted to the regular local fare of Tom Mix and Rin Tin Tin. There was no television in Brazil in those days. She had in fact always thought that her dreams were of ancient Egypt rather than Pompeii. But after her two visits to the ruined Roman seaside resort, a flood of detailed memories came back to her, and in 1973 she recorded sixteen hours of these memories on tape, which will one day form the basis of a full-length book.

I wondered if she had ever read Bulwer-Lytton's *Last Days of Pompeii*, or any of the Roman novels received by the Brazilian automatic writing medium Francisco Candido Xavier. She had, she told me, recently picked up a copy of the former, but given it up half way.

'It wasn't like that at all,' she commented. It does not seem likely that her memories of Pompeii were put there by anything she had read. Women, she assured me, were not the meek and passive creatures depicted in Bulwer-Lytton's book. 'We used to run everything in those days!'

On their way back to Brazil (after Leo had had some difficulty in dragging his wife away from Pompeii), the couple stopped off in Spain. Having identified the site of one past life, Celia was determined to locate another. She never managed to discover a particular place she recognised as easily as Pompeii or Ischia, but she felt quite at home in the dry countryside around Granada, and was flattered when a shop assistant refused to believe she was a Brazilian. '¡Parece más una española que yo!' the woman said. ('You look more Spanish than I do!') On several other occasions she would be greeted by Spaniards with the question 'But aren't you a *mora*—a gypsy?' As far as she was concerned, of course, she was. Or had been.

Readers may have concluded by now that Celia is no more than a hysterical, suggestible and altogether nutty member of the wealthy classes, who has nothing better to do than dream. This would be quite wrong; it is not possible to feel this way if you actually know her as well as I do. She is certainly not a typical Brazilian; women of her age and social status tend to show extreme class consciousness and do all they can to preserve, or simulate, an appearance of respectability and culture. Celia, however, could not care less about social conventions. Her high society friends regard her as a colourful eccentric, vivacious and uninhibited but never vulgar or crude, though they are impressed by her fearless character. Once, she spotted a suspicious-looking prowler outside her house, and rather than call the police or her husband, she took her own revolver, stuck it in the astonished man's back and marched him over a mile to the nearest police station. Brazilian women do not normally do such things.

There is no ready explanation as to how the daughter of a rich and respectable family (her father was a senior government official) should grow into a reincarnation of a Spanish gypsy or a trollop from Pompeii, which Celia freely admits she was, in great detail. Hers is the kind of experience that seems to cross the border from the merely abnormal into the totally paranormal. She accepts reincarnation as a matter of course, though she has not the slightest interest in the religious or metaphysical aspects of this much-debated subject. As far as she is concerned, her present life is merely one stage in the long personal process of evolution through trial, error and experience. She is aware of the fact that in this lifetime she has been happily married for the first time, to a man she has known several times before. Her delightful daughter does not resemble her in the least; she is a quiet and well-balanced girl whose presence in the family home seems to bring her lively extrovert parents together and calm them down.

Celia is a very practical person, an efficient organiser of social and charitable functions, and the most popular teacher at the ballet school where she gives lessons in Spanish dancing. She has little interest in the paranormal as such, though she accepts the basic principles of Spiritism. She takes a realistic attitude towards her own experience, feeling that she was born this time round into a family that gave her a chance to improve on her licentious former lives, although this took some time; to make an excellent marriage and raise a daughter whose virtues are as noticeable as her own shortcomings, to do some useful social work and generally become more aware of the purpose of life, death and rebirth.

Reincarnation, as I shall show in later chapters, is no longer a branch of the occult, but a subject now undergoing serious and systematic research, though the general public is still unaware of this. When it has been widely accepted as a fact,

there will be no more need to speculate as to whether we survive bodily death or not. We could hardly reincarnate if we
didn't.

I mention these two cases from my own experience to show
how the paranormal is there for anybody who looks for it.
Looking for it may take time and patience; few of Celia's
friends have any idea of the real story of her life, and Luiz
Antonio Gasparetto does not advertise his drawing sessions in
the local paper. But once you set out to look for such cases, you
eventually find them. Readers can do a simple experiment:
interrogate twenty of your friends tactfully, and the chances
are that at least one will have had an experience as interesting,
and as inexplicable by normal methods, as either Luiz or Celia.
If not, they will be able to put you in touch with somebody who
has.

It is perfectly natural for people to doubt the existence of the
psi world—the world of the paranormal—simply because they
have never come across it. Quite often, even when we do come
across it, we easily convince ourselves that we were mistaken.
Most of us have a deeply rooted aversion to any situation that
forces us to revise our concept of the order of the universe,
assuming we ever had one. This is quite natural and probably
a healthy factor in a balanced society. It is also quite natural
that others should go to the other extreme and see flying
saucers every time they look out of the window.

When I was first put onto the trail of Luiz, the artist, by a
very good friend who seems to me to be over-inclined to see
flying saucers, I refused to believe at first that he did what she
said he did. This was because my friend had previously told me
about a number of other phenomena that turned out to have
a normal explanation when I looked into them further. But
after I had seen Luiz at work, I had to let the facts speak for
themselves. What he did was simply not normal. Nor has
Celia's life been normal.

Ninety-nine per cent of all allegedly paranormal facts may
have a normal explanation, though I doubt if this is so. That

would still leave one per cent, the validity of which is not affected. A forged banknote does not make a real one any less real.

Now, let us take a quick look at just a few of the paranormal facts that have been reliably reported over the last hundred years or so. It is important to agree that psi events really *do* happen quite often before we get down to thinking about ways in which they *could* happen. When I say that these things really do happen, all I mean is that the evidence for them, while it may not be unshakeable, has not yet been successfully shaken. As I have said before, there are no certainties nowadays, only degrees of probability.

Paranormal, or psi, phenomena can be classified into two general categories; physical and mental. When a person seems to provoke one or the other we call him or her a medium. Luiz, the artist, is a physical effects medium, whereas my friend Celia produces evidence for purely mental phenomena. Physical psi phenomena are much rarer than mental ones, and though physical mediums sometimes produce mental phenomena, the reverse is rarely the case.

The greatest of all modern physical mediums was the amazing Daniel Dunglas Home, whose reputation has survived more or less intact since his death in 1886 at the age of fifty-three. The most (though not the first) distinguished scientist to investigate psi phenomena was Sir William Crookes (1832–1919); therefore Crookes's laboratory sessions with Home are of exceptional value. Crookes spent only about four years of his long and active life looking into what he called the 'phenomena of Spiritualism', but in that time he managed to observe and record more such phenomena than most subsequent researchers have been able to manage in a lifetime.

He studied at least a dozen mediums, finding some to be fraudulent. He was once visited by a black gentleman who claimed to be able to handle a red-hot iron. So he could, and did. But, Crookes records, 'the house was pervaded for hours afterwards with the smell of roast negro'.[2]

Home, with whom Crookes had twenty-nine sittings between 1870 and 1873, was the most cooperative of mediums. 'Take every precaution you can devise,' he told Crookes. 'Don't consider my feelings. I shall not be offended.' Many of the sessions were held in Crookes's own house, with members of his family and some friends present. Crookes did his best to persuade other scientists to come and watch, but most refused. Sir William Huggins, a fellow-Fellow of the Royal Society, did come to one session, but the general establishment attitude was much the same as that of T. H. Huxley towards similar research by the London Dialectical Society.*

'Supposing these phenomena to be true,' said Huxley, 'they do not interest me.'[3] The same Huxley had written earlier that the world is 'full of untold novelties for him who has the eyes to see them'.[4]

You could never tell what might happen when Home was on top form, and so many astonishing things did happen that Crookes had to classify them under 13 headings. Here we have almost every psi phenomenon in the book: rappings, levitations of objects (also of Crookes's wife!), alteration in the weight of inert bodies, luminous materialisations, direct writing by hands visible or invisible, plus such Home specialities as making an accordion play inside a closed cage or handling burning coals —without leaving a smell of roast Home in the house.

The best account of paranormal physical phenomena ever recorded is the one published by the Hon. Everard Feilding, Hereward Carrington and W. W. Baggally after their dozen 1908 sessions with Eusapia Palladino, the only physical medium who deserves to be mentioned in the same breath as D. D. Home. Nobody has yet managed to shake their evidence, which lists no less than 470 separate inexplicable phenomena as having

* Just as, almost exactly a hundred years later, Professor John Taylor of King's College, University of London, had difficulty in persuading some of his colleagues to watch his metal-bending experiments. 'Any scientist who investigates Uri Geller is not worth his salt', Taylor was told by Sir George Porter, director of the Royal Institution of Great Britain.

taken place under conditions that made fraud or deception the least likely of explanations.[5]

Feilding, a member of an aristocratic Roman Catholic family, is hardly likely to have had much interest in proving the reality of phenomena in which the spirits of the departed might be taking part. He had, in his own words, 'a fairly complete education at the hands of fraudulent mediums', and he cannot have been much impressed by the reputation of Eusapia, a temperamental Neapolitan who had been regularly investigated since 1892 by some very distinguished men, such as Aksakof, Richet, Myers, Lodge, Flammarion, Bergson, and Pierre and Marie Curie. She had equally regularly been caught cheating in between bouts of apparently genuine physical mediumship.

Feilding's colleagues were both experienced investigators with wide knowledge of conjuring. Baggally came to the sessions convinced that there was no such thing as paranormal physical phenomena, while only the year before Carrington had published a book called *The Physical Phenomena of Spiritualism, Fraudulent and Genuine*, giving a vivid picture of the high degree of skill fraudulent mediums had reached by then, and describing a number of amazingly intricate tricks in minute detail. As for Feilding himself, Dr E. J. Dingwall has called him 'one of the noblest characters I ever met' as well as 'the most acute and well balanced investigator'.[6] Such words from the most experienced investigator of this century, and the most devastating critic both of mediums and of other investigators, amount to a kind of official decoration.

The stage was surely set for the definitive explosion of the Palladino myth. The Feilding team set new standards for investigations of this type; they prepared the séance room themselves, weighing and measuring everything in it, they only brought the medium in when sessions were due to begin, and they hired a shorthand writer to take down every word they said while the séances were in progress. The verbatim minute-by-minute account of what went on during these séances runs for over 200 printed pages, and includes accounts not only of what was stated to be happening but also of what each investigator was doing at the time. It is the thoroughness of this report as much as the phenomena described that makes it so important.

And what phenomena! Feilding found, to his surprise and delight, that the tighter the controls he imposed—the tightness depending on what kind of mood the lady was in—the better the quality of phenomena; 1908 was certainly vintage Palladino year.

The séance table would jump about and rise into the air. Loud raps would be heard on it, and also from the curtained-off cabinets behind the medium's chair. The investigators were touched by unseen hands. A cold breeze would blow from the direction of Eusapia's brow. A guitar string was plucked behind the curtain. A handbell was carried out of the cabinet. Four reef knots tied round Eusapia's leg were untied. Blue, green and yellow lights flashed. At one point, what looked alarmingly like a human head was seen to peer through the curtains. (Some sort of light was on throughout all the sessions except for brief intervals.) On another occasion the small table inside the cabinet burst through the curtains, levitated itself over Eusapia's shoulder and tried to climb onto the main table. Both the medium's hands and feet were being held at the time. Here is just one example of the way the main table (weight: 10 lb. 8 oz. or 4.75 kilos) levitated while the medium was under full control by all three investigators:

10.23 p.m. *Complete levitation of the table.*

Feilding. *I had my hands on the floor between her legs and the table legs. Her feet and the whole of her dress were in between my hands.*

Carrington. *My left hand on her right knee, her right hand being on the top of my left hand and did not leave it.*

Baggally. *My right hand was on her left knee, her left hand on the top of my right hand. My foot was away from her foot, but F. had complete control of her feet.*

This is a description of just one of forty-five table levitations and over 400 other phenomena. It takes a little working out as to whose hand or foot was where, but it is fairly clear that Palladino's were usually where they should have been.

One of the most interesting aspects of the whole series of sessions was the way in which the three experienced and initially sceptical investigators reacted to what they saw, heard and felt. 'The mind confronted with an obviously absurd isolated fact merely rebels,' Feilding comments, though after 470 obviously absurd facts he was no longer able to rebel. He makes it very clear how unwilling he was to admit the reality of the paranormal.

'With great intellectual reluctance,' he writes, 'we are of the opinion that we have witnessed in the presence of Eusapia Palladino the action of some telekinetic force, the nature and origin of which we cannot attempt to specify, through which, without the introduction of either accomplices, apparatus, or manual dexterity, she is able to produce movements of, and percussive and other sounds in, objects at a distance from her and unconnected with her in any apparent physical manner, and also to produce matter, or the appearance of matter, without any determinable source of supply.'

This is the syntax of an intelligent man choosing his words carefully as he attempts to describe the indescribable, and to come to terms with the psi world. Feilding was honest enough to admit that he was *intellectually* convinced that the phenomena had really taken place long before he was also *emotionally* convinced. His colleague Carrington vividly expresses how they all felt during the early sessions when he says that 'the incidents seemed to roll off our minds' and that 'we lapsed back into scepticism' on the morning after each of the first four or five sessions. Over and over again we find such phrases in their report as 'I was consequently forced to the conclusion that these phenomena were absolutely genuine', 'one or two of the phenomena occurred under what I was forced to regard as ideal conditions of control', 'absolute conviction . . .', 'complete certainty . . .'

They hated to have to admit it, but the phenomena *were real.*

No court of law could reject evidence of the quality of that presented by Feilding and his colleagues after the 1908 Palladino sessions in Naples. We shall be lucky if we ever get evidence for psi phenomena as detailed and convincing as this.

There have been no physical-effects mediums quite in the Home-Palladino class, with the possible exception of the enigmatic Brazilian Carmine Mirabelli, who died in 1951. Had he ever been properly investigated, he might have qualified as one of the Big Three, but as it is his reputation must remain in some doubt.

Turning now to the mental phenomena of mediumship, we find that plenty of evidence for telepathy, clairvoyance and precognition had been collected long before the Rhines began demonstrating them in the Duke University laboratory with their dice and Zener cards.

The greatest of the modern mental-effects mediums was Mrs Leonora E. Piper of Boston, who flourished between about 1885 and 1915, though she lived until 1950. She was investigated very thoroughly by such men as the physicist (Sir) Oliver Lodge, the psychologist William James, and Richard Hodgson of the SPR, who published over 450 pages of reports on her in the society's *Proceedings*.

At a series of sessions beginning in March 1892, Mrs Piper produced a steady stream of information purporting to come from a young lawyer called George Pellew, who had died accidentally the previous month, aged thirty-two. This material is generally regarded by those who have studied it as some of the best evidence ever recorded for the survival of death by a human personality.

Mrs Piper convinced Lodge of survival and the possibility of communication with the departed at some sessions held in Cambridge (England) with Frederic Myers in 1889–90, producing apparent messages from two of Lodge's deceased relatives. (This was long before Lodge became widely known as a champion of survival, and also several years before his greatest scientific achievement, the demonstration of wireless transmission, which he, and not Marconi, was the first to do in public.)

It was also Mrs Piper who led William James to declare that through her trances knowledge appeared that she could not have gained 'by the ordinary waking use of her eyes and ears and wits'. At one session, she told him that his Aunt Kate had just died, and that he would receive the news when he got home. James went home an hour later to find a telegram informing him that Aunt Kate had indeed just died, at almost exactly the time Mrs Piper said she had. The helpful medium also used her abilities to locate a bank book that had been mislaid by a member of James's family. James is often quoted as saying that 'if you wish to upset the law that all crows are black, you mustn't seek to show that no crows are; it is enough if you prove one single crow to be white'. Less often quoted is what he said next: 'My own white crow is Mrs Piper.'[7]

As for Richard Hodgson, he was led to declare after prolonged investigation of the amiable and cooperative Bostonian that 'I cannot profess to have any doubt but that the chief "communicators". . . are veritably the personalities that they claim to be, that they have survived the change we call death, and that they have directly communicated with us whom we call living, through Mrs Piper's entranced organism'.[8]

Talents comparable to hers were displayed by a number of British mediums, including Gladys Osborne Leonard, Winifred Coombe Tennant (who used the pseudonym Mrs Willett), Bertha Harris and the Irish-born Eileen Garrett.

Mrs Leonard was investigated for more than forty years by members of the SPR. One of her specialities was the 'book test', in which she would go into trance and tell her client to take, say, the tenth book from the left of the third shelf from the top of her bookcase at home (where Mrs Leonard had never been), open it at page 58 and find a reference there that would suggest survival after death. This happened successfully far too often for coincidence. Mrs Leonard once told a widow to look for a book the widow never knew to exist, describing the contents in detail and claiming to have gained information about it from the widow's late husband. (The book was duly found.) Many people, including some of her investigators, became convinced of the reality of life beyond the grave after sessions with Mrs Leonard.

Mrs Coombe Tennant spent much of her life in public service, as a magistrate and Justice of the Peace. She was the first British woman delegate to the League of Nations Assembly. As 'Mrs Willett', she was one of the team (joined for a time by Mrs Piper) who helped assemble the well-known series of messages purporting to come from the spirits of F. W. H. Myers, one of the SPR founders, and several of his colleagues. The interesting feature of the 'Myers cross-correspondences', which went on for some thirty years, is that bits of information would be produced by different mediums, usually by automatic writing, which would only make sense when put together and read as a single message. Often the mediums concerned were in different countries, neither having known Myers or each other personally. We shall never get to the bottom of this mystery, since much of the original material is no longer available. What has been published offers solid evidence for paranormal communication between living minds, and very possibly between dead ones and living ones. Many of those who were most closely connected with the material at the time it was produced came to the conclusion that it really did come from the discarnate Myers and his psi friends.

Bertha Harris, the London Spiritualist medium, is less well-known than she deserves to be. She herself has published a delightful account of her remarkable abilities and some of the great men, including Churchill and de Gaulle, who benefited from them.[9] I have two reasons for feeling especially grateful to her. One is that at my first session with her in 1973 I was fully satisfied for the first time that a good medium can spontaneously produce knowledge of a sitter which she could not have gained by any normal means. Personal experience of paranormal phenomena is essential if one is to reach emotional as well as intellectual conviction regarding them. The other reason is that, thanks to Mrs Harris, I have something in common with Sir William Crookes, which is a flattering thought. Bertha began her work as a medium at an early age, and had a number of sittings with Crookes in 1917.

Eileen Garrett, originator of the Parapsychology Foundation and author of a number of books, is too well known to need much comment here. She was thoroughly researched by many investigators—notably Lawrence LeShan and Andrija Puharich —from the time she and Bertha Harris were fellow students at the London College of Psychic Science. Mrs Garrett, who died in 1971, is possibly the only medium in history ever to have commissioned a full investigation of herself.

Before we leave mental mediumship, mention should be made of Edgar Cayce, probably the most influential medium of this century. Cayce provided a staggering amount of well documented evidence for telepathy, clairvoyance and precognition through more than 14,000 'readings' given to people often hundreds of miles from where he lay in trance. His work is impressive for its sheer volume, its consistency, and for the wide variety of information he kept producing for some forty years up to his death in 1945. This ranged from precise medical diagnoses and dietary advice (it was from Cayce that I learned to make potato-peel soup!) to occult revelations about reincarnation, ancient Egypt, Atlantis and the Essenes.

Unlike most mental mediums, Cayce never claimed to be controlled by a 'spirit guide', and although some of his religious exhortations may have come from his own subconscious, the source of the greater part of the knowledge he produced while in trance has never been satisfactorily identified. The greatest mystery about him is why he was never properly investigated. Dr Rhine tried without success to test him under controlled conditions, but no psi research organisation seems to have taken much notice of him either before or after his death. We shall hear more from Cayce later in this book.

It may be asked why, in view of all the evidence, of which the above pages contain only a tiny sample, there should still be any doubt regarding the mental and physical phenomena I have mentioned. There are at least five good reasons why this is so:

First: people tend to ignore published facts or to reject them. I cannot blame them in either case—it is possible to live a long and useful life without worrying about the mysteries of the psi world. But I do blame people who *deny* established facts without having studied them. There is one school today that thinks evidence for a psi event should be considered worthless if there is any possible alternative explanation, however wildly far-fetched. If this line of reasoning were to be used in the courts, no criminal would ever go to jail.

Second: people familiar with the facts often deny them because they have a vested interest in doing so, usually a religious or a political one. If the main thesis of this book is ever proved true, one of its possible side effects is that it will help do away with most religions, as well as Marxist dialectical materialism, with one fell swoop. I face this prospect with some amusement, and fully expect to be torn to pieces by Marxist and Catholic alike. I only hope my dismemberment will be followed by hypotheses more accurate than mine, though I do not think this is likely from either extremist camp. I have nothing to say to Catholics, who know everything already, but Marxist readers might like to reflect upon Lenin's observation that 'the human intellect has discovered much that was unknown in nature and will discover much more, thereby ever increasing its power over her', and also Marx's remark that scientific research 'captures only the false appearance of things', an observation confirmed by some of the findings of twentieth-century physics.

Third: very little time is given nowadays to tackling the mysteries of the psi world on a full-time basis. This is a job for specialists, and most qualified people are already too busy. There is not more than a handful of full-time psi researchers anywhere in the world today, and never has been.* If the same single-minded devotion were given to the subject as is given

* W. G. Roll estimates the number at thirty.

daily to the well-financed perfection of toothpaste or bombs, great dents would be made in the frontiers of human knowledge.

The fourth reason is the most interesting of all, for it concerns the investigator himself.

In January 1899, Charles Richet addressed the SPR on what he called the conditions of certainty. His remarks in 1899 make an interesting comparison with those of Feilding and Carrington quoted earlier in this chapter.

At the moment when these facts take place, they seem to us certain, and we are willing to proclaim them openly. But when we return to ourselves, when we feel the irresistible influence of our environment, when our friends all laugh at our credulity; then we are almost disarmed, and we begin to doubt. May it not all have been an illusion? May I not have been grossly deceived? I *saw*, no doubt; but did I see aright? . . . And then, as the moment of the experiment becomes more remote, that experiment which once seemed so conclusive gets to seem more and more uncertain, and we end by letting ourselves be persuaded that we have been the victims of a trick.

Our own conviction—the conviction of men who have seen—ought properly to convince other people; but, by a curious inversion of roles, it is *their* conviction, the negative conviction of people who have *not* seen, and who ought not, one would think, to speak on the matter, which weakens and ultimately destroys our own conviction. This phenomenon occurred in my case with such intensity that scarcely a fortnight after witnessing the experiments with Eusapia Palladino, at Milan (1892), I had persuaded myself that there had been nothing beyond fraud and illusion.*[10]

Finally, it is sad but true that human beings have an instinctive aversion to really new ideas. They can be a serious threat to our precious security; and insecurity, with all the aggressive

* Punctuation slightly altered from original.

behaviour that goes with it, is probably the leading disease of our times.

The Greeks, as always, had a word for it: *misoneism*, or hatred (*miso-*) for the new (*neos*). Dr Walter Leaf, a leading brain of the SPR, seems to have said the last word on the subject back in 1895:

> A new idea . . . means a modification of brain-substance; but all living beings tend to resist anything that causes an expenditure of energy, and therefore anything that tends to modify their organs. This resistance to change, among other effects, produces in the region of thought a secondary form of 'positivism' . . . Scientific positivism is the progressive adaptation of the intelligence solely and entirely to the facts of experience; this operates to the good of the species.
>
> But there is another sort of positivism which may be called that of the individual economy; this urges the individual to avoid the necessity of new and painful adaptations of the intellect involving expenditure of energy, and therefore operates hurtfully to progress. A man conscious that he is a factor in the advance of humanity will always be subject to the opposition of these two sorts of positivism, and is tempted to confound with scientific positivism that which is only the expression of his own individual desire to avoid painful effort.
>
> The psychical enquirer must endeavour, in the first place, to accept as fact nothing but fact, but at the same time he must not shirk the painful effort to adapt his mind, by gradual steps, from ideas already familiar, to those which are new, and that with the least possible waste of intellectual energy.[11]

The BBC broadcasts an interesting and useful programme on its World Service called *New Ideas*. In all the years I have listened to this programme, I have never heard a really new idea, merely refinements of old ones—better seat belts for cars, better invalid carriages, and so on. All very admirable, but scarcely ever radically new.

What happens to people who have *really* new ideas?

We all know what happened to Galileo when he had the cheek to prove, among other things, that masses of unequal weight fell with equal velocity, and that the earth moved round the sun, although everybody else at the time knew perfectly well that both claims were nonsense. (Yet we still use such nonsensical words as 'sunrise' and 'sunset'.)

We know the outbursts of scorn, hostility or plain apathy that greeted Harvey and his blood circulation theory, Lister and his antiseptics, Paré and his stitches, Pasteur and his germs, Jenner and his vaccinations, Mesmer and his whatever-it-was, Braid and his hypnosis, Hahnemann and his homeopathy, Edison and his phonograph, Bell and his telephone, Langley and his aeroplane and Freud with his psychoanalysis.

'More fancies, more blunders, more unfounded hypotheses, more gratuitous fictions', grumbled the *Edinburgh Review* in 1803 when Thomas Young proved his wave theory of light. (Proved, mind you, not suggested.) The same learned journal urged the public to put Thomas Gray in a strait-jacket for claiming that railways were a practical proposition. Sir Humphry Davy hooted with laughter at the idea that London could be lighted with, of all things, gas! Stephenson was assured that locomotives could never go more than 12 mph. The French Academy of Sciences refused to listen to Arago's wild ideas about 'wireless telegraphy'.

Baron Georges Cuvier, founder of comparative anatomy, was given a skeleton in 1823 that had been found in the Rhine mud by a geologist aptly named Boué. He refused to take it seriously and simply threw the thing away. Two years later, a British archaeologist named McEnery discovered worked flints and extinct animal remains at Kent's Hole Cavern. The Geological Society rejected papers on his findings in 1840 and 1854, and he was only finally vindicated in 1869.

Have things improved for innovators in this century?

Einstein was forced from his homeland by a régime that believed the cosmos to be packed with eternal ice (a new idea, admittedly). Teilhard de Chardin was given the Galileo treatment by a church that welcomes new ideas the way ducks' backs welcome water. The British Astronomer Royal declared space travel to be 'utter bilge' the very year before Yuri Gagarin orbited merrily round the earth in Vostok I on April 12th 1961, and found it to be blue. British officials told Frank Whittle to stop wasting time trying to invent the jet engine, which he went ahead and did in 1937. The harmless Immanuel Velikovsky was threatened with the loss of his right to publish; Wilhelm Reich was literally persecuted to death by the U.S. Government; George de la Warr was ruined by a British court case; and more recently the Soviet psi researcher Eduard K. Naumov was sent to Siberia for the crime of putting 'international cooperation' in his field into practice. As for the unfortunate psychics, the Brazilian healer Arigó was twice sentenced to prison, while the Frenchman Alalouf has been harassed by the law most of his life—healing being apparently illegal in France except at Lourdes. Anybody with a truly original idea even today is advised to keep quiet about it.

But the problem with psi phenomena is that any explanation for them *must be truly original*. Therefore, it will probably be rejected. This has led many psi researchers into an attitude of such extreme caution that one feels they are scared stiff by the idea of actually discovering anything new.

And yet, somehow, psi research has become an officially recognised branch of scientific endeavour, at least in the U.S. After some energetic lobbying from the anthropologist Margaret Mead (whose own field was not accepted as a science in the last century), the American Association for the Advancement of Science accepted the affiliation of the Parapsychological Association—psi's professional body—in 1969. It was over a hundred years since Robert Hare had tried in vain to interest the same outfit in the phenomena of Spiritualism, and forty years after the Rhines had become the first qualified scientists to devote their lives to full-time study of psi phenomena. Better late than never.

It would be nice for researchers if psi phenomena happened more often, and if we had more people around like Home and

Palladino to lift tables and Mrs Piper to produce information from discarnate sources. Indeed, really good psi phenomena (by which I mean events for which no normal explanation seems more probable than a paranormal one, and for which the evidence has not been shaken) happen so seldom that many find it easier to assume that they never really happen at all. But not all scientists feel the same way as Prof. Wald's anonymous colleague mentioned in the Introduction.

'Rarity has nothing to do with reality,' says the astronomer V. A. Firsoff, who takes a lively and creative interest in psi. 'One elephant is just as real as a hundred elephants, and quite sufficient to establish the existence of elephants.' He points out that nobody has observed a supernova in our galaxy since Kepler's time, though modern telescopes reveal that they exist in other galaxies. 'They would still be there if these telescopes did not exist.'[12]

One Palladino, then, is as real as a hundred Palladinos, and enough to establish the existence of physical psi phenomena. Likewise, Mrs Piper established the reality of mental ones. If astronomy developed thanks to better telescopes, psi research grew mainly thanks to better researchers. In the following chapter, we meet some of the intrepid few—physicists, chemists and biologists as well as mystics and a French schoolmaster—who have rushed in where the Establishment has feared to tread, and who have tried to serve their fellow men by sketching out maps of unknown areas of the human condition.

Chapter 4

VENTURES INTO THE PSI WORLD

Nature seems reluctant to reveal her secrets to the intellectually arrogant. BURR

The sphere of my vision now began to widen . . . Next, I could distinctly perceive the walls of the house. At first they seemed very dark and opaque; but soon became brighter, and then transparent; and presently I could see the walls of the adjoining dwelling. These also immediately became light, and vanished—melting like clouds before my advancing vision. I could now see the objects, the furniture, and persons, in the adjoining house as easily as those in the room where I was situated . . . But my perceptions still flowed on! The broad surface of the earth, for many hundred miles, before the sweep of my vision—describing nearly a semicircle—became transparent as the purest water . . . and I saw the brains, the viscera, and the complete anatomy of animals that were (at that moment) sleeping or prowling about in the forests of the Eastern Hemisphere, hundreds and even thousands of miles from the room in which I was making these observations.

THIS sounds like a modern description of what is now known as an out-of-body experience, or OOBE. But it is not. It is how an almost illiterate young American described his first 'flight through space' after being 'magnetised', or what we would now call hypnotised, by the village tailor. It happened on New Year's Day, 1844.[1]

The young man's name was Andrew Jackson Davis. He was born in 1826 in Orange County, New York State, the son of a shoemaker and weaver who also went haymaking at harvest time. Both his parents were probably illiterate, and Andrew's formal education lasted exactly five months, after which he could just about read, write and do simple sums. As far as he could recall later, he had read nothing but a story called *The Three Spaniards* up to the age of twenty-one. Then, instead of reading another book he produced one of his own.

He went on to write a total of twenty-seven volumes, containing more than ten thousand pages. At the age of sixty, he gave up writing and became qualified as a medical doctor with a degree from the U.S. Medical College of New York. Known during his long lifetime (he died in 1910 at the age of eighty-three) as the Seer of Poughkeepsie, after a village where he lived as a youth, Davis was one of the earliest and certainly the most influential of explorers in the psi world of the mid nineteenth century.

His first psi experience was in 1843, when a wandering mesmerist named Dr J. S. Grimes gave a lecture in Poughkeepsie on 'animal magnetism', the term coined in about 1779 by the Viennese doctor Franz Anton Mesmer (1734–1815) to describe what later developed into hypnotism. Grimes offered to 'magnetise' members of the audience, and though he failed to alter young Andrew's state of consciousness he had more luck with William Levingston, the local tailor. He in turn later managed to get Davis into what must have been a deep trance state.

'The boy exhibited powers of clairvoyance which were truly surprising,' Levingston recalled. He could read newspapers and tell the time while blindfolded, and most surprising of all, he could tell people what was wrong with them without making anything like a conventional examination. As a clairvoyant medical diagnostician, he anticipated Edgar Cayce by sixty years.

But this was not to be his main work. While in trance, Davis announced one day that he was to dictate a book. Instructions were given for a certain Dr S. S. Lyon to do the magnetising and the Rev. William Fishbough to write down what he said in his altered state. Davis accordingly moved to New York, where at 92 Greene Street, Manhattan, he gave a total of 157 discourses under hypnosis between November 1845 and January

1847 which were published in that year as *The Principles of Nature, her Divine Revelations and a Voice to Mankind. A treatise in three parts. By and through Andrew Jackson Davis, the Poughkeepsie Seer and Clairvoyant.* Within eight years, he had followed up this 800-page work with his best-known production, the five-volume (2135-page) *The Great Harmonia,* subtitled 'A Philosophical Revelation of the Natural, Spiritual and Celestial Universe'.

Modern Spiritualism is usually thought to have begun in 1848, with the rappings in the Fox family homes in Hydesville and Rochester, N.Y. that were followed by messages from all kinds of spirits. If this is so, Davis was certainly Spiritualism's John the Baptist. There may have been others, followers of the Swedish scientist-mystic Emanuel Swedenborg (1688–1772), probably the first theologian of modern times to claim receipt of direct revelations from the spirit world. Emma Hardinge, a historian of early Spiritualism in the U.S., claims to have been shown a document dated about 1830 compiled by members of the Shaker sect, revealing that in the year 1848 'mines of treasure' were to be found, and 'floods of spiritual light were to descend from the heavens'. It may be just a coincidence that gold was discovered in California in 1848 (hence the Gold Rush and the forty-niners) in the same year that the spirits introduced themselves to the world from Hydesville. The Shakers, who had been in the U.S. since 1776, were also reported to have experienced most of what later became standard Spiritualist phenomena—rappings, table movements, visions, trances and clairvoyant states.[2]

If it was the Fox girls who first drew public attention to the more dramatic side-effects of Spiritualism, it was Davis who first spelled out the principles behind this new philosophy-religion. His main thesis was that the spirit world is a *real place,* neither the heaven nor the hell of traditional Christianity, but simply this world spiritualised, in which men and women go on living in their spirit bodies and continue to seek progress and perfection.

'The Great Positive Mind as a cause,' Davis wrote, 'develops

Nature as an Effect, to produce the Human Spirit as an ultimate.' He was one of the first writers to attempt a scientific description of God ('The Divine Mind is Positive and Nature is Negative'), who is even referred to as 'the great Nucleus, around which the infinite expansion of substances gathers into progressive forms and orders'. As for mind, this is '*an actual substance*'. It interacts with physical matter by means of electricity and magnetism, and when our bodies are damaged, it is the spirit, through the mind, that comes to the rescue. 'In a word, the spirit rebuilds, remodels and does everything necessary according to anatomical principles to keep the organism entire.'

Such ideas were somewhat ahead of the times, as was Davis's revelation that 'the human brain repeats in its foetal progress the entire plan of organic formation' or his more easily verifiable assertion, in March 1846, that there were nine planets in our system, not seven, apart from Earth. (Neptune was discovered later that year and Pluto only in 1930.) Little was known about electromagnetism at that time; Oersted had only discovered it in 1820, and nobody had suggested it could have anything to do with the shaping of our bodies. As for the suggestion that mind or spirit were actual substances, a claim which I hope this book will help establish, the world had to wait until very recently for any evidence that this could be the case.

No normal explanation has ever been found, or even suggested, for the source of Davis's extraordinary literary output. He remains the most baffling and impressive figure of the early Spiritualist movement, and is long overdue for reappraisal.[3,4]

It is seldom mentioned by critics of Spiritualism that successful attempts to test its phenomena scientifically were made within a few years of the movement's birth. Spiritualism spread like wildfire throughout most of the U.S. after the 1848 rappings, growing so popular that in 1854 an attempt was made to have Congress mount an official investigation of the phenomena attached to it. The motion was literally laughed into oblivion, but by this time three eminent Americans had begun their own independent researches. Two were scientists, probably the first to investigate psi phenomena anywhere on a scientific basis, while the third was none other than the Chief Justice of the New York Supreme Court.

First off the mark was the latter, Judge J. W. Edmonds, who began his inquiries in January 1851. Two years later, he had become, in his own words, 'a firm believer in the reality of spiritual intercourse'. He had witnessed several hundred phenomena over this period, and to crown it all his nine-year-old daughter Laura suddenly blossomed into a xenoglossy medium, speaking nine or ten foreign languages she had never studied, for up to an hour at a time. Judge Edmonds soon joined the swelling ranks of Spiritualists, and was eventually to become a popular lecturer, packing the country's largest halls with his talks on the subject.

The first American scientist to tackle the psi world was Professor Robert Hare, M.D., a graduate of both Harvard and Yale, and Chemistry Professor at Pennsylvania University. In 1853, he set out to bring whatever influence he possessed 'to the attempt to stem the tide of "popular madness" which in defiance of reason and science was fast setting in favour of the gross delusion called Spiritualism'.

Unlike most sceptics then or now, Hare decided to give the gross delusion a fair trial and to examine it with all the resources at his disposal. In his investigations, he used a number of mechanical appliances, anticipating in many respects the work of Crookes by almost twenty years. He used a lever device to assure himself that it was possible to increase the weight on a scale when the medium's hand was placed on the short end of the lever, which was scientifically inexplicable. He had his mediums rest their hands on top of brass billiard balls placed on zinc plates, to show that tables could move about without the medium touching them directly or being able to control their movement consciously. At one session, Hare himself lay flat on a table which not only took off the ground, but began to beat time to some music that was being played. He also received messages from a dead brother and a dead cousin

82 THE INDEFINITE BOUNDARY

he had scarcely known. On a journey to Montreal with one of his star mediums, he was treated to some of the playful antics of spirits, who kept hiding his keys and personal belongings and materialising them in unexpected places. Once, in a hotel bedroom, one of his pieces of equipment came out of a locked bag and hung itself on the frame of his bed, and his billiard balls fell in a shower on top of his head.

In 1855, Hare published his findings.[5] His book was a great success, four editions appearing in two years. The publishers advertised it as *Spiritualism Scientifically Demonstrated*, and Hare, instead of debunking this 'popular madness' and 'gross delusion', warmly embraced it, becoming the most distinguished convert to the faith with the possible exception of the Socialist pioneer Robert Owen. Hare tried to interest the American Association for the Advancement of Science in his findings, but was refused a hearing. At the meeting he was to have addressed, a paper was read instead on why roosters crow between midnight and one a.m. (The reason: a wave of electricity passes over the earth at that hour and wakes them up.)

It was Hare, incidentally, who made the interesting discovery that just as there are people who are able to provoke paranormal phenomena (mediums), so there are others who are able to prevent them. (Anti-mediums?) After one successful séance, Hare brought a confirmed sceptic into the room and found that nothing more happened. When he later asked the spirits why, they spelled out the answer at once: 'We could not do so, because he (the sceptic) was himself a counter or antagonist medium, and his presence annulled the power of the medium.' If we can cancel out the effects of an ordinary magnetic field, it is reasonable to suppose we can also cancel the effects of a mediumistic field. This may explain why nothing paranormal ever seems to happen to the really dedicated sceptic.

The second prominent American scientist to look into Spiritualism was Professor James J. Mapes, an agricultural chemist with a string of academic qualifications and memberships of learned societies to his name. He began his researches soon after Hare, impressed by the number of his friends who seemed to think there was something to be learned from the spirit world.

The spirits decided to cooperate, and at one of Mapes's first sessions they gave him detailed instructions, telling him to assemble a group of twelve people consisting of 'six positive and six negative minds'. (It is curious how often the terminology of electricity and magnetism keeps turning up in Spiritualist research of this period.) Mapes managed to get twelve friends together to form a circle and agree to hold twenty weekly meetings, as the spirits insisted. He had some trouble in keeping the circle together at first, for nothing memorable happened during the first eighteen meetings, after some apparent early successes in which the spirits had spelled out answers to *unspoken* questions and Mapes had felt unseen hands touching his legs.

But the group's patience was rewarded on the last two planned sessions. The spirits obliged with their full repertory, as messages were written on sheets of paper under the table, chairs were pulled back with people sitting on them, musical instruments played themselves, and a handful of coins thrown on to the floor stacked itself neatly inside a tumbler. The members of the circle, some of whom had only stuck it out because of their respect for Mapes, went on meeting regularly for the next *four years*. Moreover, Mapes's own wife suddenly seemed to have mediumship thrust upon her, and began to produce several thousand water-colours of high quality, apparently inspired by her spirit guides. Like Edmonds and Hare, Mapes ended up by joining the Spiritualists instead of beating them.

American spirits at this time seem to have been more interested in research than the researchers themselves. It was the spirits who designed and ordered the construction of what may have been the world's first psi research laboratories. These were built in the gardens of one Jonathan Koons, a farmer in Athens County, Ohio, and his neighbour John Tippie. Little is known about the latter, but thanks to the tireless Emma Hardinge we know enough about Koons to wish he had been more thoroughly investigated at the time.

After building his lab, Koons was instructed by the boys upstairs to build a 'spirit machine', which sounds very much like a primitive electromagnetic battery. It was, says Miss Hardinge, 'a somewhat complex arrangement of zinc and copper, serving the purpose, as the spirits alleged, of collecting and focalising the magnetic aura used in the manifestations'. She continues: 'This novel battery was placed upon a long wooden table, by the side of several (musical) instruments . . . and a variety of toys. Two drums of different sizes were slung up on a high frame, and a round table was so placed as to come into contact with the square wooden one supporting the instruments. The mediums usually sat in a semicircle about the round table, and the visitors were accommodated, to the number of twenty or more, on benches at the back of the first circle.'

The two drums were apparently fastened with copper wires upon wooden supporters at the head of the main table, which in turn was 'intersected with copper wires wrapped with zinc' and some copper plates cut in the form of doves with little bells attached ('which the spirits sometimes ring') were also hung from the wooden supporters.

Miss Hardinge does her best to explain what all this apparatus was for, though she was obviously not quite sure herself. 'It is said that the spirits, in their communion with earth, manifest through two primitive elements; namely, first an electromagnetic element of which the spiritual body is composed; next, a physical aura, which emanates from the medium, or can be collected from material substance, analogous, it is supposed, to the element of vitality.'

The Koons spirit machine was apparently used to collect and retain the 'electricity' of the sitters for the spirits to put to their own purposes, and it had to be 'charged' before demonstrations of spirit activity could be given. This was usually done by loud bangs on the drums by the spirits themselves (who perhaps had Othello's 'spirit-stirring drum' in mind!), followed by all sorts of other alarming noises. 'In this process,' said an eye-witness, 'the large table and the log house itself shook like a tree in a gale of wind.'

Once sessions were under way, the spirits would play tunes, write messages, materialise hands to be shaken ('deathly cold, but firm and solid as ordinary hands'), manipulate pieces of sandpaper that had been steeped in phosphorous, and even fire pistols over the heads of the audience. A thoroughly enjoyable time was had by all, especially the playful spirits. But it all came to an end when the Koons's unenlightened neighbours invaded his property, burned his log cabin to the ground and drove him out of Athens County.

It was *chez* Koons that Katie King, one of the most durable spirits in psi history, made her first reported materialisations. She was thought to be the daughter of the seventeenth century buccaneer Sir Henry Morgan (also known as John King), and was later to achieve fame through her association with Crookes in London. John and Katie have purported to 'control' dozens of other mediums, and apparently still do; Katie turned up quite recently at a séance in Italy. John, who was Eusapia Palladino's supposed guide, made his début in 1850 with the remarkable Davenport brothers, Ira and William, whose fame once rivalled that of D. D. Home.

Spiritualism was born in the United States, but it was not long before reports of the new wonders attached to it reached Europe, mostly through accounts of travellers to London and Paris, and soon there were regular séances under way all over the continent as far east as tsarist St Petersburg.

Isolated accounts of attempts to investigate psi phenomena in Europe survive from 1854, when Count Agénor de Gasparin reported on some table-turning experiments in Switzerland.[6] This had already become a popular pastime, for in the following year the Paris Academy of Sciences took an official stand against Spiritualism and the paranormal in general. (Without, of course, troubling to examine either.) Gasparin decided that the phenomena attached to Spiritualism did indeed exist, and that the human will could act at a distance on inert matter, but he rejected the notion that the spirits had anything to do with it.

His findings were followed in 1855 by those of his colleague Professor Marc Thury of the Academy of Geneva, who also went for a materialistic explanation of psi phenomena, postulating the existence of something he called the *psychode* that pervades all matter, like the hypothetical ether.[7]

There were three basic attitudes to be taken at this period: first, to welcome the phenomena with open arms and become a Spiritualist; second, to ignore them and denounce anybody who believed in them as an idiot; and third, to make a sincere and detached effort to find out exactly what was going on. The position is still much the same today.

One Frenchman who took the third of the above attitudes was a calm and practically-minded schoolteacher named Léon Rivail (1804–1869), author of a number of books on education, arithmetic and grammar. Educated in Protestant Switzerland, Rivail had a thorough grounding in the physical sciences and, as far as is known, no interest at all in anything connected with the occult. As Anna Blackwell, who translated some of his later works into English, wrote: 'He looked more like a German than a Frenchman. Energetic and persevering, but of a temperament that was calm, cautious, and unimaginative almost to coldness, incredulous by nature and by education; a close, logical reasoner, and eminently practical in thought and deed; he was equally free from mysticism and from enthusiasm.'

Table-rapping séances soon became a regular social activity in the Paris of the Second Empire. Emperor Napoleon III held sessions at Versailles, and society would visit Madame de Girardin's fashionable *salon* to see what the spirits had to say. With scarcely a table remaining unturned from Montmarte to the Champs-Elysées, as a contemporary journalist put it, it was inevitable that sooner or later Prof. Rivail would find himself face to face with a message being spelled out by the spirits. The process was a laborious one; sitters would stretch out their hands on the table surface, fingers touching each other's, and

the table would then tilt or rap a leg on the floor when somebody called out a certain letter. Pedro McGregor tells us what
happened next:

> Although the query Who is there? was inevitably an-
> swered, via the raps, as Spirits of those you call dead, no-
> body really troubled to follow up the implications of this
> reply. Despite the presence of the highly cultured and the
> learned, no one bothered to go beyond establishing the mere
> presence of 'the dead' and wondering at the extraordinary
> knowledge of personal trivia relating to the spectators. The
> ladies were in transports over the recovery of some lost
> object, the discovery of some secret concerning a lover; the
> men were eager, half defensive and half impressed, part scorn-
> ful and part in awe, to know about their past and future.
> Nobody concerned themselves with the consequences except
> Professor Rivail.[8]

It was ironic, says McGregor, that the reaction against
materialism in the age of Marx, Comte and Darwin 'was to
be started by matter itself—matter moving about, giving signs
of "life", controlled by an intelligence, all in a manner completely at variance with all known physical laws!' Before long,
Rivail found he was receiving messages from the spirit world
that went beyond routine trivia and seemed to be dictating a
whole new system of knowledge to him. He was also informed
through the tables that his name in a former life had been
Allan Kardec, and it was under that pseudonym that he should
write books containing a summary of what the spirits had to
tell him.

So Rivail became Kardec, publishing five books and two
shorter works between 1857 and his death twelve years later
in which he codified the doctrine he called Spiritism.[9] He also
founded, edited and wrote most of a monthly magazine, La
Revue Spirite, until he died. In his introduction to his first book,
he explained why he preferred the term Spiritism to Spiritualism; followers of the latter, he said, merely opposed materialism and believed that there was something more than mere

matter in man; whereas Spiritists actually accepted the reality
of discarnate (spirit) entities who were in constant touch with
us. The two terms are nowadays almost interchangeable. Spiritism, however, refers specifically to the teachings contained in
the works of Kardec.

The essence of his writings on Spiritism is that there are two
worlds: the visible or corporeal and the invisible or spiritual.
(The latter is what we now call the psi world.) These worlds
contain material and 'incorporeal' beings respectively. Stripping
the word *spirit* of all metaphysical connotations, Kardec's
sources define it as 'quintessentialised matter, but matter existing in a state which has no analogue within the circle of
your comprehension, and so ethereal that it could not be perceived by your senses'. In other words, though not material in
our accepted sense, spirit is an actual substance, a state of
matter we are not *normally* able to perceive. When we do perceive it, through what is misleadingly known as ESP (extrasensory perception), we describe the experience as *paranormal*.
This word simply means 'outside the range of normal experience, or not explicable by accepted scientific methods'.

Spirit, being a real thing, must be somewhere, and Kardec
tells us where it is and how it got there. Man, he says, is made
up of a material body, a soul (or incarnated spirit), and a 'sort
of semi-material envelope' called a perispirit (*peri-* indicates
encircling or enclosing), which serves as intermediary between
pure spirit and the physical body. When a baby is born, it
temporarily assumes a perishable material form, and when this
is destroyed by bodily death the spirit becomes free of it. The
soul lives on, retaining its perispiritual form which can occasionally be made visible to us. Spirit, Kardec insists, is no abstract
conception, but 'a real, circumscribed being'.

The purpose of earthly life is to evolve towards perfection,
and we return to earth as often as we have to in order to
attain perfection. Our incarnations are always progressive;
what we are now is the sum of what we have been, done and
thought in previous lives. This is essentially the *karma* of the
Buddhists, though Kardec firmly opposes the idea of metem-

psychosis; transmigration of souls from human to animal, plant, or other forms of life.

Kardec insisted that Spiritism was a philosophy and a science as well as a religion; Christianity restored to its original purity and stripped of all encumbrances in the form of churches or priests. 'As a practical science, it consists of the relations that are established between ourselves and the spirits; as a philosophy, it comprises all the moral consequences emanating from those relations,' he explained. And as a religion, it differs from most others by being wholly free from mysticism; it is a faith claiming to be based *exclusively* upon scientifically demonstrated fact.

As a working hypothesis for the operations of the psi world, Kardec's books are unequalled except perhaps by those of the Brazilian medium Chico Xavier, to be discussed in Chapter Seven. Anybody interested in parapsychology who has not read *The Spirits' Book* and *The Mediums' Book* has missed a gold mine. These are written in the form of questions (from Kardec) and answers (by the spirits), plus comments on the answers by Kardec. There is scarcely a question regarding the whole phenomenon of life and death to which an answer is not attempted, though the spirits make it clear that they do not know everything, and Kardec is honest enough to point out when he feels they must be wrong.

He was well aware of the problem of fraud. Would-be fraudulent mediums can learn a good many tricks from him, and probably have. Kardec tells you how to make fake raps on a séance table by clicking your thumbnails together, which can be very effective in a quiet room if the table is thin and resonant. He also tells you how to levitate a table by strapping a rod under each arm, getting the front ends of them under the edge of the table, and simply lifting your outstretched arms. As for the problem of sorting out the good spirits from the bad, he gives a number of useful tips.

This is really quite simple. The quality of the communication tells you what kind of spirit produced it, just as the quality of a book tells you something of its author. Kardec classifies spirit communications into four categories: coarse, frivolous, serious and instructive. The first two are produced by spirits who enjoy fooling about and interfering with their more serious-minded colleagues, while the third comes from spirits who mean well but often get lost in elaborate verbiage, just as earthly writers do when they are not sure of their subject. It is the fourth category that contains material of value.

Intelligent non-Spiritists frequently complain that spirit communications are trivial. One can make exactly the same complaint about writing by human beings. Supposing a visitor from another planet dropped in one day on a bookshop in London or New York, being in too much of a hurry to examine the whole stock and only having time to dematerialise half a dozen books and take them home with him. Looking through, shall we say, guides to rural Belgium or books of vegetarian recipes, he might wonder how 'earth literature' ever won its reputation. If another visitor from the same planet spent a little longer in the earth-bookstore and selected volumes of Homer, Plato, Shakespeare and Einstein, he would probably be far more impressed.

So why not judge spirit-inspired writings by the same standards? The works of Andrew Jackson Davis, Allan Kardec, Stainton Moses and Chico Xavier can hardly be considered trivial by anybody who has actually read them. These are some of the men whose books come under Kardec's fourth category, of communications that are *instructive*, and anybody who spends a little time in spirit-bookstores may be pleasantly surprised at the quality and the usefulness of the writing he can find there, if he looks for it.

By 1869, the year Kardec died, Spiritualism was well entrenched throughout Europe. In the same year, members of the London Dialectical Society embarked on a series of forty séances, publishing their report in 1871 and coming to much the same conclusions as Gasparin and Thury; there was an unknown force, and it was sometimes directed by some sort of intelligence. (This was the group that Huxley refused to have anything to do with.)

Here, William Crookes enters the scene, probably the most significant single event in the whole history of psi research.

His entry was welcomed by the scientific establishment. 'Ho ho,' they said in their clubs, 'young Willie will soon expose all this nonsense!' But young Willie (still under forty) did just the opposite; he announced that most of the 'phenomena called Spiritual', as he described them, were real. Nobody would have doubted his word as a scientist on any other matter, but although he wrote up his findings in great detail and promptly published them, the old boys in their clubs took the easy way out and began to cast doubts on his sanity.

'It is impossible, and therefore can't be,' they grumbled.

'I never said it was possible,' Crookes stormed in reply, 'I only said it was true!'

His report on his findings with D. D. Home alone should have represented an official seal of approval on the basic physical phenomena of the psi world. In addition to Home, Crookes examined a dozen other mediums including Kate Fox of Hydesville fame and the controversial Florence Cook, in whose presence he testified to the materialisation of Katie King. Critics of his researches have seized on this single episode in an attempt to discredit his overall contribution to psi by suggesting that he was having an affair with Florence (who got married *during* the period she was being researched!) and conniving with her in order to preserve her professional reputation as a medium. Some evidence for the Crookes-Cook duplicity or fraud theory has been well presented by E. J. Dingwall[10] and rather less well, though more maliciously, by Trevor H. Hall;[11] so readers who are interested enough can judge for themselves. I regard their case as not proven, and even if proven it would not shake the validity of the Home reports. At least, nobody has yet suggested that Crookes was having an affair with *him*.

Though he did so much to establish paranormal facts, Crookes could be sharply critical of Spiritualists. If, he said, they 'would but attend to the teachings of their own prophets, they would no longer have to complain of the hostile attitude of Science'. He went on to quote some lines from the American

poet Thomas Lake Harris, an important figure in the early
Spiritualist movement:

> The nearer to the practical men keep—
> The less they deal in vague and abstract things
> The less they deal in huge mysterious words—
> The mightier is their power . . .
> Facts are the basis of philosophy;
> Philosophy the harmony of facts
> Seen in their right relation.

I note that this reference was expurgated from the collection
of Crookes's writings published in London by the Psychic Book
Club.[12]

The founding of the Society for Psychical Research (SPR) in
1882 was a major step forward in the attempt to fit the paranormal into a scientific context. Scientists and scholars like
William Barrett, Henry Sidgwick and F. W. H. Myers joined
forces with Spiritualists in an effort to establish the facts behind the phenomena once and for all. The Spiritualists were
actually in the majority on the first SPR council (13 out of
19), but within a few years most of them had resigned when
they felt that scientific investigation threatened them with the
loss of their faith. These included the Rev. W. Stainton Moses,
himself a medium and author of some of the most readable
automatic writing ever produced.[13] Perhaps the Spiritualists
were too hasty in resigning, for some of the most active SPR
members were eventually to become strong believers in human
survival. Among these were scientists (Barrett, Crookes and
Lodge) and intellectuals like Myers, who was extremely sceptical in his youth but was eventually convinced by the evidence.
The SPR got off to a flying start, with Myers and his energetic friend Edmund Gurney tearing up and down the country
in search of material to collect and publish. And how they
published! Over 4,000 pages of Proceedings in the first ten
years alone. (We are lucky today if we get 100 pages a year.)
Myers and his friends were young (mostly in their thirties),

active and inexperienced. They learned as they went along, and they made their mistakes, but they laid the foundations of a building that still stands today, though some feel it could use a new coat of paint and perhaps a few additional wings.

The SPR has sometimes given the impression that it is only prepared to investigate phenomena that present themselves on its doorstep during office hours, but its overall record is far from negative. I do not agree with Colin Wilson that 'it has failed to make any general impact'.[14]

Mrs K. M. Goldney, a senior SPR official and one of Britain's leading psi researchers, has pointed out that 'it is in the SPR *Proceedings* that by far the best evidence—the *only* really worthwhile evidence—in favour of Spiritualist claims is to be found . . .'[15] I would not agree that it is the only such evidence, but the best it surely is, both for mental and physical psi phenomena. Take telepathy, for instance; but for the SPR we would not even have the word for it, not to mention the volumes of evidence.

The American SPR was founded in 1885, and for a time there was full cooperation on the international psi research scene. The American and British societies were actually merged for a time, and the latter welcomed many foreigners as presidents—William James, W. F. Prince and Gardner Murphy from the U.S., Richet, Bergson and Flammarion (an old friend of Kardec) from France, and Hans Driesch from Germany. Earlier in this century, researchers with the old Myers gung-ho spirit would comb the world in search of good material. Feilding would dash off to Hungary in pursuit of a poltergeist, Dingwall must have examined almost every medium in the world from Ossowiecki in Warsaw to Margery Crandon in Boston, while Driesch and Besterman ventured as far afield as Brazil on the trail of the mysterious Mirabelli.

Things are different today. The French have almost dropped psi research altogether, and the great tradition of Richet, Osty and the earlier pioneers of the study of the mind (Pierre Janet, Alfred Binet, Auguste Voisin, J. M. Charcot, and many others) has died. Indeed, French science came close to dying altogether; after the Joliot-Curies' joint Nobel Prize in 1935 it was thirty years before a Frenchman won another in the sciences.

There has been some cooperation recently between Western and Soviet psi researchers, despite the imprisonment in March 1974 of the latters' leading spokesman, Eduard Naumov, but on the whole international solidarity on the psi front is far weaker than it was at the end of the nineteenth century. Nobody has bothered to translate much of the work of such outstanding researchers as Willem Tenhaeff of Holland, or Hans Bender of Germany, into English. Hernani G. Andrade's extremely original psi matter theories, first published in 1958, remained hidden behind the barrier of the Portuguese language until he brought out a brief summary of them in English in 1973.

Between 1950 and 1970, Americans won more than half of *all* Nobel prizes awarded in the sciences. (I am sorry to keep harping on Nobel prizes, but laymen like myself do like to assume that they mean something.) The United States has also moved into a secure lead in the field of psi research. The American SPR publishes much fine original material; wealthy patrons such as Eileen Garrett and Chester Carlson, the inventor of xerography, have financed the kind of large-scale projects without which useful results can hardly be expected in any form of research. There are few countries in the world today where scientists as respectable as the physicist Gerald Feinberg can risk being seen in public with people like Uri Geller.

I hope it has become evident in this chapter that there *is* evidence for the reality of psi phenomena, indeed that they have been proved scientifically over and over again. As to the question of whether the spirits have anything to do with them, it must be remembered that ours is the age of probabilities, not of certainties, but even so the spiritistic hypothesis is still the only one that fits *all* the facts. In the following chapter, I hope to show that more recent advances into the psi world have tended to support the earlier findings of men like Hare, Crookes and Feilding, and that the spiritistic hypothesis, as parapsychologists like to call it, is still looking pretty good today.

'Where have the phenomena our forbears investigated disappeared to, and why?' Mrs Goldney lamented in 1972. Her lamentation was premature; a glance at some contemporary publications shows that people are still claiming to do things that would have surprised even Home or Palladino. More to the point is to wonder where the great researchers have disappeared to, and why.

Remember Hereward Carrington's remark quoted in the previous chapter about how the incidents he and his colleagues witnessed with Palladino 'seemed to roll off our minds', and how the researchers 'lapsed back into scepticism' after each of the first few sessions, until the phenomena came so thick and fast that they could no longer be ignored? 'The old wall of belief must be broken down by much battering,' a friend of Crookes's once wrote to him. It is up to researchers to do the battering.

The phenomena are still happening today, but we have developed immunity to them. Lapsing back into scepticism is a natural human reaction. This state of affairs will probably continue until a *general theory* emerges that makes some sense out of the bewildering miscellany of psi phenomena that are reported every day, only to roll off the public mind the day after.*

By the end of this book, I hope the outline of such a general theory will have emerged. Meanwhile, there is still some battering to be done at those old walls of belief, so back to the battering ram and once more into the breach . . .

* 'I think that not only is the Spiritualistic hypothesis justified as a working theory, but it is, in fact, the only one capable of rationally explaining the facts,' said Carrington after the Palladino sessions. Later, however, he became less sure, as his own evidence once again seemed to roll off his mind.

Chapter 5

THE EVIDENCE CONVERGES

Good sense travels on the well-worn paths; genius, never. And that is why the crowd, not altogether without reason, is so ready to treat great men as lunatics. LOMBROSO

'MY one aim in life is that this great truth, the return and communication of the dead, shall be brought home to a material world which needs it so badly.'

Psi research is like police work in many respects, and if any man could have convinced us all of the reality of the psi world, that man was surely Sir Arthur Conan Doyle, creator of the sharpest observer and most logical reasoner in all literature, Sherlock Holmes. Doyle, who made the remark quoted above, was no mean detective himself; he secured the release of at least two people who had been wrongly convicted, after making his own study of the evidence, and he was a witty and eloquent speaker as well as one of the most popular writers of all time.

He was a lapsed Roman Catholic of Irish descent who declared his agnosticism early in life. 'I do not admit that any faith, but only pure reason is needed to get the idea of God and also to evolve a sufficient moral law for our needs,' he wrote to a friend. He saw faith as 'a very dangerous thing'. Supposing, he said, that he had one 'real and earnest faith', and his neighbour had another. 'Then we have as a result inquisitions, persecutions, religious wars, family feuds, and all the other fearful results which have so long plagued humanity.'[1]

Doyle became a Spiritualist after discovering the psi world for himself. He spent much of the latter part of his life campaigning for it at his own expense, travelling 50,000 miles and lecturing to a quarter of a million people, but he was no more successful in getting the psi world across than Kardec had been, or Crookes, or anybody else. However eminent the man who

declared that there *was* another world, it was always preferable to cast doubts on his judgment, or just ignore him. The
great weakness of most early psi researchers was that they had
no *theory* to back up the facts they claimed to have observed.
It has been said that facts without a theory are like an army
without a general, and we still have today a horde of facts
running amok in all directions for lack of even a working hypothesis to keep them in line.

The main reason for all this confusion is that most psi research
in the past has depended on human testimony, and humans are
fallible. In 1974, the Automobile Association showed a film of
a crossroads collision involving three vehicles to an audience
of six professional observers (including two policemen and Grand
Prix ace Stirling Moss) and six members of the public of above
average intelligence. When asked to describe exactly what they
saw after seeing the film, the experts scored only four points
(out of sixty) more than the laymen, and the only witness who
scored full marks was one of the latter group. Then the AA
repeated the experiment, but sent a new team of laymen to
a psychotherapist for a week's training in ways to increase perception. The contest was held again, with a different panel of
experts, and the trained laymen beat the professionals hands
down, scoring almost full marks. The psychotherapist Lawrence
Barnes concluded that the results offered 'scientifically valid
evidence that it really is possible for people to train themselves
to be better witnesses'.[2]

I know from my own experience just how fallible human
testimony can be. While I was investigating a poltergeist case
in São Paulo in 1973, described in my previous book, a series
of inexplicable events took place early one morning. As soon as
I could, I set about taking statements from the other people in
the house, one of whom had been upstairs when the events
began with a four-legged stool sliding down the stairs into the
room where I was sleeping on a sofa. Shortly after this, a drawer
full of clothes had flown out of a bedroom chest, through an
open window and into the back yard below. Nobody was able
to agree as to who was exactly where at the time of either

incident. Luckily I had managed to turn on my tape recorder at the moment the stool reached the bottom of the stairs, and listening to the tape afterwards I was able to establish everybody's approximate movements and positions. This was very important, as it showed that nobody could have been in the bedroom when the drawer flew out of the window. But for my own taped evidence I would still be in some doubt today as to what really happened.

If the psi world is ever going to be proved to exist to everyone's satisfaction, the crucial evidence will come from the laboratory, not the testimony of a medium or an investigator. The latters' contribution may be useful, but it will never be able to settle the issue.

The simplest way to prove the existence of spirit bodies would surely be to take photographs of them, or somehow make them repeatedly visible. I have seen scores of photos of alleged spirits, some of which look very convincing indeed, while others look more like humans wearing sheets. But I cannot say I am yet emotionally convinced that spirit forms have yet been photographed. In 1897, a French doctor named Hippolyte Baraduc published a book that contained a great many odd-looking photographs of very poor quality, which the author claimed to represent the human soul. With admirable devotion to the cause of science, Baraduc later took several pictures of his wife immediately after her death, and his prints show what look like large lumps of cotton wool floating above her corpse. He also took a picture of his teenage son, who died in 1907, after he had been placed in a coffin. Again, the print shows clouds of misty something-or-other almost blotting out the body. Baraduc was thought to be an honest man, though he failed to convince the world that he had photographed spirit bodies. I cannot imagine what kind of man would deliberately fake such experiments with members of his own family, and though Baraduc's evidence is poorly presented, it should not be overlooked.[3]

A few years later, a much more thoroughly researched volume appeared in London entitled *The Human Atmosphere*, later changed to *The Human Aura*. Its author, Dr Walter J. Kilner, a hospital electrician, claimed he was actually able to see the famous human aura of the mystics and occultists, with the aid of a screen system containing a solution of dicyanin dye. Unfortunately he never managed to take a photograph of an aura, and it was found that many other people saw nothing at all unusual when they tried to repeat his methods.

Interest in Kilner's experiments were revived when 'Kirlian photography' became a popular hobby in psi research circles around the year 1970. This process, named after the Russian couple who rediscovered it in 1939, seemed to show what might be the human aura in glorious colour under easily repeatable conditions. By making contact prints of leaves, fingertips and other objects, it was possible because of the high frequencies used, to see something on the developed film that was invisible to the naked eye. The fact that the process was simple and repeatable gave researchers new heart, especially those who were despairing of ever getting anywhere with human mediums or non-repeatable spontaneous phenomena.

Kirlian devices are becoming almost as popular as ouija boards once were, as the standard do-it-yourself home psi pastime. They may encourage people to observe facts rather than develop empirical occult theories based on messages from the unseen or their own subconscious. The whole point of the Kirlian process is not that it reveals a corona, or sort of aura, around living or non-living objects, but that this corona can appear to vary from moment to moment under certain conditions.

Psi historian J. Fraser Nicol has pointed out that there are many similarities between modern Kirlian pictures and old French experiments from way back in the nineteenth century, when no high-frequency sources were used. He mentions one gruesome experiment in which a French photographer cut the hand off a corpse and found that by heating it to body temperature he got results on film similar to those obtained from a living person's hand.[4]

For the rest of this chapter, I shall survey some of the work done and ideas put forward in this century by conventional scientists working in traditional areas, and see what help they can be in our hunt for the elusive spirit.

DRIESCH'S SOMETHING ELSE

'There is a natural body, and there is a spiritual body,' wrote St Paul.[5] How's that for a working hypothesis?

For a supplementary hypothesis as to how the two bodies unite, we turn to Allan Kardec's *Genesis* (1868), where we find the following—slightly condensed and paraphrased:

> *Spirit is attracted to matter by an irresistible force from the moment of conception. But spirit cannot act upon matter directly without an intermediary, the semi-material perispirit body that belongs to both matter and spirit. Under the influence of the vital-material principle of the embryo, the perispirit unites itself molecule by molecule to the body in formation, thus enabling the spirit to take root in the embryo as a plant takes root in the soil. When the embryo reaches its full development, the union is complete and the being is born to external life. At birth, the spirit forgets its memories of past existences, though sometimes it will retain intuitions of past times, like memories of fugitive dreams. However, it retains its latent faculties which enable it to shape its current life-plan and add to its overall store of experience.*

At the start of the twentieth century, the German embryologist Hans Driesch came to the conclusion that life could not be explained away in terms of physics and chemistry alone. Materialistic explanations for biological phenomena were not enough. 'The mechanistic, or rather summative theory of life is unable to account for the facts of embryology, heredity and organic movement,' he said after some twenty years' thought on the subject.[6]

There could be no doubt that the forces of matter were at work in the organism. But, he insisted, 'something else is at work in it also, directing the material forces without changing the amount of energy'. He suggested the word *entelechy* for this 'something else', from the Greek *entelekhia*, complete reality. Driesch saw this as a 'unifying, mind-like something', a vital force that urged an organism towards self-fulfilment. Its function, he thought, was essentially an ordering rather than a creative one. Driesch's idea came to be associated with the theory of *vitalism*, and to many it smacked too much of occultism, a hangover from such obviously outdated ideas as Mesmer's animal magnetism and Reichenbach's odyle.

Mesmer had been convinced that there was a property in all living matter ('animal magnetism') which could be controlled by people such as himself and put to use for healing purposes. Reichenbach, the German scientist who discovered creosote, had no more luck than Mesmer in winning universal acceptance for his version of the mysterious force, which he called the *odyle* or *od*. He insisted that this was not the same as Mesmer's animal magnetism, but since nobody was sure what Mesmer's thing had been in the first place, Reichenbach met with equally little sympathy.

A worse fate was in store in this century for Wilhelm Reich, a Freudian psychiatrist who came up with yet another word for the elusive life force. This was *orgone* energy, and Reich died in prison after being sentenced in 1956 for selling machinery designed to manipulate something the U.S. Government ruled not to exist. It was sad to see a scientist, however eccentric, being literally hounded to death in the twentieth century, though Reich's cranky behaviour did little to establish public confidence in his sanity. It is no argument to claim, as some do, that just because Galileo etc., were persecuted it follows that anybody challenging the scientific establishment must be right. (There is quite a Reich revival now under way, and it is possible that his ideas may prove useful when examined by researchers more cool-headed than himself.)

There was nothing cranky about Driesch, yet his entelechy failed to interest biologists of his time. It is dismissed in a sharp little footnote in one of the standard textbooks, D'Arcy

Thompson's *On Growth and Form* (1917). 'I fail to see how *this* Entelechy is shown to be peculiarly or specifically related to the *living* organism,' Thompson sniffed. He pointed out that it had always been known that the biological whole was different from the sum of its parts, but made no attempt to explain why this should be.

Driesch himself had no idea how his entelechy worked. He merely hit upon what seemed a hypothetical explanation for observed fact, which is what research scientists are supposed to do. He was just unlucky that nobody subsequently confirmed it.

LODGE'S FORMATIVE PRINCIPLE

'We cannot understand anything fully and completely in terms of matter alone,' said one of Britain's leading physicists, Sir Oliver Lodge, in 1924. 'It is evident,' he added, 'that there exists a formative principle, which is able to deal with the atoms of matter, or rather with the more complex molecules into which the atoms have already grouped themselves: and thus, by aid of the energy which these molecules receive from the sun, non-material entities are able to manifest themselves familiarly in association with matter.'[7]

Lodge was one of the first scientists to suggest that physical matter is actually shaped, controlled and organised by a non-material component. 'The shape of the human body depends on the *formative organising principle*, and not on the aliment provided,' he said. (My italics.)

Lodge was a pioneer in many fields. On August 14th 1894, he gave the first public demonstration of radio telegraphy at the British Association meeting in Oxford, a year before Marconi did the same thing and walked off with all the credit. (According to Lodge's biographer W. P. Jolly, Marconi even used a Lodge coherer in his early demonstrations!)[8]

Having invented radio, Lodge promptly dashed off to a Mediterranean island to investigate Eusapia Palladino with his friends Myers and Richet. To him, scientific and psychical research were part of a single quest for knowledge about the human condition, and he saw no need to keep them apart. He was one of the earliest members of the SPR, and was one of the first to suggest that telepathy could be tested by card guessing, working out a mathematical formula for assessing scoring rates ten years before J. B. Rhine was born.

Lodge's prolonged investigations of mediums, notably Mrs Piper and Mrs Leonard, convinced him that some form of intelligence survived the death of the body, a conviction strongly reinforced when his son Raymond was killed in World War I and almost immediately appeared to communicate with his father from the other side.[9] He saw intelligence as something that could exist independent of physical matter, acting directly on 'the Ether' and only indirectly on matter. This is almost pure Kardec. 'In justification for this,' Lodge explained, 'I wish to say, as a physicist, that most, possibly all, of our actions on matter are exerted through the Ether: some obviously, like propulsion by electric motors, others less conspicuously, but just as really, wherever force crosses empty space. For atoms are never in contact.'[7]

Replace Lodge's *Ether* with Kardec's perispirit and H. G. Andrade's biological organising model (to be introduced in a later chapter), and we have a prophetic view, expressed fifty years ago, of the way in which modern researchers are trying to understand the psi world and its relation with our physical one.

CARINGTON'S PSYCHON SYSTEM

Whately Carington was a scientist and pioneer aviator who spent much of his life in the full-time study of psi phenomena. He died in 1947 after spending many years in appalling poverty, rejecting lucrative job offers in order to devote himself to his vocation. His valuable work on statistical assessment of psi phenomena made him almost wear out his right arm grinding out calculations on a primitive machine, until the SPR took pity on him and bought him an electric one. One of his special passions was telepathy, the subject of a book he published two years before his death.[10]

'It is the fact of telepathy (unless you can explain it in physical terms—which you can't!) that breaks across the frontiers of the physical world and opens up the psychical,' he wrote. In the course of his study of the mind, through which telepathy must operate, he put forward the idea that the mind might have component bits of its own, which he called *psychons*.

He suggested that psychons could be subdivided into images and *sensa*; a sensum being a psychon produced when physical stimuli are applied to our sense organs, such as when light rays fall on the eye or sound waves strike the ear drum. The *image* is what is left after the sensum has been registered. Sensa and images, Carington thought, might turn out to be the *sole* components of the mind, and might be reducible to something similar to the atoms of chemical elements.

He saw the mind as a 'psychon system' in much the same sense that a body is a 'cell system'. Psychons, he said, were linked together into groups and subgroups by forces of association, much as cells are linked by adhesive forces and atoms by electrical ones. This is one of the earliest presentations of the idea that our minds, being real things, must have some sort of structure. They must be made of something, and since they are not material they must be made of non-matter, or what we now call psi matter.

Carington seemed to be hovering around a hypothesis of psi matter without ever managing to state it. One reason for his hesitation was that he was unable to stomach the idea of reincarnation. His attitude to this crucial aspect of the interaction of psi and physical worlds was much the same as that of Myers before him. There was, Carington complained, 'not a shred of worthwhile evidence in its favour', and not even its most ardent supporters could give 'any reasonable account of what it is that is reincarnated'. He was quite right in 1945, but he is no longer right in this respect today. There are now several volumes of worthwhile evidence, and I shall be giving an account, hopefully a 'reasonable' one, of just what is reincarnated in a later chapter.

THE FIELDS OF SPACE

Before we look at any more psi theories, we should touch on the subject of magnetic fields for the benefit of non-scientific readers, since they are going to play an important part in these theories.

They are invisible, but it is easy to represent them in such a way that you can see how they work. This is done by taking a magnet, placing a sheet of stiff paper over it and then sprinkling some iron filings on the paper. The filings immediately arrange themselves around the edge of a clearly recognisable space, forming what is called a spectrum. This spectrum represents the field of magnetic force set up by the magnet. We cannot see the actual field itself, but thanks to our iron filings we can see a *material representation* of it.

Technically, a magnetic field is a condition in a region of space established by the presence of a magnet, or an electric current, in which magnetic force can be detected at every point in it. When an electric charge is in motion, it sets up what is called an electromagnetic field, and when such a charge is not in motion the field it sets up is called an electrostatic one.

Every effect has a cause. A magnetic field is an effect, and it is caused by a magnet, or by an electric charge in motion. An intelligent effect must have an intelligent cause, and a psi effect will have what we must call a psi cause until we find out more about it. There have been a number of field theories put forward by parapsychologists in recent years, but little attention seems to have been paid to the search for the *cause* behind the effects.

This is understandable, because psi researchers have enough trouble getting people to believe that psi effects really exist in the first place, leaving them little time to figure out possible causes. Also, an effect can have a number of possible causes. A train smash is an effect apparently caused by two trains, but the real cause may be one or other of the drivers, a signalman, a sleeping cow, or the Marx brothers ripping up the line.

The scientific establishment is sometimes blamed for not

dropping whatever it is doing to chase after psi causes or verify psi effects, and though there are certainly faults on both sides, a little modest diplomacy from the psi side might make more impression on science than strident proclamations of unverifiable inspirations. If Einstein, for instance, had said a few kind words about Reich's orgone theory, Reich's unhappy life might have taken a different course. Einstein is said to have been quite interested at first when the two men did meet, but Reich must have played his cards wrong because Einstein later refused to have anything more to do with him.

BURR'S LIFE-FIELDS

Sometimes pioneers can be so modest that their discoveries can be overlooked even in these days of instant communication around the global village. This is very nearly what happened to Harold Saxton Burr.

A former anatomy professor at Yale medical school, he published a total of ninety-three scientific papers between 1916 and 1956, including several from 1935 onwards on what he called his Electrodynamic Theory of Life. But it was not until 1972 that he published his first book[11] and his discoveries first became known to the general public. Burr's major discovery, published in 1935, was that all living things are surrounded by a measurable electromagnetic field. This not only is determined by the atomic structure of living matter, but also organises it. 'It determines and is determined by the components', as he put it. 'It must be the mechanism, the outcome of whose activity is wholeness, organisation and continuity.'[12] Burr paid tribute to Driesch's entelechy, which he regarded as 'brilliant', even if it could not be scientifically demonstrated. He considered his own theory as comparable to it, with the great advantage that his could be measured very precisely, with voltmeters he helped design himself.

Burr's is a practical theory. By studying his electrodynamic or L- (for life) fields, he claimed he could establish the precise moment of ovulation in a woman, detect malignant tumours,

predict when individuals would feel 'at their best' or below par',
and even map out the direction in which the nervous system
of a frog was to grow—*before it happened.* He speculated that
his method might be used in the future to measure such states
as grief, anger or love by electrical means.

One day, we may be able to answer the old question 'How
much do you really love me?' with the precise statement
'Forty-three point eight millivolts, my dear.'

Burr gives detailed instructions for measuring L-fields, pointing out that it is easier to learn to operate a voltmeter than an
X-ray machine or an electrocardiogram. It is not the measure-
ments themselves of the field around our bodies that reveal
important information, but the variations between readings
taken either from different parts of the body or at different
times from the same area. (The Burr fields should not be confused, as they often are, with the Kirlian effect. It is most
unlikely that the two have much to do with each other.)

'A modest approach to an understanding of the Universe
does not impair human dignity—it enhances it,' Burr writes.
'Moreover, it is the only approach likely to succeed, because
Nature seems reluctant to reveal her secrets to the intellectually
arrogant.'

Burr made no extravagant claims for his L-field theory. He
did point out that it seemed to establish man as an integral
part of the universe and subject to its laws, but he certainly
never claimed that 'science reveals the soul' as was suggested
in a book published almost simultaneously with his own.[18]

In this book, author Edward W. Russell gives a lively and
exciting account of Burr's work and includes many ideas of his
own; much of the book being devoted to right-wing political
propaganda. He makes a useful bid to develop Burr's ideas in
other areas, putting forward the hypothesis of thought-fields
(T-fields), which are somewhat reminiscent of Carington's psychon systems. No doubt encouraged by the fact that Burr's
fields were demonstrable and measurable, not merely hypothetical, Russell suggests that his T-fields might account for
several phenomena still considered paranormal. According to

him, T-fields can 'anchor' themselves onto material objects and stay there until picked up and 'read' by people with the right degree of sensitivity. This might well be an explanation for the workings of psychometry (obtaining information through an inanimate object of its owner or handler), the haunting of buildings, and the process of blessing or cursing places or people.

The most exciting thing about these L- and T-fields is that they present the idea of living beings as actually controlled by a non-material entity. Russell points out that there is no need to suppose that L-fields cease to exist when the bodies they have helped organise die and decompose. Nor is there any reason to suppose that T-fields fade away with time.

SMYTHIES, WASSERMANN AND ROLL

are not a firm of architects or solicitors, but three individuals who have made important contributions to general psi theory. In 1951, Dr J. R. Smythies published a stimulating article in which he put forward the idea of a universe of *seven* dimensions in which the mind, or psyche, is 'an organised *material* entity located in higher dimensional space'.[14] Things (like minds) do not have to be immaterial to be invisible, he says. 'They may be on the other side of a dimensional interface.'

Louisa Rhine has suggested that since it takes energy to direct energy, nervous energy (which directs muscular energy, which in turn moves physical objects) should be directed by 'mental energy'.[15] If our minds, or part of them, are out there in dimensions four through seven, there must be some way they interact. Smythies notes that there remains a gap between psi phenomena and anything that can enable them to operate in the physical world. This is where our various field theories are probably going to be useful. They look like the only way out of our inter-dimensional psi dilemma. We are not likely to get anywhere in terms of only three space dimensions.

In 1956, Dr G. D. Wassermann put forward his idea of psi fields at a symposium on ESP promoted by the Ciba Foundation.

These fields are set up by unimaginably tiny energy quanta, even smaller than any quantum a physical field can absorb. They can interact with physical fields and exist with them in bound states, and Wassermann also postulates M-, P- and B-fields to account respectively for morphogenesis (the development of the structure of a living being), psychological behaviour, and clairvoyance. Telepathy, for instance, would happen when the B-field of a sender interacts with a psi field, which in turn interacts with the B-field of a receiver. He comes up with an ingenious explanation of how precognition, the toughest of all psi nuts to crack, might take place. He imagines a series of physical energy fields, each destined to cause a determined event to happen, somehow becoming duplicated by another group of fields that can convey the information about the event to the human brain. In this way the owner of the brain can perceive an event before it happens. Wassermann's ideas run into the same problem as those of other people—except Smythies—mentioned in this chapter: they do not take extra space dimensions into account. To talk of precognition, for instance, in terms of 3D space seems impossible. Yet precognition happens.

In 1964, William G. Roll introduced his psi field, defining it as 'the region of space in which psi phenomena are detectable'. It can exist either in a free state or bound with physical fields. It can receive isomorphic representations, or duplicate impressions, of physical and mental events, and these impressions can remain after the causes that formed them have terminated. The psi field can also produce duplicate impressions of itself both in other psi fields and in physical ones.[16]

Roll edits a bulletin called *Theta*, which is devoted to the question of survival of death, and has personally witnessed some dramatic poltergeist action, but he is very cautious when it comes to getting mixed up with the spirits. Like Wassermann, he suggests that many phenomena can be explained by field interaction, making it unnecessary to bring in discarnate entities, ghosts, spirits or whatever. 'The idea that a person's ESP abilities can be understood in terms of fields surrounding his body does not necessarily imply an extrasomatic self,' he insists.

Here we run into the reincarnation problem again. If it can be shown (and I propose to have a good try) that something *does* appear to reincarnate, and that this something may resemble what Roll (and many others) see as a field structure, or a representation of one, also that such fields can be measured and made visible, then this whole confusing subject may begin to make sense at last.*

SOULE IS FORME

'Mysteriously though man's spirit may seem to move, and high as its destiny may sometimes prove to be, it is *born* in living matter, and the biologist can therefore claim it as part of his domain.'

It seems right to end this chapter with the views of a biologist, especially one who wrote a book with the provocative title *Biology of the Spirit*.[17] The author, Professor Edmund W. Sinnott, was a colleague and collaborator of Dr Burr at Yale, and must have been familiar with the L-field, though he makes no reference to it in the book mentioned. But he makes many references to what he calls a Principle of Organisation in all nature, as suggested by the 'upwards, purposeful thrust of life, which continually opposes the downward drag of matters'.

This principle, he says, brings order out of randomness, spirit out of matter, and personality out of neutral and impersonal stuff. His own experience of watching the way things grow led him to conclude that neither the vitalistic nor the mechanistic approaches were sufficient to explain why protoplasm made organisms rather than formless structures. Nor was Sinnott satisfied by the 'organistic' approach; merely re-

* For those interested in reading more about psi fields, I recommend Gardner Murphy's 1945 essay, probably the first to bring field theory into psi research;[18] Sir Alister Hardy's observations on the relation between evolution and telepathy;[19] R. H. Thouless on psychokinesis[20] and anything relevant by G. N. M. Tyrrell, C. D. Broad, H. H. Price and Arthur Koestler.

cognising that living things have an organising capacity and leaving it at that, admitting that a problem exists but making no attempt to trace its cause. 'The organicist is bound, I think, to be agnostic in his biology in that he simply does not know whence this strange organising power originates,' Sinnott says. (Nor does anyone else.)

Higher biological problems, he insists, are expressions of life, and biologists should try and sort them out themselves rather than pass them on to psychologists or theologians. 'Shakespeare was a living organism, Lincoln a protoplasmic system, Moses and Michelangelo were complex aggregations of proteins. But they were more than these things alone. In their material substance, as in that of every great and gifted man, there somehow came to birth high qualities that the student of matter would never suspect were latent in it, qualities rising out of that deep centre where life and matter and energy are inextricably mingled.'

On the trail of his elusive organising principle, Sinnott decided it must exist at the primary level of the cell, where life seems to begin. The character of the organism, he says, must somehow be *prefigured* in the living cells from which it grows. 'Something inherent in the entire mass (of cells), something residing in its fundamental genetic constitution, keeps (the organism) marching steadily forward to a precise culmination. The nature of this "something" that coordinates the multifarious activities of growth into a harmonious whole, that directs them on a steady course, is the greatest mystery of biology.'

Sinnott stresses the fact that man is a goal-seeking individual, who shows more signs of being *pulled* than pushed. He is drawn forward towards something he feels to pre-exist, rather than merely being pushed from behind. He criticises psychologists for putting too much stress on man's background and overlooking the more positive approach of helping him shape his future by mental processes. 'Human history,' he says, 'has been moulded by the aspirations of that minority of individuals who had the capacity to *want* something very much.'

And he quotes a thought-provoking couplet from a poem
Edmund Spenser wrote in 1596:

> For of the soule the bodie forme doth take:
> For soule is forme, and doth the bodie make.

Science cannot yet explain the basic facts of life. When we
find scientists taking refuge in words and phrases like 'something else', 'unknown force', 'formative principle' and complaining that nothing can be understood any longer in terms
of matter alone, it seems clear that the scientists themselves
realise this. And when A. N. Whitehead, asks: 'What is the
sense of talking about a mechanical explanation when you do
not know what you mean by mechanics?', we are led to wonder
if there is any sense in trying to do anything except sit back
and wait for a revelation.*

I am suspicious of revelations when they come expressed in
unreadable prose, but I am not suspicious of the human mind.
It is the most valuable thing on earth, responsible for everything we do, from lifting a finger to building a pyramid. Pocket
calculators were not available when Einstein worked out his
horrifically complex equations. So what did he do? He closed
his eyes and let the figures 'dance about' in front of him, as he
put it. All inspiration is occult in that it comes from a hidden
source. Yet we do not classify Einstein as an occultist, because
most of his inspirations have been proved true. (Not all: in
1939 he was telling President Roosevelt that atomic bombs
would probably be too heavy to be carried by air!)

'Scientific caution and humility are not enough,' psychologist William McDougall once said. 'A certain boldness also is
required, a readiness to grasp a vast range of converging evidence, each item of which, standing alone, can lead us nowhere.'

So now let us throw aside scientific caution, of which I never
had much to start with, and crash the barrier in between
us and that fourth dimension . . .

* Gurdjieff has clarified the situation further by assuring us that we
do not even understand the meaning of the word *understand*.

Chapter 6

A ROMANCE OF MANY DIMENSIONS

The boundary between the two states—the known and the unknown
—is still substantial, but it is wearing thin in places . . . LODGE

AT 11 a.m. on December 17th 1877, a German physicist-astronomer named Johann Zoellner saw four knots tie themselves in a piece of string the ends of which had previously been joined together and sealed. From this experience, plus many similar ones, Zoellner concluded that intelligent beings were able to intervene on our earth plane; and since they were certainly not here to begin with, they must come from somewhere else, or another dimension of space.

In the course of some thirty sessions with the American medium Henry Slade, Zoellner claimed to confirm the reality of almost all the phenomena to which Crookes had given his seal of approval a few years previously. In the presence of several of his colleagues at Leipzig University, including G. T. Fechner and W. P. Weber, Zoellner recorded such feats as the dematerialisation and reappearance of a table weighing 4·5 kilos, which vanished for about five minutes before emerging upside down from the ceiling and crashing to the floor, hitting both Slade and himself on the head in the process.

During one session, Zoellner's bed moved itself two feet from the wall and a heavy wooden screen near it split into two. During others, handbells rang, accordions played themselves, a full bookcase got the shudders, footprints appeared in bowls of flour and on smoked sheets of paper, somebody's coat was unbuttoned by an unseen hand, showers of water emerged from thin air, candles lit themselves and jumped up and down, and mysterious rays of light shone from nowhere. A fully materialised hand even appeared on one occasion and allowed Zoellner to shake it.

In addition to all this fun, messages would appear on slates held under the table, even on previously sealed ones that Slade never touched, or so Zoellner thought. Slade also correctly named the dates and values of three coins that Zoellner had sealed in a box; whereupon the coins appeared on a slate held under the table, while two bits of pencil turned up inside the still sealed box. It was events like these (which were very probably tricks) that suggested to Zoellner that matter could pass through matter, and since this was impossible in a three-dimensional world, there just had to be a fourth dimension of space.

To check his theory, Zoellner set up a number of experiments. He had two wooden rings made, from different kinds of wood, and he threaded them on a length of dried gut, the ends of which he sealed together to form a continuous loop. During a session held on May 9th 1878, the wooden rings left the gut loop and were found encircling the central leg of a table, there being no way this could have happened normally (without considerable clandestine carpentry from Slade), since the leg splayed out into three feet. Meanwhile, two knots appeared on the gut loop, through which another continuous loop of leather somehow threaded itself.

Slade, in whose presence all these things were said to have taken place, was a highly controversial character. A London court had convicted him of fraud in 1876 and sentenced him to three months' imprisonment, though the sentence was annulled. C. C. Massey, a barrister who translated Zoellner's intriguing book,[1] points out that Slade was not given a fair trial, one of the chief prosecution witnesses, the conjuror J. N. Maskelyne, testifying against him without ever having seen him in action. Slade later offered his accuser, Professor E. Ray Lankester, six sessions in the professor's own home under any control conditions. No reply.

Zoellner immediately offered to examine Slade in his Leipzig home and did so. He usually only told Slade what he wanted him to do at the time, with no advance warning, giving him little chance to set up any fraudulent devices. Either the phenomena happened as reported, or Zoellner was one of the most gullible idiots in history, as many still believe. Or, of course, Slade was a highly skilled illusionist, which on the evidence seems possible.*

Samuel Bellachini, Kaiser Wilhelm I's court conjuror, signed a sworn statement in December 1877 that he was unable to explain what he saw Slade doing by traditional conjuring methods. Yet Slade was subsequently caught cheating on a number of occasions, and his career ended in disgrace. Like other mediums, true or false (Mary Showers, Kate Fox, Margery Crandon), he took to the bottle, and he died penniless and forgotten.

Conjurors are always shooting their mouths off about how they can easily repeat allegedly paranormal feats of mediums and psychics, though they seldom actually bother to prove it. One of the few who did, and got away with it (even convincing Alfred R. Wallace that he was a medium), was S. J. Davey, who performed slate-writing stunts similar to those of Slade.†

Even if Slade was a total phoney, it is quite possible that Zoellner came to the right conclusions. In 1954 his ideas about multi-dimensional space received an unexpected boost from German physicist Pascual Jordan, a sometime associate of Niels Bohr and Werner Heisenberg.

Jordan recommended a re-examination of Zoellner's theory according to which 'the distance of two atoms and the intensity of their interaction, in our three-dimensional space' could be regarded as 'projections of similar magnitudes from a space of four dimensions'. There was, Jordan said, just no way of explaining away some psi phenomena within a framework of 3D

---

* Aksakof even suggested that Zoellner was the medium, not Slade!
† Would-be mediums can find out exactly how to do them in *Proc. SPR* vol. 8 (pp. 253–310). Not all magicians can explain everything, however. In June 1975, Uri Geller produced both physical and mental phenomena for members of the Society of American Magicians, even causing a steel fork to *explode*! The magicians failed to spot any form of trickery.

reality. Moreover, there were definitely no undiscovered physical processes (except maybe in meson physics) which might be
linked with psi experience. Scientists seldom use words like
'definitely' nowadays, and cynics may think that anything
categorically stated by a scientist is bound to be proved wrong
sooner or later, just as we journalists will never believe anything until it has been officially denied. However . . .

'It is genuinely possible', Jordan went on, 'that if we wish
to take into account the facts of our experience which are not
included within the framework of our three-dimensional reality,
we must broaden our basic concepts of the reality of three-
dimensional space as we now know it, and habitually conceive of
it. Zoellner was thinking somewhat along these same lines when,
attempting to explain spiritualist phenomena, he outlined the
hypothesis of four-dimensional space.' Jordan made it clear that
he was not suggesting Zoellner was right. ('Indeed, things are
not that simple.') But he did say he thought it would be interesting and rewarding to speculate along the lines of his hypothesis. 'His idea is worth pursuing,' he said, 'and may lead to
some clarification of these elemental facts.'[2]

Let us pursue it.

FLATMAN

Einstein said that we are living in a 4D space-time continuum,
in which our three dimensions of space are joined by one of
time. But what Zoellner was talking about, and what I am talking about here, is a fourth dimension of *space*. This will already
be familiar to students of Gurdjieff and Ouspensky, especially
the latter's *Tertium Organum*.

It is said that any translation into words is a betrayal of
reality, and this is especially true of non-physical or psi reality.
Describing or understanding hyperspace (or 4D space) is almost
impossible for an inhabitant of a 3D world. But even if I cannot describe it and you cannot understand it, let us agree that
it can exist, indeed that *it must exist*.

The best way to begin to grasp the idea of another space dimension is to try and imagine the relationship between ourselves and a being of one *less* dimension than our own three.

At the beginning of this century, a British clergyman named Edwin A. Abbott published a book called *Flatland*, subtitled *A Romance of Many Dimensions*. It is about a 2D world in which, or rather *on* which, flat creatures slide around without any means of moving off their flat surface, not suspecting that they can do such a thing.

Flatlanders come in various shapes and sizes, according to their social status. Women, the lowest of the low, are straight lines. Soldiers, workers and the middle classes are triangles, the gentry are squares, while the nobility have five or six sides. The highest class of all is the priesthood, whose members have so many sides that they appear to be circular!

One day, our hero (an anonymous Square) has a paranormal experience. He is visited by a thing from upper space which he assumes to be a circle, since that is what it looks like from underneath. But it turns out to be a sphere, which picks him up and takes him for a ride into the exciting third dimension. Square is made to realise that there *is* another dimension, which he can only describe as 'upwards, not northwards'. When Square gets back from his terrifying ride in the flying sphere, he tries to pass the news on to his fellow Flatmen, but everybody just laughs at him and the priests sentence him to life imprisonment for disturbing the peace.

Flatland achieved little success. Contemporary reviewers found it 'clever' and 'mind-broadening', but also 'morally tedious' and 'desperately facetious'. James R. Newman, who rescued the book from oblivion, comments that although it is too long, not funny, and 'its didacticism is awful', it is nonetheless based on an original idea and 'suggests certain remarkably prophetic analogies applicable to relativity theory'.[3]

How does it feel to be Flatman? There he is, like a shadow projected on a flat ground that is as real and finite to him as spaceship Earth is to us. A line drawn in front of Flatman is like a brick wall to us. To him, circles and squares are like spheres and cubes to us, and he can no more escape from inside a square under his own steam than we can get out of a locked windowless room without a key to the door.

Now, suppose that some modern Gulliver discovers Flatland, and peers down from his great height at all the little Flatmen sliding around on its surface, none of them aware of Gulliver's presence because they have no conception of *upwards*. Gulliver might amuse himself by bending down, peeling a Flatman off the ground and dropping him inside a square. Flatman will be petrified with fear. How would you feel if you suddenly found yourself inside a room with no doors or windows, like the man who got bricked up in Poe's *Cask of Amontillado*, and had no idea how you got there?

Noticing Flatman sliding around in panic, Gulliver takes pity on him, scoops him up and puts him back outside his square-prison. Flatman then rushes off to found a psychical research society, convinced that he has had a paranormal experience that should be investigated fully, but of course the priests lock him up as a menace to society.

This may sound 'desperately facetious', but many living creatures on this earth are little more advanced in their think-ing than Flatman. A worm eating his way steadily through your favourite book would be very alarmed if you opened the book suddenly at the page he had just reached. He might climb out of his tunnel, turn round and start burrowing his way downwards, back to the beginning of the book, unaware that when you shut the book again he will in fact be burrowing what we call upwards. (Or sideways, when you put the book back on the shelf.)

There is said to be a tribe of Indians in the Amazon region who have no word in their language for any number higher than three. How would we explain to them such things as eighty-six point four, the square root of minus one or the fourth dimension?

To us, these Indians seem ignorant. To somebody out there, we probably seem just the same.

HYPERSPACE

I may have come up against another dimension on two occasions. One (to be described fully in a later chapter) was in the afternoon of September 24th 1974, in a slum area of the Brazilian town of Carapicuiba, when I was bombarded with stones that did not seem to come from a 3D source. The other was in October 1973, while I was helping investigate the poltergeist mentioned in the previous chapter, also to be described in more detail.

The events of that morning were very confusing. At about seven, I had half woken up enough to see and hear the girl who slept in the back upstairs bedroom leave the house to go to work. She assured me later that day that she closed her bedroom door, as she always did. I dropped off to sleep again (I had been up half the night), and was woken up properly a few minutes later by the stool sliding down the stairs. The second girl in the house was still in her bedroom, so she later assured us, and as my tape recording seemed to indicate, for the back bedroom door would not open without a loud creak.

Now the point is that the stool had definitely been in its normal place on top of the wardrobe in the *back* bedroom when the first girl had left it and gone out to work. And the bedroom door *had not been opened*. It is scarcely conceivable that the second girl could have slunk into the back bedroom, climbed on the bed, fetched the stool down and thrown it downstairs just to amuse me. But she could not have gone back into the room less than a minute later to throw the drawer of clothing out of the window, because by then I was wide awake and if that door had been opened, the staircase well would have been flooded with sunlight. I would certainly have noticed that, as at the very moment the drawer was heard to fall I was fiddling with the light meter of my camera to take an accurate reading.

I am forced to the conclusion that the stool very probably came through a closed door, or at least that it left the back bedroom without that door being opened. In other words, it must have been whipped into hyperspace and immediately out again on to the staircase.

Had this been the only incident of its kind on this case, I might well have let it 'roll off my mind' just as Eusapia Palladino's feats rolled off those of the Feilding team in 1908. But the stool and drawer incidents of that morning were merely two of a series that had plagued the family concerned for six years, in four different homes. Even if girl two had been helping the poltergeist now and then (we never established that she did), she could not have produced all the phenomena. Some took place while she was either out of the house or under close observation, and several involved the movement of objects out of closed drawers or cupboards.

There are no normal explanations for this, and only two paranormal ones that I can think of. One is that there is some power that can dematerialise an object, atom by atom, and put it all together somewhere else. The amount of energy required to do this would be so enormous that, if lost in our dimension, we would certainly be aware of the fact. The other is that hyperspace exists, and some intelligent source is able to move objects into and out of it under certain fortunately rare circumstances. This seems to me by far the most likely hypothesis. I am not saying it is possible, but that it seems probable.

Most attempts so far to come to terms with the psi world have met with failure, simply because they have not taken hyperspace into account. This leaves us with two options: either we try to sketch out a theory that fits what seem to be known facts, or we simply to forget about the whole business. Whichever option we choose, the facts remain. They do not go away even if they do roll off our minds.

Crookes touched briefly on the dimension problem in his 1898 address to the British Association. Recalling his researches, he said: 'I was like some two-dimensional being who might stand at the singular point of a Riemann's surface,* and thus find himself in infinitesimal and inexplicable contact with a plane of existence not his own.' Had Crookes read Abbott's *Flatland*

* See Glossary.

when it came out a few years later, he might well have understood just how Square had felt when he was visited by the
Sphere.

Some critics may spend the rest of their lives searching for
hypothetical ways in which Crookes, Hare, Zoellner, Richet,
Lodge and all the rest *could* have been deluded, dishonest or
just mad. But much of the evidence these men have produced
remains unshaken.

Now we shall turn to a theory by a Brazilian scientist that
supports their evidence. (Readers with a scientific training might
like to have a look at the Appendix at this point. Readers without one need not worry if they find the following section incomprehensible; it is a bit technical, but its essential points
will be repeated in more palatable form later in the book.)

ANDRADE'S MODEL OF THE PSI ATOM

Matter is made of atoms. The word comes from the Greek
atomos, meaning indivisible, and although the atom is now
known to be far from indivisible, it is still regarded as the basic
building block of physical matter, with its nucleus and orbiting electrons.

If physical matter has an atomic structure, psi matter should
have something parallel. We already have various models of
the atom (by atom in this section I mean the physical atom),
and Andrade has chosen the familiar Rutherford-Bohr model to
serve as a starting-point for his psi atom model, which he included in his 1958 book. The R-B model is a very simple affair
by modern standards of physics, with its neutron and proton in
the middle and its electrons orbiting neatly round it like planets
round a sun. Now that about 200 sub-atomic particles have
been discovered, or postulated, and with the electron behaving,
as has been said, like a particle and a wave on alternate days of
the week, the R-B model may not mean very much any more.
But it still serves a useful purpose as a theoretical model.

Niels Bohr is said to have made his contribution to the R-B
model after receiving inspiration in a dream. Andrade's psi atom

model was arrived at by more conventional methods, after many years of scientific observation and reflection. One source of his theory was that old favourite of the science class, the paramecium. This is a single-cell protozoan, one of the most elementary forms of life that is large enough to observe comfortably. Compared in size to such things as atomic particles or viruses, it is absolutely enormous, being about a fifteenth of a millimetre long. The paramecium lives, moves and has being. It gobbles up bacteria when it can, and it reacts to attacks from external agents. When it bumps into an obstacle, it tries to get round it. In three essential respects, it is just like any other living being.

First, it has vitality. It coordinates the physical, chemical and biological activities of what we call a living being. Next, it has perception, because it is able to react to stimuli from its surroundings. It also has some sort of memory of previous stimuli, which it retains just as all living beings retain all memories. Finally, it has a kind of intelligence, because it is irritable or able to offer a response to stimuli.

Taking vitality, perception-memory and intelligence as the three basic components of the paramecium (and every other living creature), Andrade ascribed an elementary psi particle to each, or rather to the *quantum* of each. Quantum here means the lowest possible fraction, with a fixed and constant value, of each of these basic components.

For the quantum of vitality, he proposed the name *bion*, for that of perception-memory, *percepton*, and for that of intelligence, *intelecton*. The latter two psi particles form the nucleus of the psi atom, while the bion corresponds to the electron.

The bion is the agent that vitalises physical matter. It can be either free or captive. In their free state, bions form the cosmic store of what has been called the vital fluid, or the universal *prana*. They can be attracted and directed in the form of vital currents; and they can be absorbed, emitted, condensed and stored in a similar way to electricity. When bions are in a captive state, they are used to animate organised cells, vitalising the protoplasm and gravitating around the nucleus of the psi atom.

The seas and forests of the world, with their continuous cycles of birth, growth, death, decomposition and rebirth, are leading sources of bionic energy. Some people, known as magnetic or spiritual healers, seem to be able to tap this source. They can generate bionic currents and channel them into diseased organisms. Perhaps this is what Mesmer was trying to do.

Every science student knows that an electric charge in motion sets up a magnetic field. Andrade hypothesises that bions set up what he calls a *biomagnetic* field, or BMF for short. His BMF may be a similar idea to Burr's L-field, and it certainly meets Sinnott's requirement for a vitalising force operating at cell level.

The idea of an organising field linked to organic molecules is not new. In an experiment published in 1960, scientist Paul Weiss took some chicken embryos eight to fourteen days old, cut bits of tissue from them, mangled the bits up and strained them through nylon mesh. Then he transplanted his scrambled tissue back on to the embryos and found that organ-forming cells obligingly regrouped themselves and formed the organs they were supposed to form in the first place. Weiss found he could produce normal embryonic kidneys with scrambled kidney tissue from *different* embryos. He felt that his experiment suggested that when, for instance, a batch of skin cells that had never formed a feather were grouped together, a *field* was set up that led them to grow according to a specific programme.[4]

Weiss's work seems to show that cells behave rather like the iron filings sprinkled on to a card placed over a bar magnet which I mentioned earlier, only of course in three dimensions instead of two. The process of growth begins to look like the representation or the materialisation of a field. It is now known that cells will adjust themselves to new positions if you interfere with an embryo early enough; you can even cut one in half and grow two animals in some cases. But you cannot mess around with an embryo after a certain point in its growth. It does not seem to be a case of each separate cell knowing where it has to go, but of *all cells together* obeying some unseen master plan.

Commenting on Weiss's work, Jacques Bergier has said that if it could be repeated, it would hardly be possible to deny the existence of an organising field. A chicken feather not being intelligent *per se*, its cells could hardly be reassembled by its soul or its consciousness. The reassembly must have been done by physical or chemical forces, and Bergier thought physicists and chemists ought to be able to identify them. In these organising fields, he said, lay one of the great secrets of life, and once scientists had found the link between physics and biology, the mathematicians could take over and work out the details. Bergier suggested the word *viton* for the particles that carried the organising field to Weiss's chicken cells.[5] The only essential difference between Bergier's viton and Andrade's bion is that the latter must have four dimensions. More about that in a moment.

Bergier has also suggested that since it is by no means certain that the cause of evolution is biological at all, there might exist what he calls a 'space-time evolutionary field in which cells deflect in the same way as the needle of a magnet deflects towards the north pole in the magnetic field'.[6] The cell, he says, is surrounded by 'an aura of information' which serves as an organising field.

Now for a quick look at the two other psi particles of Andrade's model psi atom, starting with the percepton, the corpuscle that has the faculty of perceiving stimuli and registering them. This is what Andrade calls a particle of *pre-sensory perception*. It bears much the same relation to our mind and its actions as particles of paint to a finished masterpiece. It preserves the memory of all experience, and helps build up the fund of knowledge that we acquire. It is rather like a sensitised film that registers and stores the stimuli it perceives in their natural sequence, giving rise to the sense of duration that living beings feel, enabling them to situate themselves simultaneously in time and space. It is, in effect, a constantly expanding multi-dimensional historical continuum.

Being receptive to any stimulus, the percepton's energetic nature must be neutral, like that of the neutron. The last of

Andrade's psi particles is the active and positively-charged *intelecton*, which corresponds to the proton. This quantum of intelligence is the seat of thought, discernment and will, the mystic's 'divine spark'. It can only function fully when associated with a percepton, its fellow component particle of the psi atom nucleus, which Andrade calls the *psion*. Around this elementary nucleus, the positive charge of the intelectons sets up a field and captures a bion which then orbits round it, thereby setting up a four-dimensional orbital layer.

Readers who are beginning to feel confused have no need to worry about the fact that bions, intelectons and perceptons are invisible to us. Atoms are largely invisible as well, as I have said. Using the most elaborate equipment, we can make up photographs of atoms by reconstructing their wavefronts, but we have no hope of seeing exactly what one atom really looks like with our own eyes. (A group of ten carbon atoms, for instance, measures 23 *billionths* of an inch in diameter.) We are never likely to be able to grab hold of a single electron and have a good look at it, not to mention all those weird sub-particles the physicists keep inventing nowadays.

Nobody has ever seen a virus, even under a microscope, yet physicists tell us that if it were possible to enlarge a particle to the size of a glass marble, a virus would be about as big as the moon in comparison. They also tell us that if the nucleus of an atom were the size of a pea, and were placed in the middle of a sports stadium, the nearest electron would be whizzing around somewhere at the top of the grandstand. If we can accept this kind of information, we should also be able to accept the idea that our minds are made of component particles. Whether we can see them or not is beside the point.

'Electricity,' Bertrand Russell said, 'is not a thing, like St Paul's Cathedral; it is a way in which things behave. When we have told how things behave when they are electrified, and under what circumstances they are electrified, we have told all there is to tell.' So it is, in a way, with the atom, both the physical and the psi ones. The Rutherford-Bohr model was only a way of representing 'a way in which things behave'.

Andrade's psi atom model is a way of suggesting how our psi component, or spirit, behaves.

All we need at this stage is to think of psi matter as real stuff, with a composition analogous to that of physical matter. The essential difference between the atom and the psi atom is that the latter is four-dimensional, interacting with physical matter through a biomagnetic field.

Just as the shadow of a man on a wall is a 2D representation of a 3D object, so is the same man, according to Andrade's theory, a 3D representation of something that exists in four or more dimensions. If we accept this idea of hyperspace, we may well ask where exactly is it? The answer is—right here. Hyperspace is superimposed on our own space, and our psi bodies are at least partly in it all the time, though we are normally insulated from its effects. We are 'encapsulated entities', as Gardner Murphy puts it. Cleavage between individuals, he suggests, may be no more than a question of biological organisation. When we have flashes of what is called ESP, we are spontaneously bursting out of our little capsules and making contact with something larger.

This leads us towards the concept of a collective subconscious mind, about which C. G. Jung has written a great deal. Man, for all his encapsulation, is not an entirely closed system. There are ways out, but experiences of them are usually so baffling or frightening that man hastens back into his capsule. Pascual Jordan was prepared to assume, with all sorts of reservations, that if hyperspace exists, then objects far apart in our world can be brought close together much as one can put two dots on a piece of paper and bend the paper so that the two dots touch.

My own experience has convinced me of the reality of telepathy, which is one of the commonest ways we can break out of our capsules.

One evening in 1972, when I was living in Rio de Janeiro, I was visited by a neighbour who had just had a rather alarming psychic experience. He had been in a prolonged session of deep yoga meditation, when blue flashes had started going off in the room (witnessed by a friend) and he had suddenly been im-

pelled to write automatically. The message he received involved
me, and sounded rather threatening, so he came straight over
to talk about it.

'Heavens!' I said, when I had heard the facts. 'I don't know
what to suggest. We must ask Pedro.' Pedro McGregor, the
medium and author I have already mentioned, was a good friend
of mine, but it was late at night and I decided to wait until
morning before calling him.

A few minutes later, the phone rang. I heard loud rock
music coming through the receiver, then Pedro's voice.

'Hullo,' he said. 'What's the problem?' Later, he told me that
he had been in the middle of a lively party with his teenage
children, and had simply been 'hit in the head' by a message
to call me.

On January 11th 1973, I was having a farewell party at another neighbour's house, which I left at about 9.30 p.m. to fetch
something from my house. As it happened, I had lent Pedro
some books I was very anxious to get back, but I had not managed to do so. I was packing for a trip to Europe, after which I
had planned to move to São Paulo.

As I unlocked my front door, the phone was ringing. It was
Pedro, asking if he could come over and return my books. I
thought he might have been ringing my number all evening,
but he assured me he had not.

On February 23rd 1973, I flew to London after a short trip
to Bulgaria. The flight was three hours late because of a strike
somewhere. Pedro, who was also in London at the time, knew
I was due back that evening, but he did not know the flight
was delayed. As I walked through the door of my parents'
London home, the phone rang. It was Pedro calling from a hotel,
where he was in the middle of dinner. He had not called previously that evening.

'Just wanted to say hullo,' he said.

When this sort of thing happens to you three times in as
many months, the chance-coincidence hypothesis begins to look
improbable.

BLACK HOLES AND BLACK BOXES

Telepathy may be one of the doors through which we can
catch a glimpse of hyperspace, but it tells us little about the
nature of the hyperspatial world. In the course of his cheerful
book on Black Holes, through which he assures us we are all
going to disappear sooner or later, John Taylor refers to what he
calls Superspace.

'It has no past or future, nor any dimensions. It is a lace-
work of worm holes, forming and disappearing, constantly in
motion but never advancing or retreating. It is full of ceaseless
activity yet overall it is static and timeless.'[7] If all science
can tell us about hyperspace (the prefix super- is more trendy
nowadays but means much the same as hyper-), is that it is a
lace-work of worm holes, I would rather it was left undefined.
We shall find more suitable ways of describing it when we get
there.

One practical researcher who caught a tantalising glimpse of
hyperspace was the British engineer and inventor George de la
Warr, who died in 1969. Born in 1904, he worked for many
years as a consultant to private firms and public authorities.
Around 1936, while still active in public service, he and his
wife Marjorie began experimenting in their Oxford home into
various ways of treating disease by radiation, and for the next
thirty years a startling series of claims was made, almost all of
them totally ignored. With the aid of devices that became
known as Black Boxes, the de la Warrs claimed they could treat
disease in absent patients by radiating at them through a blood
sample. They also claimed to be able to prospect for minerals
with the use of their various cameras, and they produced a
series of photographs of what were thought to be radiations
from minerals, tap water, and even animal and human embryos.
In 1950, de la Warr apparently produced a photograph of his
own wedding (in 1929) by mentalising the event over blood
specimens of himself and his wife. He also photographed the
future, producing recognisable pictures of the same one-, two-,
three- and six-month human embryo *on the same day*. This

astonishing series of pictures, which has been published,[8] offers striking evidence in support of Andrade's hypothetical biological organising model described in the Appendix of this book.

De la Warr made numerous other discoveries, but he was plagued all his life by the fact that results were not always repeatable, especially when a sceptical scientist or reporter was standing nearby and demanding proof of his extraordinary claims. (Remember Robert Hare and his 'anti-mediums' in Chapter 4?) De la Warr produced evidence for everything he claimed, and he did his best to cooperate with the scientific establishment. When he was hauled into court by a dissatisfied purchaser of one of his black boxes, he was as baffled as anyone else by the fact that some of his inventions only seemed to work when he or his wife (or a few trained assistants) were operating them, and not always even then.

There were in fact two different instruments that became known as 'black boxes'. One was for diagnosis, and the other (also known as the 'camera') was for treatment. The former looked, to the layman, like an almost empty box with a lot of dials and a rubber pad in one corner. To make a diagnosis, the operator would rub a finger on the rubber pad, altering the dials until the finger seemed to 'stick', which would indicate the 'vibration' rate of the problem to be treated. The basic idea is that every disease has a 'wave-form', and once the diagnostic instrument's dials had been set correctly, they would indicate 'resonance', which would be felt by the operator's finger on the pad.

De la Warr never claimed he could *cure* disease. Leonard P. Corte, a director of the Delawarr Laboratories in Oxford, explains: 'What has been suggested is that specific response may be obtained in the living cell which might enable it to naturally repel a disease state.'[9] According to Mr Corte, only eight people have been able to use the treatment camera with repeatable results. It seems that George de la Warr's successes were due as much to his mind as to his machinery, and that he was well aware of this himself.

I met him briefly in 1957, when he gave a lecture to a large and generally sympathetic audience in Cambridge. At question time, a nuclear physicist from Harwell got up and said that although he could not quite understand what de la Warr was doing, he could find no fault with his scientific approach to his work, and nor could he doubt his honesty and sincerity. De la Warr gave me the impression of somebody who knows he is on to something new and exciting, but is not quite sure what.

His most startling claim of all was that he was able to 'tune in' on either the past *or the future* by way of what he called the fundamental rays of the multi-dimensional magnetic spectrum. To do this, he used a specially-built spiral aerial, a representation in three dimensions of what he felt to be the *double* vortex of energy emitted by the atoms of all matter, living or not, and existing or at least originating in a dimension other than our own.

The history of science is full of coincidences. The most famous of all is the simultaneous concept of natural selection presented by Wallace and Darwin in 1858. Faraday and Henry discovered electromagnetic induction within months of each other, in England and the U.S. respectively. Lobachevsky in Russia and Janos Bolyai in Hungary worked out the basic concepts of non-Euclidian geometry at the same time. Newton and Leibnitz both discovered the calculus, and Lodge and Marconi both demonstrated wireless telegraphy independently.

All this may prove is that similar causes tend to produce similar effects. There must be scores of people bashing their brains out all round the world today trying to solve the same problem in any given field of science. If two of them solve it at the same time, this may look like a coincidence and lead to arguments as to who gets the Nobel Prize, but it may be no more than a sort of academic survival of the fastest as well as the fittest.

Even so, the ideas of Andrade and de la Warr coincide remarkably closely, although neither had heard of the other in the latter's lifetime. At about the time de la Warr was pondering on the implications of his double vortex, Andrade was working out his idea of a biological organising model (BOM for short), the term he uses for the form in which psi matter interacts with physical matter to regulate the growth of a living being. Andrade decided that the BOM must be a kind of permanent historical model, existing in its own space, and conserving the whole biological experience of its species in a multidimensional space-time structure. When it interacts, by mutual attraction, with a living cell, it forces the embryo to develop along lines that recapitulate the whole story of evolution of the cell's particular species. The BOM is just as real as a physical body, but is made up of four-dimensional psi atoms, elements and molecules which are stepped down to three dimensions by a process similar to that of holography. (This is the process of reproducing images by reconstructing their wavefronts, as a laser beam can record a diffraction pattern from which a 3D image can be projected onto a flat surface.)

De la Warr believed that everything was linked in a fifth dimension (four space plus one time) in the framework he called the multidimensional magnetic spectrum. He represented this in 3D in the form of a diabolo, a toy consisting of a spinning top in the form of two solid cones joined at their apexes. He insisted that this was only a *representation* of the spectrum in 3D; since we have no means of perceiving anything with more than three dimensions, we could have no idea as to what it really looked like.

To represent his BOM in 3D, Andrade illustrated it for his 1958 book in the form of two cones, joined at the bases rather than at the apexes as in de la Warr's model. The top cone is the *psi component*, with the astral body at its base. The other cone is the space-time continuum structure of the entity concerned. Both cones are aligned along a time axis, and in between the bases of the two cones, like the filling in a sandwich, comes the temporary physical body. The vital and astral bodies together correspond more or less to what Kardec called the perispirit body, the means by which spirit and body come together. When the physical body dies, according to Andrade, these vital and astral components come together and remain in a latent state, waiting to reincarnate or evolve elsewhere. At the moment of conception, the BOM connects itself to the fertilised egg by the tip of its lower cone and takes over control of the growth of the future embryo, guiding it through the whole history of its species towards maturity, while the upper cone directs a similar recapitulation of the individual's soul history.

Thus, a new-born baby is a new materialisation of two separate entities: a physical body descended from those of its parents and ancestors according to the laws of genetics, and a psi body descended from *itself*.

In the Introduction to this book I promised to present theories by two Brazilians regarding the psi world. In this chapter I have tried to give some idea of the first, and in the following chapter we shall see to what extent the views of a spirit support those of a scientist.

We do not know exactly who this spirit is, or was. He is known to his large reading public by the pseudonym 'André Luiz', but whatever his true identity, he has left us the most laboriously detailed description of the psi world yet written in any language, and since almost none of this is available in English I shall attempt to summarise it at some length.

Chapter 7

THE LITTLE RED FISH

The Cosmos is what it is, and Revelation can do no more than reveal it. Holiness itself must be a reflection of a reality beyond the veil. If this be so, then Science has come not to destroy but to fulfil; Religion must needs evolve into Knowledge . . . MYERS

IN 1943, Francisco Candido Xavier began to write his nineteenth book. It was published the following year under the title *Nosso Lar* (Our Home), and it is still in print, about 150,000 copies having been sold. It was followed over the years by no less than eight sequels, forming one gigantic novel of 2,459 pages; one of the longest ever written and certainly among the most intriguing for at least three reasons:

First, like everything 'Chico' Xavier (as everybody in Brazil knows him) has ever written, it was apparently dictated by a discarnate spirit, in this case a man about whom almost nothing is known except that he was a doctor on earth and he calls himself 'André Luiz'.

Second, the nine parts of the novel (usually referred to as the *Nosso Lar* series) show a remarkable consistency of style, as if they had all been written consecutively, although by 1957, when the last of them was completed, Chico's tireless right hand had pencilled the manuscripts of forty-seven other books from at least ten other purported spirits.

Third, and most important of all, the series contains a huge mass of information that we cannot possibly expect Chico to have obtained from any normal source. His formal education ended at primary level in 1923, when he was thirteen, and yet the *Nosso Lar* series shows clear signs of having been written by somebody with a professional knowledge of medicine, especially anatomy, and far more than the average layman's familiarity with physics, chemistry, biology, embryology, psychology and the history of evolution. Moreover, the books reveal a complete mastery of the Portuguese language, superior to that of many a Brazilian who has been through a university education. I have translated hundreds of pages of Portuguese, from legal documents and economic reports to full-length books on a wide variety of subjects, yet I have never come across passages as difficult as many of those to be found in the *Nosso Lar* collection.

In addition to the nine novels, the collection contains three more books; a brief anthology of phrases that distil the essence of André Luiz's moral teaching (*Agenda Cristã*) and two works of straight science which to date have baffled Spiritists and scientists alike (*Evolução em Dois Mundos* and *Mecanismos de Mediunidade*) summarising the scientific information contained in the nine novels in a form that reads like a series of lecture notes. The whole *Nosso Lar* series is listed in the bibliography at the end of this book. I shall not give individual references here because few readers are likely to be able to read the originals of this gigantic work, only a small portion of which is available in English.

Chico Xavier was born in 1910 in Pedro Leopoldo, a small town in the state of Minas Gerais. His mother died when he was five, and after a rather unhappy childhood Chico went to work in a textile factory at the age of eleven, two years before he finished school. At seventeen, he attended his first Spiritist meeting (he was raised as a Catholic), and on July 8th 1927 he went into a trance and wrote down a seventeen-page message on themes from the gospels, which was signed 'A Friendly Spirit'.

From 1931 to 1961, Chico worked full-time for the government in a succession of humble posts, and his only income today is his official pension, which amounts to about £40 a month. He has never accepted a penny for any of the books he has written, and he refuses to claim any credit for the authorship of them. In 1974, he described himself to me as 'a medium who received the contents of these books from the Spiritual Entities who are the true authors.'[1]

Though he has been showered with honours, including the freedom of most of Brazil's leading cities, Chico's life is a model of Christian humility. He gives all he has, and asks for nothing in return. When I first met him in 1973, he was signing copies of his books at a public ceremony in São Bernardo do Campo, just across the street from Brazil's Volkswagen plant. The ceremony began at about 3 p.m., ending long after midnight only when the last visitor had received an autograph, a red rose and a few kind words from the tireless Chico.

The works he has 'received' include contemporary and historical novels, poetry, children's stories, essays, a history of Brazil, and numerous works of Spiritist philosophy and teachings. Of all this vast output, for which more than 600 spirits seem to be responsible, it is the *Nosso Lar* collection that holds the attention of the more educated of his fans. For as with any of the lasting works of literature, there is something there for everyone.

Perhaps it is misleading to call them novels. Though they are written in the accepted style of Brazilian romantic fiction, with all the adjective-laden sentimentality this entails, they are quite clearly meant to be true, if in an allegorical rather than a literal sense, as with Bunyan's *Pilgrim's Progress*. *Nosso Lar* might indeed be called *The Spirit's Progress*. The plot is very simple: André Luiz, who narrates all nine novels in the series in the first person, dies at the beginning of the first book and shortly thereafter returns to his senses to find himself in 'the next world'. For the next two thousand pages or so, he describes the world he finds himself in, and how it constantly interacts with ours. In the tradition of Plato, Virgil and Dante, the books take the form of instruction from, or dialogues with, a series of wise and amiable spirit guides, who take every opportunity to plunge into a three-page paragraph that examines some aspect or other of the human condition in exhaustive and often highly technical detail.

André Luiz soon realises that the next world is no heaven. It is much like this one, and God is as remote a mystery to its citizens as he is to us. 'Death is merely a change of clothing,' one of his guides tells him. 'We are what we are!' The transition from flesh to spirit certainly 'broadens our concepts', but all we find after physical death is 'the paradise or the hell we ourselves have created'. André is warned not to expect any miracles, for there are no such things either in our world or the next. Everything that happens, however surprising it may seem, represents the working of the Law. 'We are not miraculous creations destined to adorn some cardboard paradise,' André is told, 'we are sons of God and heirs to the centuries, conquering values from experience to experience and millenium to millenium.'

The first and most important lesson André learns is that man is immortal. He is born into flesh ('dense matter') over and over again in order to acquire total experience and strive towards the point when he will no longer need to reincarnate, but can move on elsewhere to a sphere about which André can tell us nothing except that it is beyond his comprehension. He does, however, indicate that there are worlds apart from ours. Our galaxy, he says, is merely one of countless cities in a country whose size we cannot calculate, though he does estimate that it would take a radio wave travelling at the speed of light a thousand earth-centuries to pass around it. He hints at the existence of other 'cities' on Betelgeuse (527 light years from earth), in what he calls the Orion district, and also on Canopus, Arcturus and Antares.

All this vast work of creation, of which our world is a barely perceptible detail, is the work of Superior Intelligence, which irradiates corpuscles of mental energy. These in turn are condensed by spiritually-directed electromagnetic waves into sub-atomic dimensions, without loss of motion, to be transformed into what we call dense nuclear mass. 'All matter is essentially energy made visible,' André remarks, and it all emanates from a divine source even he cannot comprehend. But he is quite clear with regard to the main purpose of all life. This is to evolve as individual members of a vast community, and to evolve we must turn the evil we are doing into the good we should be doing. Creation is not only a Great Thought but also a Great Molecule. It obeys the orientation of some inconceivably remote Intelligent Principle, and it operates along rigidly scientific lines, with all matter being directed by the *pre-existent mental mould*. This reminds us of Driesch's 'something else' that directs material forces, Lodge's 'formative organising principle' and Andrade's 'biological organising model'.

Evolution is taking place all the time on innumerable different levels. Once a planet has served its purpose, it undergoes a process of 'atomic collapse' and is remade into a new celestial dwelling place. In the case of our own little planet Earth, evolution has been going on ever since we were no more than tiny cellular organisms bobbing about in the sea. These maintained and multiplied themselves by the process of schizogenesis, forming sponges in which the rudimentary spiritual principle learned to dominate autonomous cells, imposing the idea of obedience and collectivity. Next, the nervous system began to evolve with the jellyfish, then the worm and the Batrachia, as living things learned to support themselves on dry land rather than wait for nourishment to float their way. The spiritual impulse moved on 'from mere impulse to irritability, from irritability to sensation, from sensation to instinct, and from instinct to reason.' Victorious humanity has been emerging over the last few dozen centuries from a state of primary bestiality, but it is quite clear that we have a very long way still to go. We are still in the state of transition between 'primitive animality and human spirituality', and a brief look at the world of the late twentieth century is enough to show aspects of both at work. For all our sophisticated scientific, artistic and cultural achievements, we still have torture, terrorism and starvation. We are only half way to our final goal, if that.

Discussions about evolution and the ultimate purpose of life tend to become a bit nebulous, and André Luiz constantly apologises for not knowing more about them. Yet when he turns to his own subject—medicine—he could hardly be more precise. Some of the most astonishing passages in his books are those that deal with such routine events as birth and death, but as seen from a highly original viewpoint—that of a spirit who is occasionally able to 'condense himself' down to our plane in order to be able to see into people's bodies, like a human X-ray. Listen to this:

'I looked at the sick man ready to discarnate.* I noted in detail that the soul was slowly withdrawing itself through isolated organic points. I was astonished to see a focus of dimming light right in the centre of the cranium; a candle flickering to the soft undulations of the wind, filling the whole encephalic region . . . The scientific picture was simply stupefying; I was able to identify the nine organ-systems of the human machine: the osseous framework, the musculature, the blood circulation, the blood purifying apparatus consubstantiated by the lungs and kidneys, the lymphatic system, the digestive machinery, the nervous system, the hormone glands and the sense organs . . . The blood circulation was like the movement of vitalising channels in that small world of bones, flesh, water and residues. Millions of microscopic organisms came and went in the impoverished current of red globules . . . Larger elements of the microbian flora became tiny boats carrying hundreds of minuscule beasts, invading all of the organised nuclei . . . And as the invading microbes were consolidating themselves in certain cellular regions, something was slowly detaching itself from the zone under attack, as if a still new mould were being expelled from a worn-out and aged form.' André watches the dying man's mental waves trying to regain control of his organs, but to no avail, as 'all his cellular complexes caused attrition among themselves and the bacteria seemed to enjoy the right to multiply increasingly and unchecked.'

'Thus,' André concludes, 'I saw that discarnation takes place bit by bit, which taught me a useful lesson.' His ever-present guide points out the departing spirit, which they can both clearly see, reminding him that the human body is like a machine constructed 'in the subtle mould of the preexistent spiritual body', invariably operated by the mind while it is incarnate. Upon death, this spiritual body separates itself from

* See Glossary.

the flesh molecule by molecule, though it remains what it always was—a mould or model that will be used again to shape a new foetus in its next attempt at evolution down on earth.

Long before 'Visible Man' kits were put on the market, André and his spirit friends had what sounds like life-size versions of them for use in their anatomy classes. André describes his first impressions of the human body as he saw it in a way he had never seen it before:

'The heart was like a big bird in its nest of arteries twined round the tree of the lungs; the liver was a vibrant condenser, the stomach and intestines were technical digestors and the kidneys were a complex filtering apparatus . . . My greatest interest was focused on the endocrine system, in which the glands stood out in configurations of light. The pineal, the hypophysis, the thyroid, the parathyroids, the thymus, suprarenals, pancreas and genetic sacs stood out perfectly against the living background of the perispiritual centres that combined with each other in the subtlest of nervous ramifications, singularly adjusted through the plexuses, with each centre emitting its own radiations and the group forming a harmonious whole . . .'

The centres he refers to are described in great detail more than once in the *Nosso Lar* series. There are seven of them; the coronal, cerebral, laryngeal, cardiac, splenic, gastric and genetic, and they correspond closely to the traditional *chakras* or *padmas* familiar to students of Yoga, being located respectively on the top of the head, between the eyebrows, on the throat, near the heart, belly and spleen, and at the base of the spine. 'Our body of rarefied matter,' says André's guide, 'is intimately ruled by seven centres of force, which work together in the ramifications of the plexuses. As they vibrate in tune with each other, upon the influx of directing power from the mind, they establish for our use a vehicle of electric cells, which we may define as an electromagnetic field in which thought vibrates in a closed circuit. Our mental position determines the specific weight of our spiritual envelope (the perispirit body) and consequently its respective habitat. Mere problem of vibration rate.' After death, he adds, the growth of mental influx depends upon the experience we have acquired and filed away in the archives of our spirit memory.

André Luiz again and again refers to the mind in terms of electricity and magnetism. It is, he says, 'an incessant generator of power, through the positive and negative wires of sentiment and thought, producing the word—an electromagnetic discharge regulated by the voice'. It is 'an entity placed between inferior and superior forces', receptive to the influence of each.

'Switches and conductors are at work throughout the cellular cosmos, elements of emission and reception. The mind orients this microscopic universe, in which billions of multiform corpuscles and energies are devoted to its service. From it, there emanate the currents of the will, determining a vast network of stimuli, reacting to the demands of the external scene or attending to suggestions from interior zones. Placed as it is between objective and subjective, it is compelled by Divine Law to learn, verify, choose, repel, accept, collect, preserve, enrich and illuminate itself, and always to progress. From the objective plane it receives the attritions and influences of direct struggle; from the subjective sphere it absorbs the inspiration . . . of the discarnate or incarnate intelligences in tune with it, and the results of its own mental creations.'

The mind is like a three-storey castle, with its subconscious, conscious and superconscious levels. André sees these in order as the residence of automatic impulses and living summary of services carried out; the storehouse of our present qualities and conquests; and the 'house of superior notions indicating the heights we are to achieve'. The upper floor is the important one, representing our future (the other two representing past and present) and in our often misguided efforts to evolve, we often fall down stairs and get stuck on the middle floor!

The brain, naturally, is the physical seat of the mind. 'In the nervous system, we have the initial brain, repository of instinctive movements and seat of subconscious activity; we see it as the basement of individuality where we store all experience and register the smallest facts of life. In the motor cortex region, the intermediary zone between the frontal lobes and the nerves, we have the developed brain, substantiating the motor energies the mind needs for manifestations in (the present). At the level of the frontal lobes, still closed to the investigation of the world's scientists, there lie materials of sublime order which we shall gradually conquer in our effort to ascend, representing the noblest part of our divine evolving organism.'

All our memories remain in the subconscious for ever. We do not retain conscious memories of past lives as a rule, simply because the brain could not stand the strain of dealing with more than one life at a time. However, our stored past-life memories are constantly guiding our thoughts and tendencies, giving rise to what André calls *conditioned reflexes of the spirit*. Psychiatric treatment, he says, is impossible without taking spiritual factors into account. Our mental aberrations are often, if not always, due to damage done to our perispirit in a past life. The phrase 'psychic surgery' appears in a book he dictated in 1954, some years before anybody had heard of José Arigó or Tony Agpaoa. The mind, says André, can and should be operated on in order to have its balance restored, like the body. 'Later, human science will evolve in psychic surgery . . . the earthly doctor will disembowel a mental labyrinth as easily as he now removes a diseased appendix.' He will also be able to 'examine an emission of optimism or confidence, sadness or desperation, fixing their density and limits just as he can now separate and study the radiation of the uranium atom.'

Freud is mentioned in five of the books, sometimes at great length. André's spirit guides seem to agree that he was a well-intentioned explorer of the origins of mental disease, but insist that he would have been more successful had he taken reincarnation and the law of *karma* into account. It is all very well classifying the psychoses and attributing them all to sexual frustration, but 'arabesques of gold on the sands of Sahara would not make the desert any less arid'. Mental disease requires understanding and treatment, not mere fine words.

'Inferiority complexes, repression, the libido and the emergence of the subconscious are not factors acquired in the short space of one earthly existence,' André is told, 'but characteristics of the personality emerging from past experiences.'

The subconscious is indeed the expanded basement of our memories, the repository of emotions, desires, impulses and tendencies that are not projected onto the screen of immediate actions. However, it extends far beyond the limited time zone in which a physical apparatus moves. It represents the stratification of all struggles and the resulting mental and emotive acquisitions after the use of several bodies. What the theories of Freud lacked, then, was the notion of reincarnation principles and a knowledge of the real location of nervous disturbances, which can rarely be traced to the common biological field, but almost always to the preexistent perispirit body, bearer of serious congenital disturbances, because of deficiencies of a moral nature, cultivated with fierce tenacity by the newly-reincarnated one in previous existences. The psychoses of sex, the innate tendencies to delinquency so well studied by Lombroso, extravagant desires and often lamentable and dangerous eccentricities— represent forms of the spiritual patrimony of the infirm, a patrimony that reemerges from afar through ignorance or the voluntary relaxation of the personality in disharmonic circles.

Attributing all human follies to sex, says another guide, would be like trying to study the sun solely by a ray of light filtering through a crack in a roof !

Having paid his respects to Freud, André Luiz makes some observations on behaviour that might be addressed to followers of the behaviourism of Messrs Watson & Skinner. The nerves, motor zone and frontal lobes of the brain, he says, are 'fields of fixation', and we should not get stuck in any one of them.

Anybody confined to one at the expense of the others will hold up his overall development. 'A creature stationary in the region of impulses (the nerves) loses himself in a labyrinth of causes and effects, wasting time and energy; he who gives himself up totally to mechanical effort, without consulting the past or organising bases for the future, mechanises existence and deprives it of edifying light while those who seek refuge exclusively in the temple of superior notions run the risk of contemplation without action, meditation without toil, and resignation without profit.' In order for our minds to evolve, they must be balanced by making full use of each 'field of fixation'. André seems to condemn the ivory-tower saint along with the mindless stimulus-and-response automaton of the behaviourists. Life is to be lived to the full, bearing in mind that it is only a brief intermediate stage between our long past history and our even longer future one.

Elsewhere, however, he does point out that occasionally we must spend a lifetime restricted in some way in order to achieve a quality we lacked previously. I will enlarge on this point in a moment when I get on to the subject of *karma*. Incidentally, it seems that Chico Xavier himself is going through such a lifetime; he has never married and not even the Brazilian press has managed to link his name with anybody, which they certainly would have if they had had half a chance. Chico's life of monastic chastity and dedication to his work of writing make the views on sex expressed in his books even more surprising. In one, we are even treated to a close-up description of the process of fertilising an ovum. It is not quite what you find in the medical textbooks . . .

> The masculine sexual elements were racing along the natural channels in search of the ovule, as if prepared beforehand for a race of about three millimetres a minute. I was surprised to see there were millions of them, heading forward *en masse* in an impulsive instinct of sacred competition . . .

At this point André realises that his guide Alexandre is actually going to intervene from the spirit world, as occasionally happens when a particularly important rebirth is being planned and carried out.

I realised that Alexandre could see the chromosomic dispositions of all the masculine principles in motion, after closely observing the future maternal ovule, presiding over the initial work of determining the sex of the body to be organised.

After watching, deeply absorbed, the march of the minuscule competitors that formed the fecundating substance, he identified the most apt and fixed his magnetic potential on it, giving me the impression that he was helping it get ahead of its competitors and be the first to penetrate the maternal sac. The element he focused gained new energy over the others and advanced rapidly towards its target. The feminine cell that, in face of the microscopic spermatic projectile, looked like a small round world of sugar, amidogen and proteins, awaiting the vitalising ray, underwent laceration of the cuticle, like a small ship being torpedoed; then it went stiff in a singular manner, closing its tiny pores as if seeking to withdraw them into its own depths so as to receive the expected visitor face to face, preventing the entry of any of the other competitors that had lost first place in the great race.

Still under Alexandre's magnetic-luminous influx, the victorious element went on its way after crossing the periphery of the ovule, taking just over four minutes to reach the nucleus. Both forces, male and female, now formed one whole, converting themselves as I saw it into a faint focal point of light.

Working like a skilled surgeon, Alexandre next starts the process of division of the chromatin in the egg, which André confesses is a mystery to him, as it was to most people in 1945, when this was written. And now for the actual moment of reincarnation!

'Next, Alexandre adjusted the reduced form of Segismundo, which was interpenetrating with the perispiritual organism of (the mother) over that microscopic globe of light impregnated with life, and I saw this latent life beginning to move.' The initial operation, that of joining the psi body of the reincarnating Segismundo to that of his future mother, is over, having taken just fifteen minutes, and André settles down to watch the process of cell division that is to lead to the formation of the baby's embryo.

The material organism is to supply all the aliment for the basic organisation of the physical apparatus, while the reduced form of Segismundo, like a vigorous model, will act like a magnet among iron filings, giving a consistent form to its future manifestation on the stage of Earth. (My italics.)

Reincarnation, says Alexandre, means a recommencement of the whole process of evolution, starting with the amoeba. 'This is why the future body of a man may not be different in its embryonic development from the formation of a reptile or a bird. What operates the differentiation of the form is the evolutive value, contained in the perispiritual mould of the being that adopts the fluids of the flesh. Thus, upon returning to the denser sphere, which Segismundo is doing, it must recapitulate all the experiences lived through in the long drama of our perfection, even if only for a few days or hours, repeating in a rapid course the stages it has overcome and the lessons it has learned, stopping in the position at which it must carry on its apprenticeship. Soon after the microscopic form of the amoeba, the signs of the aquatic era will appear in Segismundo's foetal process, and so on through all periods of transition or stages of progress the creature has already been through on its incessant march towards perfection . . .'

André learns that reincarnation is usually an automatic process, with the spirit simply drawn to a certain parent. When the soul is more advanced, it chooses its parents with more care. Segismundo has chosen to be reborn as the son of a man he once murdered, so that they can both forgive each other and get over a bad stage of evolution. But before the sexual act that is to lead to Segismundo's rebirth takes place, the future father has a premonition that he is trying to come back and at first refuses to accept him. The spirit guides have to work on his mind for some time before he agrees to welcome 'the beggar knocking on his door' and forgive him.

Moral considerations apart, the mechanisms of reincarnation are fascinating enough. André Luiz learns that people can actually help plan their own future bodies, with the help of genetic engineers at the Reincarnation Planning Department. Here, people being reborn for a specific purpose are able to ask for physical defects that will help them develop qualities they need.

'I have to defend myself against certain temptations of my inferior nature,' says one, 'and my bad leg will help me, making me think of better things. It will be an antidote to vanity, a sentinel against the devastation of self-love.' The physical laws of heredity are fully respected, André is told over and over again, but now and then 'modifications can be impressed on matter', such as bad leg, a weak heart or more serious disabilities. I hope it will be some comfort to the millions of the physically disabled to feel that they may have asked for their disabilities themselves; some I have met seem to accept this instinctively.

To plan a new human being, the bioengineers make use of the life-size Visible Man, which fascinates André. His lengthy and detailed description of it reveals a sound knowledge of anatomy. 'From the frontal to the annular ligament of the tarsus, threads of light were to be seen symbolising the various regions of the general musculature. Some fibres, however, were more brilliant, such as those in the orbicular zone of the eyelids, the triangular zone of the lips, the great pectoral, the pectineal, and in the thenar and hypothenar prominences as far as the extensor of the fingers . . . I was struck by the perfect composition of the vessels distributed around the coeliac trunk, like small rivers of light. Outstanding was the luminosity of the upper and lower venae cavae, the external and internal jugulars, the arteries and axillary veins, the upper mesenteric and splenary arteries, the descending aorta, the iliac vessel and the ganglia of the groin.'

André sees the glands as 'small stars of life, like a rutile antenna attracting light from the Most High', each under the direction of the pineal, 'a small bluish sun that kept all the others within its field of magnetic attraction, from the hypophysis to the region of the ovaries, like our star of life, guaranteeing the cohesion and movement of its great family of planets and asteroids'.

The bioengineers seem to have a way of programming a whole body and then condensing their design into the genes. André cannot quite figure out how they do this, as he freely admits. Nor can he understand the process by which a spirit is gradually 'miniaturised' before being linked to that of its new mother. He watches this happen, and can only say that 'something was being eliminated from his form' as the guide orders him to mentalise an embryo and make himself small. It is such moments of bewilderment that make André Luiz's books so convincing; so many alleged 'spirit authors' like to appear omniscient that it is refreshing to find one who is not, and frequently admits he is not.

Yet however baffled André (and most readers) may be much of the time, those other-worldly spirit guides certainly know their jobs. The bioengineers use 'chromosome maps' to decide where they can intervene to the client's best advantage. One of them shows André his work:

'Here we have the design for a friend of mine's future reincarnation. Can you see some dark points, from the colon down to the sigmoid loop? This indicates that he will suffer from an important ulcer in this region as soon as he reaches physical majority. He chose it, though . . .' The reason he chose it was to experience the same pain that he once inflicted on a man by knifing him to death. André also learns that some advanced souls ask for physically unattractive bodies, 'thereby concealing the beauty of their souls to guarantee an efficient task'.

André is never tired of learning, and his friendly guides always seem to have a lengthy lecture ready to give him on request. One of the most intriguing of these concerns the pineal gland, which takes up a whole chapter.

From his medical student days on earth, André recalls that

this gland presided over the control of sexual instincts during childhood, then to fade away and hand over its functions to the genital glands. Not at all, says his guide; the pineal is the seat of our divine potential, although in most of us it remains asleep or 'embryonic' as he puts it.

'It is not a dead organ, as used to be supposed,' the guide goes on.

It is the gland of mental life, awakening puberty and creative forces in man's organism, then continuing to function as the most advanced laboratory of psychic elements of the earthly creature . . . During infantile development, the readjustment phase for this important centre of the pre-existent perispiritual body, the pineal seems to constitute the brake on sexual manifestations. However, there are some rectifications to be made. At the age of about fourteen, it recommences from a stationary position as to its essential attributes, to function in reincarnate man. That which represented control is now a creative fount and an escape valve. The pineal gland readjusts itself to the organic concert and reopens its marvellous worlds of sensation and impressions in the emotional sphere. It delivers itself to the recapitulation of man's sexuality, examining the inventory of passions lived in another age, now reappearing under strong impulses . . .

It presides over the nervous phenomena of emotivity, like an organ of exalted expression in the ethereal body . . . The genital glands secrete sex hormones, but the pineal gland, if I may put it this way, secretes 'psychic hormones' or 'units of force' that are to act in a positive manner in the generating of energies. The chromosomes of the seminal pouch cannot escape its absolute and determined influence . . .

It maintains ascendancy throughout the endocrine system. Connected to the mind through the electromagnetic principles of the vital field, unidentified as yet by ordinary science, it commands the subconscious forces under the direct determination of the will. The networks of nerves form telegraph lines for its immediate orders to every cellular department, and under its direction all organs' autonomous storehouses are kept supplied with psychic energy . . .

As controller of the emotive world, its position in sexual experience is basic and absolute. Generally speaking, we have all, now or in the past, debased this sacred fire of creative forces, transforming it into a relaxed magnet between inferior sensations of an animal nature. How many existences have we misspent channelling our spiritual potentials into the lowest fields of materialist pleasure? Lamentably divorced from the law of usage, we embrace emotional disorderliness, and that, my dear friend, leads us to our multi-millenary dissipation of generating energies, weighing us down with moral commitments as well as those we have wounded with our thoughtlessness and folly.

As usual, André's guides make moral considerations a matter of practical common sense. There is no preaching, no stuffing of moral teaching down unwilling throats. If we live correctly, we evolve higher and sooner. If we do not, we stay where we are. It is entirely up to us. The law is the law.

Karma, as André Luiz sees it, is merely a question of cause and effect, or action and reaction. 'The action of evil may be rapid,' he observes, 'but nobody knows how long the process of reaction may take!'. Our karma is our personal balance sheet, showing our credits and debits, and not only individuals, but also countries and institutions have such balance sheets.

So far, I have only quoted extracts from the didactic passages of the Nosso Lar series. But I must stress that nine out of the twelve books that form the collection are essentially novels, written in the style and form of popular Brazilian fiction.

In between his (or his guides') lengthy discourses on Freud, sex, the pineal gland, and so on, André Luiz invariably inserts episodes to show how his teachings are (or more often are not) put into practice, by ordinary mortal men, women and children. In many cases, these fictional episodes amount to self-contained short stories, or even short novels, the plots of which are so complex and already so condensed that I cannot hope even to summarise one here. A particularly intriguing one is set at the time of the war between Brazil and Paraguay (1865–70), containing a mass of accurate historical detail and giving the impression that the war is still going on. Another episode introduces the powerful and unforgettable character of Gregorio, a vain and rebellious spirit whom some see as a personification of what we call the devil. The description of how Gregorio is made to accept the law of personal evolution makes exciting reading.

Each of these episodes seems to have been put together in order to illustrate how the physical and spirit worlds interact. André is constantly being taken down to Earth on some special mission or other (you get here from there by 'reducing the vibration rate') usually for the purpose of helping out somebody who has asked for assistance by prayer. Prayer is no more than a form of telepathy, or the transmission of images at a distance via *fields of mental energy*, and it can be received by discarnate as well as incarnate minds. André is given a long lecture on the workings of television, and shown how the process of prayer is analogous in some ways, except that mental energy is much stronger than electricity and it not subject to our laws of material physics.

Help is given to those who seek it by direct communication between the spirit guide and the patient. André gives many fascinating descriptions of mediumistic séances as seen from the other side. He describes automatic writing sessions, materialisations, and speaking through incorporated mediums. He touches on the subject of xenoglossy, or speaking strange languages in trance, pointing out that a medium can only do this if he actually did speak the language concerned in a past existence. (Ian Stevenson, in his study of the subject, has put forward a similar idea.)[2]

The first essential for any kind of mediumistic interchange is a suitable medium. 'He needs clarity and serenity, like the crystalline mirror of a lake. Otherwise, the waves of unrest would disturb the projection of our spirituality onto earthly materiality, just as stormy waters cannot reflect the sublime images of the sky and surrounding nature.' Getting the medium into the right state of mind is described in precise technical terms:

> First, his nerve cells received a new magnetic coefficient, so that there should be no regrettable loss of the tigroid or Nissl corpuscles needed for the processes of intelligence . . . The supra-renal glands received an increase of energy, so that there could be a more rapid production of adrenalin, which we need in order to compensate for the eventual spending of nervous resources.

To produce automatic writing, the spirit simply makes contact with the medium's frontal lobes and his right hand, leaving the rest of his brain and body free. This would explain how mediums are often able to write and speak at the same time, remaining almost entirely conscious of their surroundings.

Preparations for a materialisation session are more elaborate. The room has to be ionised and disinfected with ozone to kill bacteria, or what the guides call 'expressions of inferior activity' that might harm the medium's ectoplasm. The spirits bring along their own supply of energy, gathered from plants and water, which is used to reinforce the ectoplasm exteriorised by the medium, whose physical and psi bodies have been separated by magnetic passes. The communicating entity then links himself to the medium's perispirit and appears as himself. Materialisation is a fairly complicated process, and the spirits do not go in for it without good reason—the reason usually being the same as for all other phenomena; to produce proof of the existence of a spirit world.

The spirits are all in favour of psychical research, but they have little time for negatively-minded researchers who insist upon 'normal' explanations for the effects they work so hard to produce. 'Researchers,' says a guide, 'currently known as metapsychists, are strange workers who swarm all over the field of service without producing anything fundamentally useful. They bend over the soil, count the grains of sand and the invading worms, calculate the degree of heat and study the longitude, climatic conditions and atmospheric variations. But to the surprise of more sincere workers, they forget about the seed.' Research is necessary, they insist, but not as mere entertainment for the researcher.

In one of his rare moments of humour, André Luiz describes a séance at which a spirit, with some difficulty, incorporates himself in the medium's body and delivers a forty-five minute speech exhorting the values of the spiritual life. Afterwards, the spirit's son, who is present, says it was all very interesting but not very convincing. 'He might have given us better proof of his identity!' No wonder the spirits often feel they are wasting their time trying to get through to us.

To illustrate the positive kind of research, we are told the story of a little red fish living with other bigger fish in an ornamental lake fed only by a narrow stone-lined canal. One day the red fish finds the canal, and thinks to himself how interesting it would be to explore it and see where it led to. Although he is the smallest fish in the lake (the others do nothing but eat all day and are greatly overweight) he has to go on a diet before he can squeeze through the narrow gap between the bars, but he finally makes it, and swims excitedly into a new world. He meets other fish of a kind he has never seen before, and sees all kinds of wonderful new scenery. His whole life is changed, expanded and made more enjoyable. It is all so marvellous that he feels obliged to go back to his lake and tell the other fish about it, especially when he learns that in the dry season the water on land disappears as all the rivers drain off into the sea.

He makes his way back to the lake only to find that none of the fat lazy fish even noticed his departure. Reluctantly, they allow him to describe his experiences, to which they listen without much interest, having overeaten as usual. Beyond that narrow channel, says the little red fish, there is a whole new world, with rivers bordered with flowers, and all sorts of nice friendly fish like trout, salmon, mullet and dogfish. And then there is the sea, where the scenery and vegetation are simply marvellous, and fish live in Coral Palaces instead of this rotten old muddy lake. Why don't they all come back with him and see for themselves? After losing weight, of course.

'This is all frankly impossible,' say the other fish. 'Ravings of a diseased brain. Can't you see that our lake is the centre of the Universe?' They tell him to clear off and stop trying to disturb their peace.

The little red fish leaves them sadly, and swims back to his distant coral palace, this time to settle down for good.

A few years later, there is a disastrous drought, and the ornamental lake dries up altogether. The corpses of the fat and ignorant fish lie rotting in the mud at the bottom . . .

'André Luiz's efforts,' says Emmanuel, who tells this story in his introduction to one of the Nosso Lar books, 'are like those of the little red fish, seeking to bring light to darkness . . . He is telling his former colleagues (on Earth) that there is a more intense and beautiful life, though painstaking individual betterment is needed to make the narrow crossing to the clarities of sublimation.' There are many human fish he adds, lying around waiting for free entry to paradise after they die, and expecting it to be full of miraculous wonders. (Emmanuel is Chico Xavier's chief spirit guide, who also serves as general editor of the Nosso Lar series. He has also written several excellent historical novels set in Ancient Rome, scene of one of his previous lives.)

'But,' says Emmanuel elsewhere, 'death will not give anybody a free passport to celestial bliss. It will never promote anybody compulsorily from man to angel. Each creature will pass through the customs carrying only the baggage of what he has sown, and he will learn that order and hierarchy, and the peace of edifying labour, are the immutable characteristics of the Law everywhere.' André Luiz's greatest achievement is that he strips the next world of all its metaphysical aspects and presents it as something just as real as this one. There is no sentimentality about his conception of God, who is no benevolent paternal figure waiting to pat us on the head and tell us what good boys we have been. God is the Intelligent Principle, the ultimate source of all energy, which in turn is the source of all matter.

'I don't think the diplomatic service of my church is very well received in heaven,' laments the spirit of a deceased Catholic whose priest had promised him eternal bliss surrounded by angels just because he made a small contribution to his local church. According to André Luiz, priests often have a terrible shock when they come round after death:

> They raise sumptuous basilicas, forgetting the living temple of the spirit itself. They pay homage to the Lord as the proud Romans revered the statue of Jupiter, seeking to bribe heavenly power with the material size of their offerings. Ah, but they forget the human heart, they belittle the spirit of humanity, they ignore the afflictions of the people they were sent to serve. And blind to their own folly, they still await a fantastic Heaven to enthrone their criminal vanity and their cruel laziness . . . After more than a thousand years of the teachings of Christ . . . men went into the so-called holy wars, exterminating each other in the name of Jesus, setting up the courts of the Inquisition, full of prayers, where people . . . were tormented by the thousand in the name of the charity of Our Lord. As you see, ignorance is age-old, and the mere change of dress that physical death imposes does not modify the interior of the soul. We have no automatic heaven; we have realities.

André's guides have little to say in favour of religion as it is usually practised in the Christian world. 'Theological arguments of thousands of years obstruct the channels of human intelligence as to divine realities,' they observe, and they are not fooled by all the commercialism and hypocrisy that characterises the Roman Catholic church, at least in Brazil:

> When the Mass obeys mere social convention, functioning as an exhibition of vanity or power, our collaboration invariably results in nothing. What would we have to do with an act of flattery, in which devotees of material fortune or perversity puff up the disorderly conduct of the unscrupulous? There are solemn masses dedicated to astute politicians

and magnates of gold that are in fact pure sacrileges in the name of Christ. There are also masses for souls that constitute a mockery of the pain of those who have been carried off by death, such as those ordered by ambitious relatives who sometimes even rejoice at the absence of the dead man in their eagerness to plunder his booty and rush to notaries and wills. Such masses, strongly fertilised with money, are as cold as the tombs where the disfigured flesh is exiled.

But, the guides hasten to add, if people attend mass in a true spirit of prayer and charity, they will certainly cooperate. They seem to get best results in the early morning.

The whole history of man has been that of his dual behaviour, the conflict between intelligence and the bestial impulse.

We sang hymns of praise with Krishna, learning the concept of the soul's immortality in the shade of the august trees on the crest of the Himalayas, and then we went killing and destroying down in the Ganges valley in order to enjoy and possess. We spelled out universal love with Siddartha Gautama, and we persecuted our brother in alliance with the Singhalese and Hindu warriors. In the distant times of the Sphinx we were heirs to the Knowledge, yet we went from the mysteries of initiation to bloodthirsty hostility on the banks of the Nile. With the symbolic Ark of the Hebrews, we read the commandments of Jehovah in the sacred scrolls over and over again, only to forget them in the first blast of war against the Philistines. We wept with religious emotion in Athens, and assassinated our brothers in Sparta. We admired Pythagoras the philosopher, and we followed Alexander the conqueror. In Rome, we made precious offerings in marvellous sanctuaries to the gods, exalting virtue as we unsheathed our swords minutes later in the atrium of the temple, disseminating death and enthroning crime. We wrote beautiful sentences of respect for life with Marcus Aurelius, as we ordered the killing of blameless and useful members of society.

With Jesus, the Divine Crucified One, our attitude was no

different. Over the remains of the martyrs sacrificed in the circuses, we shed rivers of blood in cruel vengeance, building bonfires of religious sectarianism. We supported arbitrary and ignominious administrators from Nero to Diocletian, because we were hungry for power, and when Constantine opened the doors of political domination to us, we converted ourselves from servers apparently faithful to the gospel into criminal arbiters of the world. Little by little we forgot the blind man of Jericho, the paralytics of Jerusalem, the children of Tiberiades, the fishermen of Capernaum, to caress the crowned heads of the victors . . .

The idea of the Kingdom of God became a fantasy of the ingenuous, as we stood at the right hand of princes eager for worldly prominence. Even today, almost twenty centuries after the cross of the Saviour, we bless bayonets and cannons, machine guns and tanks in the name of the Magnanimous Father, who makes the sun of pity shine upon just and unjust alike.

So much for the history of civilisation and religion! What can we do about it? Everything, says André Luiz; or nothing. It depends entirely on us. This world is what we have made of it, and so is the next. There are other worlds beyond the next, but it will be some time before we catch any glimpse of them. We have to do our job down here first.

It seems a depressing picture. After all these centuries, the world of the mid-twentieth century is a disagreeable, neurotic and often unbearable one. Is there no hope for us?

Of course there is. André Luiz makes it perfectly clear that each individual one of us is on an evolutionary path, and whether we go forwards or stay where we are is for us and nobody else to decide. God is patient; he must be, to put up with our behaviour.

Twentieth-century man is tired of being told that all the world's problems will be solved if we all love each other, go to church on Sunday and help old ladies across roads. André

Luiz's great virtue is that he does not tell anybody what to do, ever. He merely points out that we are caught up in the workings of a vast and unchangeable Law, and that there is no way we can escape from the consequences of our thoughts and actions. Effect follows cause, maybe in this life, maybe in the next. It is in our own interest to originate positive causes. André strips religion of all its pomp, circumstance, mystification and hypocrisy and assures us that Christian Spiritism is a matter of plain common sense, backed (as no other religion is or ever has been) by sound scientific laws.

It only remains for us to confirm those laws by conventional scientific methods. We have to do this ourselves, for the spirits are not going to give us all the answers to the great mysteries of life all at once. Both Spiritists and spirits seems to agree that it is no use our receiving knowledge unless we know what to do with it. Give a baby a book on wave mechanics and he will happily tear it to pieces, though later he may become a great scientist.

It seems to me that the best place to start confirming the Law as revealed to us by André Luiz (and others) is to establish the reality of reincarnation. As I hope to show in the following chapter, this is one field in which much research has already been done, and initial results are extremely promising. If we can establish, as I think we can, that people (or some component part of them) really are reborn over and over again, we can then move on to studying the effects of causes originated in past lives, and gradually establish the fact that we alone are in charge of the destiny of civilisation.

Chapter 8

REINCARNATION

I have been here before. ROSSETTI

IN 1974, the BBC broadcast a series of talks on the theme 'Where do we go from here?' Six men and women of different religious faiths gave their opinions on the subject of life after death, and it was interesting to hear that only one of the six accepted human survival as a matter of course, and said so plainly without getting lost in vague theological arguments. This was the controversial politician Enoch Powell, and he made the only memorable remark of the whole series when he said that it was not a case of where we go from here—we are there already! One or two of the other speakers seemed to have some intimation of immortality, but it was odd that not even Powell made any reference to the large amount of *evidence* that points to reincarnation (and therefore survival) as a highly probable *fact*.

To many intelligent people in the Western Christian world, the idea of reincarnation is still anathema. We are born, we live, we die and that's that. Death is the end of everything, and the only consolation is that we all live again in some way through the twenty-three chromosomes we present to each of our children.

Western Christians are taught at an early age that when people die they go to heaven, which is somewhere up in the sky. The main entrance is through a gate in a cloud, watched over by St Peter, who knows lots of funny stories. When we get in, we meet God, a nice old man with a beard surrounded by harp-playing angels, and all sorts of interesting people like Homer and Shakespeare, who are happy to sit around and chat with us. How such idiotic ideas ever took hold of rational minds I cannot imagine.

All children know that babies are brought by storks and dropped down chimneys, somehow without being hurt in the process. When they grow up, children find out the truth about birth, but they still retain ridiculous ideas about death, if they ever give the matter a thought until it is too late. This is strange when we consider that for at least 2,500 years the idea of rebirth has been fully accepted throughout large areas of the non-Christian world, and that in the early days of the Christian church it was taken for granted. The Bible is full of clear references to reincarnation as an established belief, and while it is true that this belief is never explicitly stated, it is never attacked or contradicted. Such remarks as 'Ye must be born again' may perhaps be considered as symbolic but there was nothing symbolic about Jesus's disciples' reactions on being asked what people were saying about their master's origins. 'Some say that thou art John the Baptist: some, Elias; and others, Jeremias, or one of the prophets.' This sounds like a plain statement of fact, based on a widely-held belief.

And what are we supposed to imply from the most grammatically intriguing statement in all literature—Jesus's 'Before Abraham was, I am'? There may have been many other such unequivocal statements in the original gospels before they were allegedly censored by the sinister Byzantine empress Theodora, after the ecumenical congress of Constantinople in 553. The purpose of this event is said to have been to lay down the new party line on reincarnation, and to demolish the teachings of Origen, the third century Christian scholar who was a follower of Plato and a firm believer in his ideas.

Plato had no doubts at all about reincarnation. 'Souls,' he said, 'are continuously born over again into this life.' He warned people that 'if you become worse, you will go to the worse souls, and if better to the better souls.' This is basically what the law of *karma* is about, and Plato's teachings remained highly influential for at least 500 years after his death. Many early Christian saints fully accepted his views; St Augustine even suggested that the third-century Roman philosopher Plotinus was Plato himself reincarnated.

Plotinus taught that the soul entered the body 'through a certain voluntary inclination' in order to acquire experience of both good and evil, and that it rose again after death to its former non-material condition. As for Origen, he states his views on the soul in the plainest possible language: 'It puts off one body, and exchanges it for a second.' It was, he said, the soul's 'previous merits or demerits' that determined the body it was in at any given time.

Such beliefs never died out altogether through centuries of Western thought, enlightenment and progress in the sciences. Schopenhauer, Kant and Hume were all prepared to take the idea of reincarnation seriously, as were an enormous number of poets and writers from Shelley, Browning and Tennyson (who was an SPR member) to John Masefield, and even to such extrovert men of action as John Buchan and General George S. Patton. It was one of the basic postulates of Allan Kardec, who never tired of repeating that Spiritism was merely a return to the original principles of Christianity.

What happened to those original principles? According to Dr Leslie Weatherhead, they began to fade away as early as 325, when Roman emperor Constantine I became converted. 'A very doubtful gain to the cause of Christ,' Weatherhead comments.

'Christianity', he says, 'became in fact a polite veneer without power or beauty . . . Paganism remained, but now it was labelled Christianity, as it is today. The religion of Christ has never recovered either, except for brief periods of revival.' Strong words from a man who was a leader of the Methodist faith in England.

'Rome yawned and accepted the fact that it was now a Christian state,' he writes,[1] and it seems most so-called Christians have been yawning ever since. Only occasionally does one of them wake up and do some original thinking, like Dr Weatherhead, or, like Andrew Jackson Davis, Allan Kardec or Stainton Moses, get woken up and have some original thinking thrust upon them.

It is rather ironic that whereas paganism, according to Dr

Four pioneer explorers of the psi world from the nineteenth century: Above—
Andrew Jackson Davis (left), the Seer of Poughkeepsie, and chemistry professor
James J. Mapes (right). Below—scientist Robert Hare (left), who joined the
Spiritualists instead of beating them, and Judge J. W. Edmonds (right) another
eminent convert to the movement.

Four of the most distinguished psi researchers of the past hundred years. Above: Hans Dreisch (left) and Nobel laureate Charles Richet. Below: Sir William Crookes (left) and Sir Oliver Lodge. All four were presidents of the Society for Psychical Research.

Allan Kardec (1804–1896), the 'calm, cautious and unimaginative' French schoolmaster whose writings inspired Brazil's most active religious movement. His main works are among the most comprehensive treatises on the psi world yet published.

Francisco Candido ('Chico') Xavier, Brazil's leading medium who has produced over 130 books in forty years of automatic writing, though he left school at thirteen. The teachings of one of his chief spirit guides are summarised in Chapter Seven.

Hernani Guimarães Andrade, Brazil's foremost psi researcher and founder of the IBPP. Scientist, teacher, author and investigator of paranormal phenomena of all types, he has formulated a detailed theory of 'psi matter' which is presented in the Appendix specially written for this book.

May 9th, 1878. Two wooden rings specially made by Leipzig physicist J. K. F. Zoellner were found to be encircling the leg of his table, leading him to conclude that matter can pass through matter via a fourth dimension of space. He may have been deceived by a clever conjurer, or he may have been right . . .

December 17th, 1877. Knots tie themselves in a piece of string sealed to Zoellner's table. Numerous other inexplicable events took place in the presence of medium Henry Slade, who in the same month was able to convince a royal conjurer that he was not using conventional conjuring methods. See Chapter Six.

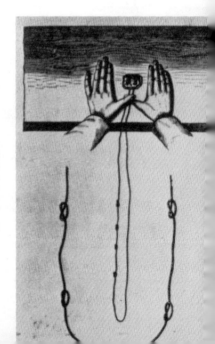

Celia, the lady from Pompeii, as a Spanish dancer and (inset) at the age of six when she first began to recall other lives. Note gipsy-like position of hands on hips.

Celia took this photo of 'her' street in Pompeii when she went there in 1970. It was the street along which she had rushed to her death when the city was destroyed.

Even as a young girl. Celia would have visions of erotic scenes . . .

Two of the wall paintings from Celia's house in Pompeii— the city's brothel. Celia 'rediscovered' them in 1971.

Photos taken by the author while Luiz Antonio Gasparetto was being filmed in June 1974 by the IBPP. Normally, he draws and paints in near-darkness . . .

Gasparetto rarely watches his hand as it flies over the paper, often producing a completed drawing in less than a minute.

Left: a vivid portrait of a child drawn in front of the author in about 30 seconds. Below: Gasparetto draws two heads at once, using both hands. He works at the same speed whether the special film lighting is on or off.

Carapicuiba, Brazil, September 1974. The author examines damage done to heavy roof tiles on two of a group of six houses. In the lower picture, several tiles have clearly been recently replaced, after three weeks of steady bombardment by an invisible assailant. It was this roof that was the target of the shower of stones thrown while the author was standing a few feet away on his first visit to the site. Local police agreed with all residents involved that no normal explanation for the attacks could be found.

Weatherhead, was labelled Christianity in the fourth century AD, in modern times the Spiritists, who carry out the teachings of Christ to the best of their abilities, which is more than can be said for most other so-called Christian faiths, find themselves being labelled pagans by both the Catholic church and *Time* magazine. (An official spokesman for the former once told me he had no statistics on the 'non-Christian sects' in Brazil, meaning the Spiritists, the people who do all the charitable social work the Catholics leave undone.)

In this century, reincarnation has been widely popularised by the trance statements of Edgar Cayce, mentioned in Chapter 3. Psi Cayce (by which I mean the personality that spoke through Cayce's body while he was in trance) first raised the subject in 1923, about twenty years after Cayce had begun his work as a full-time sleeping clairvoyant. The interesting point about his powerful advocacy of the reincarnation concept was that the waking Cayce was originally very much opposed to it.

Psi Cayce was quite capable of rattling off details of clients' previous lives dating back to 10000 BC or even earlier. He often named names, places and dates to help people locate evidence of their former lives, and much of what he said about the relationship of one incarnation to another is holding up well in the light of evidence now available—but not available in 1923.

He would often suggest that people's problems in this life were the result of wrong living in a previous one. He would give advice to children which would lead them to a new interest and a successful career. He undoubtedly did a great deal of good to thousands of people, and many still alive today will swear that they owe their health and happiness to the information he gave them about their past, present and future.

Fascinating as all this is, it offers no hard evidence for reincarnation, though some cases in the Cayce files are very convincing. So before I get down to describing how I believe the phenomenon of rebirth actually takes place, we should take a look at the hard evidence that suggests there is such a phenomenon.

In 1960, Dr Ian Stevenson published a forty-page essay on reincarnation, including a survey of the evidence for it.[2] Six years later, after a great deal of field work in several countries, he brought out a full-length work that quickly became established as the most important piece of original research since Myers' *Human Personality*.[3] Stevenson, a medical doctor and psychiatrist who heads a department of the University of Virginia medical school, would be the first to deny that he has proved reincarnation, or that he was the first to attempt such a task. Nowhere in his writings does he claim that his findings constitute final proof, and he gives full credit to his predecessors in the field. All the same, it is Stevenson who has put the subject on the psi research map as a reasonable area for further exploration.

What would constitute final proof, anyway, even of human survival? Stevenson put this question to delegates attending the Parapsychological Association's fifteenth annual convention in 1972. Most delegates agreed there was plenty of evidence for survival, but no proof, while one went so far as to say he did not think definite proof would ever be forthcoming. Dr Stevenson did not agree, saying that a perfect case of reincarnation *would* prove survival, and though none of the twenty cases he has published is perfect, I find it very difficult to resist the belief that reincarnation is the only plausible hypothesis that fits *all* the facts as presented. There may be normal explanations for each separate item of evidence (indeed, there are, and Stevenson lists them at length), but when we look at all of them together we simply run out of alternative hypotheses.

It is very important in psi research to take *all* the evidence into account when searching for hypotheses in any given area of it. This sounds obvious, but it is not always done. Take the case of Eusapia Palladino; you can easily make out a case using carefully selected evidence to prove conclusively that she was a blatant fraud. But if you read all the evidence you have to conclude that she could be both fraudulent and genuine as the mood took her. Some extremist critics have even tried to blacken D. D. Home's reputation solely on the grounds that he once got mixed up in some shady dealings that had nothing at all to do with his work as a medium. No court of law could accept this kind of argument. Can you imagine a defense counsel getting up and saying: 'My Lord, this man cannot possibly be a mass murderer, because he was once seen to help an old lady across the road.' Reincarnation, it is sometimes said, cannot be true because there are all sorts of alternative explanations for it.

Pro-reincarnationists sometimes claim, for example, that a childhood genius like Mozart must be carrying on from where he left off in his last life. This would explain his astonishing precocity, also that of the Indian mathematician Ramanujan, whose reported feats stagger my imagination far more than those of any physical-effects medium in history; or the multi-linguist Sir William Hamilton, who could speak thirteen languages by the time he was as many years old. But, Stevenson argues, too little is still known about the way the inheritance of characteristics operates. It might well be possible to account for child prodigies by rare combinations of heredity and parental encouragement. Mozart had both; his father Leopold was a good musician who gave his son every encouragement. In cases where a prodigy does something his father did not do, like Ramanujan, he might just have inherited an overall ability or a desire which his father never put into practice. Child prodigies make fascinating study, but they do not provide the best evidence for reincarnation. (Musicologists might like to pursue a passing idea of mine that if Mozart was a reincarnated composer, the only likely candidate for the latter would seem to be Pergolesi.)

The really good evidence can be divided into two groups; informational and behavioural. The first consists of bits of information produced spontaneously by children regarding supposed former lives which do not seem to have a normal source. The second, which is far harder to explain away, consists of personality traits in the child that correspond to those of the person it is purportedly a reincarnation of. These become even more intriguing when there is no direct blood relationship involved, and the possibilities of genetic inheritance consequently do not apply.

In addition to these types of evidence, we have birthmarks. These are not exciting in themselves, but they become important when they correspond to places on the body where fatal wounds are recalled as having been inflicted in a previous life. The perfect reincarnation case should offer plenty of good informational and behavioural features, plus a good big birthmark.

Stevenson did not pick out his best cases, of which he now has over a thousand, for study and publication in his book. He chose what he felt to be a fair selection, including both strong and weak cases, and some he agrees to be probably fraudulent. His twenty cases come from five countries; India, Sri Lanka, Brazil, Lebanon and the U.S. (Alaska).

One of his most interesting cases is that of Imad Elawar, from Lebanon. Its best feature is that Stevenson investigated it himself at the time, which makes it stronger than cases where information is recalled later by parents or friends. Imad produced fifty-seven pieces of information about his previous life as Ibrahim Bouhamzy, of which fifty-one proved to be correct or probable. Imad gave his former surname, the names of his uncle and several cousins, plus the name and a vivid description of his (or rather Ibrahim's) mistress. Imad, who was only five when Stevenson first interviewed him, also described and named the site of his former home, mentioning that he had a yellow car, a truck and a bus. He was correct in fourteen out of sixteen statements or recognitions made when Stevenson took him on a visit to the village he claimed to have lived in, as Ibrahim Bouhamzy, though he had almost certainly never been there before in his present lifetime. When shown a portrait of Ibrahim and asked who it was, young Imad promptly replied 'Me!'. Imad also showed behaviour traits that corresponded to those of Ibrahim, and a study of this case does not seem to lead to any probable explanation other than that of reincarnation.

Birthmarks were to be found on eight of Stevenson's twenty cases. They were especially common in cases from among the Tlingit people of Alaska, where until recently reincarnation was a well-accepted fact of life, with which birthmarks were thought to be associated. Jimmy Svenson had four of them, which Stevenson examined and found to be very similar to marks that might be left by bullet wounds. Jimmy claimed to have been shot dead in his past life as his uncle, John Cisko, who vanished two years before Jimmy's birth and was never traced. Another Tlingit, William George, apparently reincarnated as his own grandson after announcing that he would do so, and members of the family recognised marks on the baby's body that corresponded to marks Grandpa was known to have had.

Birthmarks are obviously of special interest when the supposed former personality is known to have had similar ones, or known to have died from wounds that could be expected to produce them. The case of Ravi Shankar (not the musician) from India involved a boy with a linear mark on his neck who later described how he had been murdered—by having his throat cut. Ravi produced a total of twenty-six verified statements linking himself with a boy known to have been killed in this way shortly before Ravi's birth. In the case of H. A. Wijeratne from Sri Lanka, it seemed that the murderer ended up with the birthmark: Wijeratne was born with a deformed right arm and breast, and he himself stated that this was because he had killed his wife in his last incarnation. The person he claimed to be the reincarnation of, an uncle of his, had in fact been executed—for the murder of his wife.

There are several explanations to account for some features of apparent reincarnation cases. Stevenson examines those of fraud, cryptomnesia (hidden memory), genetic memory and dramatic impersonation in detail. Yet as I have said, after reading his cases and studying several original ones researched by the IBPP (one of which is coming in a moment), I am forced to assume that children may appear to remember details of a previous life because they really do remember them, and that they behave like their former selves because they *are* their former selves.

If Stevenson's writings were the only source of information leading to such conclusions, it would be possible to dismiss them by the time-honoured method of discrediting the author. There is no need to do this, since we have several other sources of similar material, if seldom so thoroughly researched and well presented. Stevenson is not only a professional observer of human nature and a most meticulous field researcher, but also a very fine writer.

Some of his Asian cases have been researched at first hand, independently, by the Indian psychologist Hemendra Nath Banerjee, which adds greatly to their interest. Banerjee, whose findings have only recently been published outside India, began researching the field at about the same time as Stevenson, and has come up with some very good cases.[5] A Swiss researcher, Karl Muller, has provided us with much useful evidence for comparison with that of Banerjee and Stevenson.[6]

An indication of Stevenson's seriousness of approach is the fact that after his book had been out for several years, he set out to revisit *all* of his twenty cases in search of new evidence for the new edition published in 1974.[3] Seldom has such a mass of first-hand research been undertaken on any aspect of the paranormal, or so clearly presented as in this extremely important book.

Systematic research into reincarnation in Brazil began in 1967, when Stevenson read of a case in São Paulo in a German newspaper (the family involved was of German descent) and asked Hernani Guimarães Andrade to help him investigate it. The two men met on one of Stevenson's visits to Brazil and have corresponded regularly for many years. Andrade's first case, the one mentioned above, was described in my previous book along with a selection of others from the IBPP files, which now contain nearly a hundred Brazilian cases.

One of the most interesting of these, unpublished until now, is the story of Jacyra. (Pseudonyms are used, but the original material may be studied at the IBPP headquarters by accredited researchers, and the case will eventually be published in full, in English.)

In 1951, a twenty-eight-year-old man called Ronaldo committed suicide in his home in a small town in the southern-central area of Brazil. He put a spoonful of formicide into a glass of *guaraná*, a popular Brazilian soft drink, turning it dark red, took a sip and was dead a few minutes later.

In 1956, his sister Maria da Silva went to her regular Spiritist meeting with her husband Carlos. During the meeting, a medium went into a trance and apparently became incorporated by an entity claiming to be the surviving spirit of Ronaldo.

The communication was none too clear. Carlos understood it as merely a request for guidance for an earthbound entity; for Spiritists believe that former suicides remain tied to the earth plane in a state of confusion, often unaware that they are what we call dead. Maria, however, was certain that her brother's spirit was pleading for another chance to come back to earth— as her child. To settle the matter, Carlos and Maria held a private session in their own home, during which another entity came through and assured them that Ronaldo really did want to come back, but as a girl this time. He was pleading for a chance to make up for his failure in his last incarnation.

Maria was thirty-nine years old, and her husband a year older. The couple had no plans for another child, indeed, Maria had had her Fallopian tubes tied off, a clear indication that she wished to prevent further pregnancies. (Her tubes had not been cut, which makes pregnancy impossible.) But a couple of months after the second session, she was pregnant. It was a painful pregnancy; she would feel a burning sensation in her mouth and everything she ate seemed to taste of formicide. However, in October 1956 she gave birth to a plump and healthy baby girl weighing five kilos. She was named Jacyra.

By the time she was nine months old, Jacyra could both walk and talk. Like her dead uncle Ronaldo, she was cross-eyed, and her general expression reminded both her parents of him, though we must remember that they were already under the impression that she *was* him. As Spiritists, both accepted the idea of reincarnation as a matter of course, and believing their baby to be a former suicide they gave her extra special love and care.

Ronaldo's manner of death was absolutely *never* discussed in the family. Only a few close relatives knew that he had killed himself, and as far as the neighbours were concerned he had simply died suddenly. Early deaths are common in Brazil, where life expectancy is still only about 50.

When she was about a year old, Jacyra caught sight of a photograph of Ronaldo. 'Take it away!' she screamed, obviously upset by the sight of the handsome face she should never have seen before. Soon after this episode, Maria made a drink from some dark red gooseberries and gave Jacyra a glass of it. The sight of the red liquid threw the little girl into an inexplicable panic and she refused even to look at it. She reacted in this way on several subsequent occasions, once even saying she didn't want to drink 'that poison'.*

Before she was four years old, Jacyra had produced several signs of memory of a past life—as Ronaldo. As soon as she could talk fluently, she would ask Maria why she had two mothers, 'you and Grandma', and why she was supposed to call her brothers 'uncle', She remembered the house where Ronaldo had lived as a child, and recalled a number of incidents from his early life.

'Remember that time when Morena chased us, and made me hide inside a house?' she asked. Morena was a cow, and Maria did recall the incident, though she made no comment.

'And remember that time when I was running along the river bank and you kept telling me to be careful not to fall in? I never did fall in, did I?'

Maria made no reply. These memories worried her, and she

* Direct quotations are translated literally from taped testimony by those involved in the case. This applies to all original cases referred to in this book.

did nothing to encourage them. She felt that somehow they were a sign that Jacyra was in danger of following Ronaldo to an early or violent death. And she was even more worried when Jacyra sat beside her on the sofa one day and suddenly began to cry for no apparent reason, which was not like her.

'Why did I do that?' she sobbed. 'I drank that red water . . .'

Carlos recalls that he often came home at this period to find his wife in tears, after such an episode, which suggests that she would not have been making them up or putting ideas into her daughter's head. But luckily for Maria's peace of mind, this was the last such remark Jacyra was to make, with rare exceptions. From the age of four, she began to grow into a completely normal child, well above average intelligence. She did very well at school, and one day when she was seven she came home and said: 'See how well I'm doing? I'm going to be somebody in life—I don't want to be a coward any more!' On another occasion, she told her mother how glad she was to be a girl rather than a boy. Maria asked her why.

'To do what he did? I was a man, but I was a coward!' she replied.

In addition to spontaneously producing more than twenty different items of information about Ronaldo's life, Jacyra showed several behavioural features that linked her personality with his. From an early age, she showed unusual affection for Ronaldo's brother, and was heartbroken when he died in 1970 at the age of forty.

'I felt something different,' she recalled three years later, when she was seventeen. 'I'd never felt that way before in my life; it was as if a part of me had been taken away.' (H. G. Andrade, who researched this case with his IBPP colleague Carmen Marinho, was interested to learn that Ronaldo and his brother were almost identical twins.)

Jacyra also showed unusual interest in the girl to whom Ronaldo had been engaged when he died. When Jacyra was about four, the girl married somebody else.

'She won't be happy,' Jacyra observed. 'It was me she wanted!'

Carlos and Maria would always do their best to ignore such remarks, and they have insisted over and over again that they never encouraged Jacyra to recall her past incarnation in any way. They are both quite certain, as is Jacyra, that they never mentioned the real cause of Ronaldo's death in front of her. Suicide in the family is seldom discussed in front of children anywhere, and Jacyra was only told the whole story while her case was being investigated in 1973. By then, she had no trace of conscious past-life memories, and had become a totally normal teenager.

Jacyra has no complexes or hangups of any kind today, except for the fact that she still avoids drinking anything red. She still shows strong affection for her grandmother (Ronaldo's mother), whom she often visits.

'I don't think of her as Grandma at all,' she said in 1973. 'Every time I go to her house, it's as if I've been with her for a long time. It's just as if she were my mother.'

The story seems to have reached a happy ending. But the file on Jacyra is not yet closed.

'We don't close our files until either the investigator or the patient dies,' Andrade told me when I began to work for the IBPP. 'And perhaps we shouldn't even then,' he added, with a smile.

According to Spiritist beliefs, people will always have to face a repetition of a situation that led to their downfall in a previous life, so that they can overcome it, thereby upgrading their *karma* and evolving to a more enlightened state. Sometimes they fail a second time.

In the Lorenz case, researched in Brazil by Stevenson, a girl committed suicide by swallowing poison, and then apparently came back to earth as a boy, Paulo, in the same large family. Paulo's very first coherent words were: 'Take care. Children should not put things in their mouths, it may be dangerous!' Paulo Lorenz showed several similarities of behaviour to the dead sister he had never seen, and eventually, like her, he killed himself.

Though there are no signs of it as yet, it is probable that

Jacyra will one day find herself in a situation where she is faced with the idea of committing suicide. Luckily, many Spiritists who are well aware of this are in constant touch with her. Theirs is a practical religion, and at the first sign of conflict they will know what to do. Jacyra will be all right this time round . . .

What are we to make of a case like this one? Some may feel that Jacyra's parents, convinced as they were that they had a reincarnation on their hands, somehow transmitted their thoughts to baby Jacyra and caused her to produce memories and behaviour features. This would be an astonishing demonstration of telepathy, and we have no evidence that it ever works on this scale. It seems more probable that Jacyra really is Ronaldo coming round again.

One of the problems in reincarnation cases is that as soon as you think you have found a normal explanation for one, along comes another to blow your hypothesis to pieces. The Jacyra case suggests that parents' beliefs might be a factor that makes some sort of thought-transmission theory plausible, but how would this apply in cases, of which there are many, where parents had no idea of their children's former personalities? You cannot very well transmit a thought unless you have the thought to begin with.

What normal explanation, for instance, could account for the story of the lady from Pompeii in Chapter 3? Her parents were completely baffled by her early recollections, which came literally out of the blue—starting on the day she stared into the cloudless sky and seemed to move back to another life. Her behaviour and general character could not be accounted for by her inherited genes or by her comfortable environment. A sheep-farmer friend of mine has told me that recessive genes can lead to the appearance of a black sheep after several *thousand* generations of white sheep have been carefully bred, and since the laws of genetics are supposed to apply to all living creatures, they must apply to us. But can we regard people like the lady from Pompeii as no more than a black sheep, produced by a freak blend of the genes of her ancestors? I do not think so. Genes are not supposed to transmit memories.

Psi genes, however, could transmit memories. Jenö Miklós, a chemist from Timisoara, Rumania, proposes that the study of psi genetics should be given a prominent place in the general area of psi biology. Physiological functions, he says, are traceable to components of the chromosomes, so why not psi functions as well? Psi abilities, he argues, probably appeared at a certain evolutionary stage in man and have been preserved by the usual hereditary mechanisms; and there is no reason why psi genes should not be subject to the same laws of dominance, recession and crossing-over, that governs the physical genes.[7] This is a promising theory, fitting in with a widely-held general conception of human psi abilities as a kind of leftover from the days when we needed them in order to survive, a view Freud was prepared to support. Such abilities could include far-memory.

If people really do reincarnate, and I believe the evidence suggests this to be a reasonable hypothesis, it is logical to suppose that they do so according to laws as strict as all the other laws of nature. Do we all reincarnate? If so, why do all babies not start babbling away about their past lives as soon as they can talk?

A study of Miklós's psi genetics theories, if fruitful, might provide an answer eventually to the second question, though there are other lines of inquiry we can follow based on evidence we already have. No pattern has yet emerged to suggest a typical interim period, between one life and the next, though memories will presumably tend to be strongest when they are of recent events or recent previous lifetimes.

In almost every case I know of where childhood memories of past lives are very strong, the past life recalled came to a premature or violent end, often only a few years before the start of the present one. Of Stevenson's first twenty published cases, fourteen involved memories of somebody who had died unnaturally or prematurely, only two of natural deaths, while the remaining four were inconclusive. In the IBPP files, the great majority of cases with clearly identified former-life memories involve unnatural death, either by murder, accident, suicide or illness at an early age.

If the mind is an entity in its own right, it will obviously remain far more active when suddenly deprived of its physical housing, through early or violent death, than it would if it simply eased itself out of an old and tired body at the end of a natural lifespan. Old men forget even before they die, but the young do not, and time and time again we find children like Jacyra recalling past lives that ended before they should have.

We can almost state that memories of former lives in children *only* occur when the former life ended prematurely. There are exceptions, though. Two of Stevenson's cases concerned past lives that ended naturally. Maybe the people concerned had unusually active minds in their old age. Some minds can remain active for an amazing number of years; men like Bertrand Russell, Stravinsky, Shaw, Picasso and Casals were mentally active long past the age when many men are totally gaga. How can we think of minds like these suddenly ceasing to exist?

When there is enough evidence, it will be interesting to see if the proportion of children with claimed past-life memories corresponds to the number of people in any given country or area that die unnaturally. It may be that the great majority of people die natural deaths, wait a long time before coming back to earth, and retain no conscious memories of anything at all when they do. Some occult sources regard about 300 years as a typical interim period, but the time factor may not really be very important, assuming that time in the psi world is not like it is here. An earthbound spirit will presumably be more aware of earth-time and seek to reincarnate as soon as there is a vacancy. More evolved souls, existing in a different time dimension, will not be in such a hurry. As to the question of whether we all reincarnate, some believe that when a soul is sufficiently evolved, it has no need to return to earth and moves on to a higher plane of existence.

One of the most common objections to the reincarnation

theory is simply based on mathematics; there are more people alive today than there ever have been, so we cannot all be reincarnations.

We may not all be reincarnations—of human beings. I am not going to suggest that some of us were goats or pineapples last time; transmigration of souls (metempsychosis) from man to plant or animal is one subject where Spiritism flatly contradicts some traditional eastern beliefs. In fact, this question is one of the most controversial of all in both occult and Spiritist circles. In one of Chico Xavier's books, it is stated that there are something like twenty billion souls, several times the present population of earth, already in existence somewhere. Many have never incarnated at all, and still have a long time to wait. Allan Kardec, on the other hand, sees creation as a continuous process, in which we can presumably include the creation of new souls. As for metempsychosis, Kardec insists that it is the task of all living matter to evolve, and that when plants or animals die, the intelligent principle that animated them is immediately used for animating new beings.

A very quick look around us is enough to suggest that many people now alive may be going round for the first time—as humans. It is amazing what contrasts are to be found among people of a single social group. In my days of active journalism, I often had to tramp around the poorer areas of Brazil's large cities, which must be as primitive as twentieth-century living conditions can be; I am thinking of the mocambos of Recife so vividly described by the late Josué de Castro, and especially the alagados area of downtown Salvador, the very existence of which is an affront to the human race.

In places like these, you may find two neighbours who have had the same education (if any at all) and upbringing, yet who are obviously at different stages of evolution. Next door to an illiterate criminal who scarcely resembles a human being at all, you might find a man of wisdom, understanding, humanity and resignation to his present circumstances; as if he had deliberately chosen them for the good of his soul development. In 1974, I spent some time observing the behaviour of two regular bus drivers on the route to the part of São Paulo where I was then living. One drove in the standard Brazilian manner, that is, like a criminally insane caveman; while the other, an elderly black, would steer his crowded bus gently through the chaos of the city traffic with an expression of serenity you might have seen on the face of Einstein as he finally sorted out his Unified Field Theory. I cannot imagine these two drivers as belonging to the same soul generation.

Expatriates in Brazil, as elsewhere, spend much of their time complaining about their servants. I have had my share of disastrous housemaids, but Alexandrina, the black woman who looked after me for eight years in Rio de Janeiro, is one of the most evolved and adorable people I have ever known in any country. Though barely literate, and though her life has been a hard one, deprived of even what few consolations Brazilians of her class can hope for in the form of a husband and family, Alexandrina is infinitely more developed in her understanding of the realities of life, against which she bears no grudges at all, than any of my literate friends and also than myself.

Another common objection to reincarnation consists in pointing to all the people who claim to have been Napoleon or Marie Antoinette. This calls for little comment. Reincarnation has nothing to do with the creation of artificial memories based on fantasy-identification with one's historical heroes. And if Marie Antoinette really is among us again, I hope she is now a baker making cheap cake for the masses.

Some may object that the reincarnation theory makes nonsense of traditional concepts of genetics and heredity. Not at all. The human body descends from other bodies, while the mind has a genealogy of its own. It is easy to get reincarnation and heredity mixed up, especially since it seems quite common for rebirth to take place into the same family.

With all due respect to Tolstoy, all happy families are not in the least alike. Some give the impression that they have been together for centuries, having worked out most of their mutual tensions, and are almost ready to move elsewhere *en bloc*. Other families, equally happy, seem to be in the process of forming a unit, getting to know each other and gradually settling down. Yet Tolstoy was certainly right when he said that each unhappy family is unhappy after its own fashion. One cause of family unhappiness not yet recognised may be an unwelcome reincarnation.

The British, one of the least violent of peoples, may be surprised to know that they kill an average of almost two children *every day*. To be specific, a total of 4,600 children suffer 'non-accidental injuries' inflicted on them by their parents every year in Great Britain, and 700 die as a result. In addition, one British baby is permanently damaged *every day* by parental violence.[8] And this in a country with one of the world's lowest annual records for murder. (About 0.4 per 100,000—compared with 7.2 for the U.S., though these statistics are subject to various qualifications.)

To most mothers and fathers, there is nothing more beautiful and lovable than a baby, however exasperating they can be at times. The idea of hurting one, let alone wounding it permanently or killing it, is simply inconceivable. Yet there are the statistics. Some of the babies involved in all this brutality may be unwanted ones, and it should be possible to calculate roughly how many by comparing present-day statistics with those of past years when family planning advice and equipment were less readily available than they are today.*

I have evidence for another explanation that may apply to some of these unfortunate babies. Spiritists believe that some children choose to be born into families where they know there will be tensions and problems to overcome. They realise that they need such challenges for the sake of their overall evolution, but sometimes their new parents are simply not up to the task. Subconsciously, they recognise their baby as a mortal enemy from a previous life, and feel the desire for revenge. Flat-earth psychologists no doubt have other theories, but it seems they have not been able to solve the problem.

* These statistics do not appear to correspond to official figures. But for the purposes of my argument, a single damaged baby case would serve.

An extraordinary case of parent-baby conflict came to my notice in 1974. I cannot name those involved, but I have good reason to believe the story is true in its essential features. About seven years ago, a baby was born into a wealthy and socially prominent family in one of Brazil's big cities. The parents were Roman Catholics with no interest in or sympathy for Spiritist beliefs. From the very day of the baby's birth, the parents, who had other children, simply could not stand the sight of it. The mother in particular took an instant and savage hatred to her child, for reasons she was quite unable to explain. It was not deformed or ugly, but the mother just could not bear to touch it or even to be in the same room with it. It is not clear why the poor baby was not given away for adoption, but what happened was that the family built a special self-contained apartment in their large home, hired a full-time professional nurse, and had the baby brought up entirely out of their sight.

When the baby—a boy—was about six, the mother called in a Spiritist medium on the insistent advice of a close friend. As so often in Brazil, a Catholic turned to a Spiritist as a last resort. And as so often, it worked. The medium went to the house, wandered around 'picking up vibrations' and soon announced that the boy had been buried alive by the mother in a previous lifetime some centuries back. The only way out of the problem, the medium said, was for the mother to face the facts and try to make friends with her son, who wished her no evil. In fact; he wanted to give her a chance to repair the damage to her *karma* that had resulted from his previous death at her hands.

The family accordingly went off for a long holiday together, for the first time including their youngest boy. When they came home, the boy had become a normal member of the family. The mother had overcome her fear of her boy and they have lived happily ever after.

Two people who claim to have put the reincarnation concept to practical use are the British medium Joan Grant and her psychiatrist husband Denys Kelsey. Joan Grant is well known for her series of books which she herself describes as 'biographies of previous lives I have known,' dating back to ancient Egyptian times. Her husband became interested in reincarnation during World War II, when he was treating servicemen for emotional disorders. Together, they have written a book that describes how, by combining their talents, they have been able to help people by showing them how their problems originated in earlier lives.[9]

The law of *karma*, the idea that we are today the sum of our previous actions and thoughts, paying debts incurred in earlier lives, may seem no more than an attempt to impose artificial logic upon a senseless, cruel and entropic world. I do not want to get into the moral aspects of reincarnation here; either there is a purpose to our lives, or there is not. If there is, then the law of *karma* makes very good sense. This is a question everybody must sort out for himself.

Readers who are now convinced that they have lived before may want to rush off to the nearest hypnotist, ask him to regress them back as far as he can, and find out all about their previous lives.

Hold it! It is possible that hypnosis may be able to stimulate genuine past-life memories. It is certain, however, that it can also stimulate a whole lot of other things, especially dramatised fantasies that originate no further away than your subconscious. It is also certain that some of these fantasies will be very upsetting. A good friend of mine got into serious emotional trouble after a bad trip with an amateur and, in my opinion, unethical hypnotist. It took many visits to a Spiritist centre to get him out of it.

The classic case of fantasy-stimulation under hypnosis is that of 'Blanche Poynings', where it was shown that an apparent former life recalled in rich and authentic detail originated in a book the patient had read as a child and completely forgotten consciously.[10] The well-known Bridey Murphy affair shows how much confusion can arise when you start dredging for memories under hypnosis. Much of what the lady in this case recalled obviously came from her present-life subconscious, although normal explanations for all of her memories and simulated behaviour have never been produced, to my knowledge.[11]

Dr Leslie Weatherhead mentions some cases where the evidence seems stronger.[12] The most interesting is that of Annie Baker, who began to speak fluent French under hypnosis, although she claimed never to have studied this language. She named a street in Paris where she claimed to have lived at the time of the French revolution, and when a newspaper reporter went over to check, he found that no such street existed. He checked further, and found that it had existed, however, at the time of the revolution in 1789. This story was published by a popular Sunday newspaper which does a lot of checking before accepting a story with a paranormal slant.[13] (They once rejected one of mine, after giving me a long grilling. The story was absolutely true, but I could not prove it.)

This brings up the subject of xenoglossy, or the speaking of a language not learned in the current lifetime. When unlearned languages are written, I suppose the correct term would be xenography. Good cases of either are very rare. By far the best researched was that of the prolific novelist and poetess-philosopher who called herself Patience Worth, producing many volumes of colourful xenography through the mediumship of a Missouri housewife, Mrs John H. Curran. The language she wrote from 1913 to 1937 was English—but the English of the seventeenth century, which would be as difficult for us to speak today as many a foreign language. Analysing one of her books, a critic found that about 90 per cent of the words in it were Anglo-Saxon, and no single word appeared in it that had come into use later than the mid-seventeenth century, the period in which Patience claimed to have lived on earth. This case is one of the most thoroughly researched in psi history, and Miss Worth's books make enjoyable reading.[14] They may have little to do with reincarnation, but they offer strong evidence for the survival of a personality. No normal explanation for Mrs Curran's astonishing literary output has yet been found.

Xenoglossy and xenography are fascinating subjects, but I have not yet found either to be of much value in reincarnation research. I have only come across one case in which a child showed signs of the former. The little girl in question came out with a number of correct Italian words without any apparent prompting, without any member of her family being able to speak anything but Portuguese. I described this case in my previous book, and I have since learned that an Italian-born laundrywoman was in the habit of visiting the house regularly. She might have spoken some Italian on occasions, though there is no evidence that she did, and it is more likely that she did not, for Italian is very rarely heard in São Paulo despite the large number of Italian immigrants there. Even if the girl had picked up a few words from the laundrywoman, this would hardly account for many other features in the case, including a chilling account she produced spontaneously of her own death.

A pattern of some kind does seem to be emerging in cases that suggest reincarnation. Small children begin to make remarks as soon as they can talk that consistently refer to another personality than their present one. Sometimes they also seem to imitate the behaviour of somebody they can never have known in their present lives. Occasionally, they have birthmarks that seem to correspond to wounds received in past lives. It is definitely small children that give us our best evidence, and there may be much more such evidence around than many of us realise.

As soon as I became aware of this, I began to look for more evidence. I soon found that in many cases, perhaps nine out of ten, children produce no evidence at all, or if they do, their parents do not notice. Two close friends, however, told me that children of theirs had repeatedly told them that 'you aren't my real Daddy'. Too much time had elapsed in both cases for any more such information to be forthcoming. But one day, a trivial incident took place in my own home that suggested the way the best evidence is likely to turn up—spontaneously and totally unexpectedly.

Some old friends came to visit me with their ten-month-old daughter, who could neither walk nor talk intelligibly. While her father was showing her the pictures on my wall, holding her in his arms, she suddenly pointed to a Bulgarian ikon showing St Dimitri seated on his horse and skewering an enemy lying on the ground.

'Horsey!' she exclaimed loudly and clearly, with a big beaming smile.

Both her parents were rather surprised, for their little girl had never seen a horse. Nor had she spoken a recognisable word up to then, apart from 'Mama'.

On the same day, the little girl seized hold of a small red wooden horse of mine and refused to let go of it, showing no interest at all in several other brightly-coloured animals I offered her.

Some months later, I received a letter from my friends, who live in a fairly remote rural region of Brazil. I had asked them to let me know at once if their daughter showed any sign of producing information that seemed not to originate from her present life. An extract ran:

'. . . she's still keen on horses and made a curious remark the other day. We pointed out a horse to her and she turned around and said: "not horse, that a donkey", and she was right.'

I am certainly not suggesting that my friends' baby girl is a reincarnated Don Cossack on the strength of these episodes. I mention them only as examples of the way in which initial evidence has turned up in the past on what later became cases strongly suggestive of reincarnation, and also as an example of the kind of evidence that was forthcoming as soon as I set out to look for it. This was, in fact, the very first married couple I asked to provide me with reincarnation-suggestive evidence.

So if your little boy or girl suddenly tells you that you aren't his or her real Mummy or Daddy, or reacts strangely to red drinks or photos of a relative who committed suicide, or donkeys; or starts telling you all about the good old days in Pompeii —don't worry! Such memories and behaviour patterns are not likely to last more than about seven years. (André Luiz says that it takes seven years for the spirit to be fully reborn in the new physical body, and Stevenson has found that past-life memories last for an average of 6.9 years.) My friend from Pompeii is a very rare exception to the rule. Remember, however awful a past life may have been, all babies start over again from scratch. And most important of all, *they* chose *you* as parents.

Of all areas in psi research, reincarnation is the one that can really come up with an explanation of what human life is all about. So when the evidence turns up, however trivial it seems at the time, grab your tape recorder.

I was rattling back into São Paulo on a crowded bus one hot Sunday afternoon, sitting next to a woman on whose lap a rather cross little girl was dozing fitfully. The woman was talking to a man standing in the central corridor of the bus, and happened at one point to mention that somebody or other had just died. The man made suitable noises of sympathy, and there was a brief pause in their dialogue. The sleepy little girl opened her eyes.

'I know,' she said, to nobody in particular. 'I died once, too.'

Chapter 9

THE FACTS OF DEATH

There is no other side. There are only levels of apprehending a single incomprehensibly vast universe. ARTHUR FORD

A MAN dies. What then?

One day in the summer of 1889, a Kansas country doctor lay in his bed at home, suffering the final stages of typhoid fever. Feeling that the end had come, he called his family and friends to his bedside and said good-bye to them. Then, anxious to save the undertakers too much trouble, he straightened his legs and clasped his stiffening fingers over his chest. His voice faltered, his vision blurred, and he sank into unconsciousness. The village church bell began to toll for him.

For four hours he lay technically dead, without noticeable pulse or heartbeat. But every time the family doctor was about to pronounce him dead, a barely perceptible gasp would emerge from his mouth, suggesting that there might still be hope . . .

At this point the patient himself, Dr Wiltse, takes up the story.

I lost, I believe, all power of thought or knowledge of existence in absolute unconsciousness. I came again into a state of conscious existence and discovered that I was still in the body, but the body and I had no longer any interests in common. I looked in astonishment and joy for the first time upon myself—the real me, the real Ego, while the 'not me' closed in upon all sides like a sepulchre of clay.

With all the interest of a physician, I beheld the wonders of my bodily anatomy, intimately interwoven with which even tissue for tissue, was I, the living soul of that dead body. I learned that the epidermis was the outside boundary of the ultimate tissues, so to speak, of the soul. I realised my condition and reasoned calmly thus. I have died, as men term death, and yet I am as much a man as ever. I am about to get out of the body . . .

Dr Wiltse then feels himself being rocked sideways, as in a cradle, as countless little cords seem to snap, separating his Ego from the tissues of the body, starting with the feet. It is as if a stretched rubber band were contracting in the direction of the head, and finally he feels his whole self collected into the head.

'I am all in the head now, and I shall soon be free,' he thinks.
' Inside his head, Wiltse moves around his brain, before emerging between the sutures of the skull like 'the flattened edges of a bag of membranes'. Looking to himself something like a jellyfish, he then hovers around before finally breaking loose and landing on the floor, fully out of the body.

'I seemed to be translucent, of a bluish cast, and perfectly naked.'

The latter embarrasses him somewhat, since there are ladies present, but he soon realises they cannot see him, even when he almost immediately finds himself fully clothed. He sees his old physical body lying on the bed, and feels satisfied that he has died decently, with feet together and hands folded. He notices two people watching over his body; he knows they are women but does not identify them as his wife and sister. He tries to attract their attention by bowing and waving at them, but to no avail.

'Then the situation struck me as humorous and I laughed outright.'

Dr Wiltse then leaves his house and goes out into the street. Only then does he notice a small cord like a spider's web that is still apparently linking him with his dead body. He feels elated, well aware that he has died and survived, and delighted to be so alive and able to think so clearly. The rest of his long narrative takes on a dreamlike quality, reminiscent of the adventures of Er in Plato's *Republic*. Voices warn the doctor that if he goes on, he will be unable to return. He fully understands this, and after walking into a sort of black cloud he loses his senses and wakes up back in his old physical body. He is both astonished and disappointed.

'What in the world has happened to me?' he asks at once. 'Must I die again?'

Though still weak, Wiltse immediately gave an account of his experience, writing a detailed report eight weeks later which was reprinted in the SPR *Proceedings* (Vol. 8, pp. 180–94) together with lengthy sworn testimony from four eye-witnesses and a note from his doctor declaring: 'I observed his symptoms closely, and if there are any symptoms marking a patient as *in articulo mortis* that were not presented in his case, I am ignorant of them. I supposed at one time that he was actually dead as fully as I ever supposed anyone dead'.

Two interesting features of the Wiltse case are the bluish colour of his psi body and the spidery cord that linked it to his physical body. This blue colour is often mentioned in accounts of similar experiences, while the 'silver cord' is a standard feature of what are known nowadays as OOBEs, out of body experiences. Reports of these date back to ancient Egypt, but no serious study of them seems to have been made until 1929, when Hereward Carrington and Sylvan Muldoon published a book based on the experiences of the latter, a remarkable invalid who seemed to be able to pop out of the body whenever he felt like it.[1]

Even to summarise well-documented cases of OOBE trips, or astral projections as they are also called, would take the rest of this book. There can be no doubt that they happen, and they provide good evidence for the survival of death by the psi component. A very good case of OOBE is the one presented by Sir Auckland Geddes at the 1927 meeting of the Royal Medical Society. Like Wiltse's, this case was recorded at the time, in shorthand, and it involved a man who left his body on the point of death. He found himself in a sort of free-time dimension in which he could see London and Scotland at the same time, and was eventually hauled back into his physical body after being given a shot of camphor. Like Wiltse, he was disappointed at finding himself back in his old physical body again, in fact he was thoroughly annoyed!

Attempts have been made in recent years to get scientific evidence for OOBE activity under controlled lab conditions. Two cooperative astral travellers who have been investigated with apparent success are the artist Ingo Swann and writer-business-man Robert A. Monroe. The latter's account of his experiences is a most useful companion to the Carrington-Muldoon work mentioned above.[2]

According to H. G. Andrade's psi matter theory, the physical body is sandwiched into position by the two components of the psi body, the astral and the vital. The simplest way to represent this in three dimensions is to take two blocks of magnetised steel and place them each side of a sheet of metal, so that they hold it firmly in position, as long as their positive and negative poles are opposite each other. The lower surface of the top block represents the astral body, while the block itself is the 'cupola' of the spirit, the repository of a synthesis of all previous lives and the seat of the superconscious mind. The upper surface of the lower block is the vital body, and the block itself contains the biological organising model, the experience-memory component that causes the physical body to grow. The sheet of metal between the magnetised blocks is the physical body.

Take the metal sheet away, and what happens? The two blocks snap together to form a single block of steel. They have not been affected in any way by the removal of the sheet, except that they no longer have an object on which they can make their force fields visible. This is what we all are; arrangements of ordinary bits of physical matter, like carbon and hydrogen, held in place while we are incarnate by the interaction of the biomagnetic fields.

When we die, our vital and astral bodies do not exactly snap shut at once, like the two blocks of steel. Each leaves the physical corpse in its own time, before uniting with the other to form the psi body, now existing only in hyperspace and entirely free from physical matter. This psi body is now invisible, as a rule, but by no means always.

Reports of apparitions of the dead are extremely common, though most people keep quiet about them for the same reason they keep quiet about psi phenomena in general; they don't want people to think they have gone mad. Myers, a meticulous classical scholar, collected an enormous number of such reports, and for him they formed some of the best evidence for the survival of physical death. Myers, by the way, had almost nothing to say on the subject of reincarnation. He only mentioned it once in his *Human Personality* . . . ,[3] and although he found nothing in the idea that was, as he put it, 'alien to the best reason or the highest instincts of man,' he had to admit that there was simply no valid *evidence* for it. The only evidence he did mention came from a very dubious source; the French medium Hélène Smith, whose claims included being able to speak Martian language, and being herself the reincarnation of guess who? (Marie Antoinette, who else?) Myers wasted no time in demolishing this case in one of his rare outbursts of scorn. If only he had had evidence of the quality provided by Stevenson, Banerjee or Andrade, he would have gone to the ends of the earth to check it out.

Myers reckoned that about one person in ten had seen a realistic apparition of somebody who was supposed to be dead and buried, and this is indeed one of the commonest of all psi happenings. Everybody believes in ghosts, or at least admits they exist, if only in jest. Ghosts are particularly well integrated in Great Britain, where they are regarded as harmless members of society, and even as status symbols that raise property values. But what are they?

The psi body does not leave the dead physical one instantaneously. It takes its time, and as the vital body gradually unplugs itself from our dead molecules, it takes with it some of that mysterious stuff known as ectoplasm, with the aid of which it can become visible again. The question of where and when it becomes visible depends on who is polarising its psi atoms at the time. Usually this will be a relative, whose mind is fixed on the dead person, though apparitions of the dead are also common in cases where the percipient is unaware they have died.

In Brazil, where dead bodies are exposed to view during funeral services, there exists a lugubrious profession known as *vestidor de cadaver*, or corpse-dresser. His job is to get the corpse out of his pyjamas and into his best suit. It is widely believed (I'm afraid I haven't seen it) that if the dresser shouts loudly enough into the corpse's ear, telling it to loosen its arm so that he can get the jacket on, the corpse duly obliges! This would suggest that a medically dead body can retain some essential functions, and if this is so, then there must be something left in the body that can control them. It is not enough to call them reflexes and leave it at that. Of course they are reflexes, but what of? Presumably, they are reflexes of remnants of psi matter that are able to respond to stimuli.

To return to ectoplasm; this is the stuff familiar to Spiritists that is supposed to emanate from mediums in deep trance and assume recognisable human forms. The word itself was probably coined by Charles Richet, a Nobel Prize winner in medicine, who provides good evidence for the existence of this elusive substance.[4]

A simple experiment can be carried out in any school lab to show that materialisation through use of ectoplasm is not as impossible as it might seem. Take an electrolytic cell, and place two plates in it, attaching one to the positive and one to the negative electrode. The first plate should be copper and the second something almost transparent, like a fine metal mesh. By careful lighting, the second plate can be made to appear almost invisible until you switch on the current, when it will 'materialise' due to the fine layer of copper that will cover it as it is polarised by the negative electrode. When you reverse the current, it will become invisible again as the copper ions return to their original plate. Magic!!

I am not suggesting that ectoplasm can be formed as easily as this, only that a phenomenon *similar* to that of materialisation can be produced very easily. It may be that a suitable medium corresponds to the plate attached to the positive electrode in our cell, and the biomagnetic fields attached to the structure of the psi body to be materialised correspond to the other plate. Here is one way, based on Andrade's psi matter hypothesis, in which materialisations could take place:

Ectoplasm is drawn from the body of the medium by a negative bionic charge. (The bion is the electron of Andrade's psi atom.) It is attracted to the body of the psi entity waiting to materialise. When the ectoplasm makes contact with the psi entity (ghost), its charge will be neutralised, and it will be conveyed to the biomagnetic centres of the ghost's body. These centres act as fulcrums in physical space, around which the material extracted from the medium is arranged. At first, all that is visible is a vague shape, but eventually a recognisable form appears, and if conditions are right the borrowed ectoplasm can be used to materialise every cell in the psi body, which will then be able to move around and speak exactly as it did when incarnate. When the time comes for the psi person to get back to hyperspace, where he belongs, the direction of the bionic charges is inverted and the borrowed ectoplasm is reabsorbed by the medium as the ghost 'dematerialises'. Some of the ectoplasm will be lost in the transfer process, as stated in the First Principle of Thermodynamics, which may explain why mediums invariably complain of exhaustion after such sessions. We often say of some strenuous activity that 'it really takes it out of you', and in the case of materialisation mediumship this is literally true; it takes the ectoplasm out of you and it doesn't put it all back.

Brief materialisations are most common immediately after death, but if a psi person is sufficiently earthbound, it seems they can happen much later. The following incident took place in September 1974, and I have reason to believe it is essentially true. (Pseudonyms are used.)

Maritsa is a well-known ballet teacher in São Paulo, and a close friend of a lady I know well and trust. Some of her classes for teenage girls contain up to thirty pupils. To help identification, all girls at the academy where she teaches have to sew their surnames on their costumes. This also enables teachers to check that no girl is in the wrong class. One day, Maritsa was putting a large class through its paces, and she noticed a girl whose face was not familiar. Must be a new pupil, she thought, and she made a note of the name Gouveia, a fairly common Brazilian surname, stitched on the girl's T-shirt.

It was not worth stopping the class just to see if Miss Gouveia was in the wrong class, and ballet teaching being the energetic work it is, Maritsa forgot about the newcomer, after noting that she was a tall and rather pale girl who was very good at her dancing.

But after the class, Maritsa was walking along the corridor when she spotted Miss Gouveia waiting outside another classroom. Aha, she thought, she is trying to sneak in a few extra lessons. Some of the girls do that; they pay for one lesson a week and just drop in on two or three more. So Maritsa went along to the director's office and asked casually which class Miss Gouveia was supposed to be in.

The director checked the register. 'We haven't got any Gouveias here,' she replied. 'What did she look like? Perhaps she's a new girl who hasn't paid her fee yet. I must see to that.'

Maritsa described her in detail. The director stared at her amazed.

'That sounds exactly like poor Julia Gouveia,' she said. 'One of our best pupils, she was. She shot herself in January.'

Julia was not seen by any of her classmates, and Maritsa is not the sort of person to invent this kind of story. She had never seen Julia before; the previous year the girl had not been in any class of hers. If she really did see her materialised spirit, which is possible, then there must be degrees of materialisation, degrees of perception on our part, or perhaps both.

Some German friends of mine once invited a rather pompous and very highly-strung young English diplomat to lunch one day in their country home. They were sitting on the terrace outside the glass front door, when the diplomat, who was sitting facing the door, suddenly announced that it must be lunchtime.

'Not quite,' said one of my friends. 'The chicken should stay in the oven a bit longer. Sorry if you're starving!'

'Oh no, it isn't that,' the diplomat replied. 'But I thought I saw your cook waving at us through the curtains.'

The others looked at him in surprise. 'You can't have,' they said. 'We haven't got a cook.'

The Englishman, who was sceptical enough about most things material, not to mention things non-material, stuck to his story. He *had* seen a woman behind the thin lace curtains, and he gave a good description of her. When he realised that what he had really seen was a ghost, he became very embarrassed and begged everybody to keep quiet about it. (They didn't, and it is still one of their favourite stories.)

You do not have to be dead to become a ghost. There are indications that you can even become one by mistake. A very interesting example of this happening is to be found in one of Harold Sherman's many books on psi phenomena.[5] Mr Sherman is a welcome rarity; he is well developed as a medium, he takes trouble to document the strange things that happen around him, and he writes very well. His long-distance telepathy experiments with the explorer Sir Hubert Wilkins are some of the most convincing of their kind yet published.[6]

Mr Sherman and his wife returned to their Hollywood apartment at about 3 p.m. on the afternoon of Thanksgiving Day, 1941, to find a note in their box from the desk clerk.

'Mr Loose was here—will see you Sunday,' read the message, which recorded the time as 2.30 p.m. The Shermans had a date to visit their old friend Harry Loose, a retired police officer and well-known criminologist, who lived an hour's drive away in Monterey Park. The date was for Sunday, but they were not expecting a visit from him that Thursday. Assuming him to be on his way home, they waited until 3.30 before calling to apologise for having been out when he called.

Harry Loose sounded surprised when Sherman phoned. 'I haven't been out of the house today,' he said. And there were four witnesses to prove it.

Sherman immediately went to check with the desk clerk, who

had never seen Loose before. The clerk not only confirmed the message, but described what Mr Loose had been wearing and added that he had not noticed him enter the building, but had looked up and just seen him standing there. He also recalled that Mr Loose had given his spoken message with some difficulty, as if having trouble with false teeth.

Sherman again phoned Loose and told him the clerk had described him and his clothes in detail. Loose offered to discuss the incident the following Sunday, preferring not to do so on the phone.

That Sunday, Loose confessed that he had had the ability to project himself from the physical body for some years. He would lie down in his bedroom, ask his wife to make sure he was not disturbed, and off he would go on what we now call an out of body experience (OOBE). And yes, he had been dozing off around 2.30 p.m. on Thursday, after his Thanksgiving lunch.

He had also been thinking of the Shermans around this time, as they had sent him a basket of fruit for Thanksgiving.

Sherman then asked Loose to come and visit him on a week-day, instead of his usual Sunday, so that the same desk clerk could have a look at him. The following Tuesday, Loose drove into Hollywood in the old clothes he usually wore at home (but not when he visited Sherman) and went up to the desk in the hall of Sherman's apartment building.

'Oh! Good morning, Mr Loose!' the clerk said at once.

Loose asked the clerk, who by now was very interested in the affair, to describe how he had been dressed the previous Thursday. The man gave much the same description he had originally given Sherman, but said he thought Loose was wearing a lighter-coloured shirt this time. Loose confirmed this.

Sherman obtained detailed signed statements from the desk clerk and the other four people involved in the case, which is one of the most convincing examples of its kind in recent times. He gives a thirteen-page account of it in the book mentioned above, including the supporting testimony.

So much for accidental materialisations; now for deliberate ones. The most complete account of the materialisation process from the occult literature of this century, with the exception of the works of André Luiz, comes from Stewart Edward White, author of the celebrated series of 'Betty' books. Betty was his wife, who became a medium in 1919 (after buying a cheap ouija board and finding that it would spell out messages that made sense to her). Later, she took up automatic writing, and until her death in 1939 she kept up a remarkable running dialogue with a group of entities White refers to as the Invisibles. It sounds like a TV serial, but it was a great deal more exciting.

The Invisibles were a good-natured bunch of spirits who not only delivered some homely Spiritualist philosophy, but organised a complete home course in the production of psi phenomena, making it clear as they did so that even they were not too sure how such things were done! In 1922 White, Betty, and three other married couples got together for ten special meetings held over a five-week period. The purpose of these meetings, according to the Invisibles, was to give scientific demonstrations of the reality of what they called the Beta body, or what in this book I am calling the psi component or psi body.

They explained that mind and body are manifestations of a single reality—human consciousness. Spirit, linked to the body through the mind, had a definite body of its own, with weight and colour, form and substance. This was also the seat of the subconscious mind. It was just beyond the range of normal human vision, and to become visible it had to be condensed, while the retinas of onlookers' eyes were 'strengthened'. The spirit body and the human eye had to meet half way, as it were. Perhaps this is what happened in the case of the phantom ballerina quoted earlier.

Four members of the group of eight had mediumistic abilities, and the Invisibles arranged them into two groups, positive and negative, like an electric battery. (Again!) Soon, one of the women found she could leave the physical body while in trance, and the others could keep track of her, so to speak, by following the cord that linked her two bodies, psi and physical. The cord was not visible at first, but could be located because of the extreme cold it radiated. (Inexplicable cold currents of air are standard features of many séance phenomena.) When the invisible cord was pinched, the person it belonged to would feel the pinch, literally!

The psi body remained invisible for the first four sessions, but at the fifth something like phosphorescent smoke began to emanate from one of the mediums' finger tips, forming itself into a duplicate of her forearm. It stayed visible for two minutes under normal electric light. By later using coloured lights, they managed to see more of the psi body, including the face. When the medium's eyes were bandaged, her normal features would appear as if the bandage were not there. White noticed that when parts of the second body were materialised, they had a kind of inner illumination of their own. He also learned that psi bodies could only be exteriorised when attracted by another consciousness, reminding us of our electrolytic cell with its two plates. When one of the sitters asked if she could exteriorise her psi body when she was alone, she was told:

'There is always another consciousness present'![7]

With that comforting thought, we leave materialisations. They are exciting things, but until we have more evidence of the quality of White's and Sherman's, plus a lot more spontaneous cases like the ones I have mentioned here, we can only speculate as to how they happen rather than draw up rules and laws. White himself was rather disappointed by his experiences, believe it or not. He felt that such phenomena must be repeatable to order if they were to convince people in general. The Invisibles agreed, but kept complaining rather pathetically that they too were baffled by some aspects of the whole business. They were as anxious to learn how it worked as anyone else. They sounded rather like children playing around with a Junior Electromagnet Kit.

Now we come to the question of communication between ourselves and the departed. The first thing most of us do when we die, as soon as the mechanics of the process have taken place, is to have a good long rest. Those of us who accept life after

death as a natural phenomenon will probably realise we are
dead at once, when we wake up from this rest. Those of us who
do not accept survival are in for a fairly nasty experience, as
repeatedly described in gruesome detail by André Luiz. (We will
accept it, he says, when the worms start eating us!) Finally,
those who die violently or prematurely may be frozen into a
state of suspended animation lasting for days, months or even
years.

We will feel a bit befuddled when we wake up after our
post-mortem sleep. We will feel as disoriented as we do when
suffering what is known as jet-lag. This is what happens when
you arrive in Los Angeles at 6·p.m. after a direct flight from
London to find your Californian friends all fresh and ready for
an evening out, whereas to you it is two o'clock the next morning, and feels like it. Like jet travellers, the dead have to adjust
to a new time dimension.

At this point, we have no more evidence from mortals, and
we have to rely on information from supposed communicators
from the psi world, or from other occult sources. Neither can
be considered of the same quality as testimony from people like
Dr Wiltse who, as the Sunday papers would say, died and
lived to tell the amazing tale! But all evidence is evidence
whatever its quality, as any detective would agree. None of it
can be ignored. Survival evidence may often be trivial, like
evidence on a murder case. What could be more trivial than
bits of hair, blood specks on the carpet, or all the other little
details that have sent many a killer to the next world? According to the bundle-of-sticks theory, a number of weak pieces of
evidence may help build up a strong case, just as a bundle of
fragile sticks will be firmer than each individual stick. This
theory has in fact been mathematically proved.[9]

Most occult accounts of the next world make it sound so
marvellous that it is hardly surprising that communication between it and us is rare. Who needs us? But communications do
take place, either in the form of automatic writing, impressions
directed at our minds, or through the voice of a trance medium.
It is very difficult to establish what is a real communication

from the psi world and what is not, human imagination, suggestibility and credulousness being what they are, but the evidence begins to look good when we have cases of information unknown to the sitter at a séance being subsequently verified.

For instance, if the spirit of your Aunt Jemima comes through and says (or writes) that she is alive and well and everything is just lovely, this is no proof of anything. But if she tells you to look in a box hidden behind the kitchen dresser, where you will find her gold watch, which you never knew to exist, and you then go and find it there, you have a different quality of evidence.

Ah, but would it stand up in a court of law?

In 1921, James L. Chaffin died, leaving a will. Four years later one of his sons had a dream in which his father told him he had left a second will, which he would find if he looked in the lining of an old coat. This was good news, for the son in question had not done very well out of the first will, so he set about locating the garment mentioned. This was not easy, since it had been given away, but he managed to find it. Inside the lining of the coat, there was no will. But there was a message telling the finder to take out the family Bible and turn to Genesis 27. The son did this, and there was the second will. A North Carolina court accepted it, and the earlier will (1905) was reversed.[10]

Spiritists often cite this case as proof that messages from the dead can be of great practical value. But I wonder. If the Chaffin case really took place as reported, why does this sort of thing not happen more often? Surely most of us die with some business unfinished? Why do we not receive spirit messages all the time, like: 'Hullo, sorry I died, but will you pay that bill in the top drawer, and make sure Edward gets his hair cut, and, oh, don't forget to change the back tyres of the car, and . . .' and so on.

Nobody worked harder to establish the reality of human survival than Frederic Myers, both during his life and, apparently, after his own death. Before he died in 1901, Myers left a sealed message, the contents of which nobody knew but himself, and which he planned to reveal after dying. The message ran:

'If I can revisit any earthly scene, I should choose the Valley in the grounds of Hallsteads, Cumberland.'

This referred to the home in the north of England of his cousin Annie, with whom he had a powerful but frustrated Platonic love affair. The two of them had often walked together in the valley at Hallsteads, but Annie had died young and Myers desperately wanted to meet her again. It is possible that this was what made him the great researcher he was.

Not long after his death, Myers—or let's call him Psi Myers —apparently began to communicate through several different mediums at once in at least three countries. Thus began the famous series of 'cross-correspondences', so called because messages received by one medium would often only make sense when put together with words received by another. Some of the mediums had known the living Myers, and some had not. Some knew each other, and some did not. The scripts they all received make absorbing reading to anybody familiar with the Greek and Latin classics (in their original languages) plus almost the whole of English poetry from Shakspeare to Myers himself, who was a prolific minor poet. Even a summary of the scripts is fairly confusing reading, though Saltmarsh[8] and Tyrrell[11] have managed to present their essential features in a form ordinary readers should not find too indigestible.

It is quite clear that the dozen or so mediums involved were sometimes producing information they could not have received through normal sense channels. Unless, of course, telepathy is a normal channel able to operate on this scale, of which there is no evidence.

Surely one of these ladies would come up with final proof of survival at last—the contents of the sealed envelope Myers had left as a test for himself? One day, Psi Myers came through to one of his earthly scribes, Mrs A. W. Verrall, and wrote the following sentence, which is concise and clear by Psi Myers standards:

'I have long told you of the contents of the envelope. Myers' sealed envelope left with Lodge.' (Psi Myers often referred to himself in the third person.) 'You have not understood. It has in it the words from the SYMPOSIUM—about Love bridging the chasm.'

Here we have the sort of frustrating situation so common in psi research. There undoubtedly is some connection between the two messages. Hallsteads was the scene of a Platonic love affair, in which Myers must have felt a 'chasm' between himself and his beloved cousin, who was already securely married. It can also be said that a chasm and a valley are similar things. Moreover, a book written by Myers but not made public until after his death showed that he definitely *did* associate the Hallsteads valley with the concept of Platonic love as contained in Plato's *Symposium*.

But why could Psi Myers not have been more specific? All he had to say through Mrs Verrall was that he wanted to go back to Hallsteads valley, or words to that effect. That would have been enough. Why allege that the message contained *words* from Plato, when it did not? Why claim he had already revealed the contents of the message, when he had not? The evidence is too good for chance coincidence, but not good enough for solid proof. The same goes for much of the volumes of writing produced over the years by the Psi Myers group. The same also goes for a great deal of psi research in other areas.

Assuming that our dead friends do communicate with us occasionally, and there is enough good evidence to make this a reasonable hypothesis, it is quite clear that communication is not easy. Members of the Psi Myers group made this point over and over again. It was, Psi Myers wrote once, like 'dictating feebly to a reluctant and somewhat obtuse secretary, through a sheet of frosted glass'. There were many objections that strangers among the sitters deflected the material to be conveyed, and that automatic script was always apt to follow asociations in the mediums' minds over which the communicators had no control. Reading through the cross-correspondences, one gets a very strong impression that somebody is trying very hard to get through to us from the psi world, but not always succeeding. Psi Myers, in particular, would insist that he was 'trying with all the forces to prove that I am Myers'. To many of those involved in the case, he succeeded, but since much of the original material is not available for study we shall probably never get to the bottom of this mystery, which would make a fine subject for a doctorate thesis.

There were two intriguing sequels to the thirty-year series of Psi Myers scripts. The first was an entire book dictated by Psi Myers to the automatic writing medium Geraldine Cummins, which is described by Sir Oliver Lodge in his foreword as 'a genuine attempt to convey approximately true ideas' about the life hereafter. It is written in a style strongly reminiscent of Myers's, and contains many ideas that preoccupied him when alive. It also contains the news that Myers does not intend to reincarnate.[12] Pity, we need more like him.

The second was another full-length book, also dictated to Miss Cummins, purporting to be by Winifred Coombe Tennant, one of the mediums who had helped take down the Psi Myers cross-correspondences, under her pseudonym Mrs Willett. She was related to Myers by marriage, and received much of the best Psi Myers material while she was alive, and her own book gives strong evidence for the survival of a clearly identifiable personality, full of accurate (plus one or two inaccurate) references to her own life of which Miss Cummins could not be expected to have known.[13]

In all, it seems that Psi Myers and his group spent almost sixty years trying to convince us that they were still conscious and active in the next world. Most people who have studied their evidence have concluded that the survival hypothesis has to be taken seriously. The only main alternatives are fraud or mass telepathy, and neither fits all the known facts.

Finally, we have what are known in the trade as drop-in cases (because they just drop in unexpected and unannounced). These are interesting because neither the fraud nor the telepathy hypothesis seem to make much sense. What happens is that during a home Spiritist circle, an entity suddenly 'drops in' via the medium, either speaking with her voice or writing with her hand, and gives some fragments of evidence pointing to a certain identity. Sometimes droppers-in give names and personal details that can be checked, and are. Most of these cases seem to support the earthbound spirit hypothesis, which supposes that people who have died violently are likely to remain hovering around near our plane in a state of shock or confusion.

The case of the Brazilian soldier I mentioned in chapter two is a good example of a drop-in personality unknown to anybody present, who gave very full details of his identity that were promptly checked and found to be almost entirely correct. The important feature of this case, however, was that two of the items were found not to be correct. The communicator gave his rank as that of officer cadet and stated that he had been wounded, but not killed. In fact, it turned out that the soldier in question had been promoted to Lieutenant soon after the battle in which he had been killed, not merely wounded, and later promoted again to Captain. (Posthumous promotions are normal in Brazil, being a way of increasing relatives' pensions, in the case of soldiers killed on duty.)

If any telepathy or fraud were at work on this case, one would suppose that the information recalled from the original sitting would have coincided exactly with the true facts. I have never heard of incorrect information being transmitted by telepathy between two people who had no idea of the other's existence. As for fraud, a hypothesis none of the investigators on this case was able to take seriously for long, it would have been quite easy for the group concerned to unearth the true facts if they had wanted to. These points have been overlooked by some critics of this case, which in my view provides very good evidence for the survival of a human component after physical death. It is similar to, and stronger than, a number of 'drop-in' cases researched by Alan Gauld and published by the SPR.[14]

But as I have said, I am not too concerned with the problem of survival. It is going to be much easier to prove reincarnation, and that will take care of the survival problem automatically.

I must make it clear that I do not claim reincarnation to have been proved already. Nor does Ian Stevenson.

'The evidence we now have falls far short of proof,' he says. 'There is no perfect case and all the cases and all their reports have some blemishes, some of them severe ones. I do think, however, that the evidence has increased since the publication of my first book.

'Perhaps the best way of summarising my present view is this. The evidence is far from conclusive, but it is now sufficiently strong so that a rational man can believe in reincarnation on the basis of evidence instead of resting his belief on religious traditions only.'[15]

In the course of the following chapter, I shall try to suggest exactly what reincarnates, when and how.

Chapter 10

I WAS A BIOMAGNETIC FIELD
FROM HYPERSPACE

We know absolutely nothing of the universe which surrounds us.
We live in a sort of dream and have not yet understood anything
of the agitations and tumults of this dream. RICHET

*The organic world has 'been carried on to a high state of
development and has been ever kept in harmony with the
forces of external nature, by the grand law of 'survival of the
fittest', acting upon ever varying organisations. In the spiritual world, the law of the 'progression of the fittest' takes its
place, and carries on in unbroken continuity that development of the human mind which has been commenced here.*

W HEN Darwin's theory of natural selection was introduced
to a largely indifferent world at a meeting of the Linnaean
Society on July 1st 1858, some felt that a death-blow had been
struck against any sort of spiritistic hypothesis regarding evolution. Yet the man who wrote the above lines was no critic of
Darwin. On the contrary, he was the man who arrived at exactly the same conclusions at exactly the same time; conclusions that were presented at the same meeting, in one of the
most remarkable instances of simultaneous independent discovery in scientific history.

The man was Alfred Russel Wallace (1823–1913), who was
eventually to become 'more Darwinian than Darwin', as Sir
Alister Hardy has put it. And although Wallace's own book
on natural selection was simply entitled *Darwinism*, its author
was also to become one of England's leading campaigners for
the cause of Spiritualism!

In 1844, as a young schoolmaster, Wallace experimented
with hypnotism on some of his pupils, noting with interest that

he seemed to be able to merge his mind with that of a hypnotised subject. When Wallace put a lump of sugar or some salt in his own mouth, or when somebody pinched or pricked his skin, the hypnotised schoolboy would seem to react in sympathy at a distance. Wallace remained sceptical about the phenomena of Spiritualism until 1865, when he witnessed the full range of both physical and mental effects at a series of private séances at a friend's house.

He wrote the book from which the above quotation is taken in 1874[1], soon after Crookes had published his findings of his examination of D. D. Home. Wallace regarded the facts as finally proved ('characteristics of a new truth'), and wondered why, after twenty years of 'proof' from such men as Hare, Mapes, Gasparin, Thury—and now the brilliant young William Crookes, any further proof were needed. 'But why more confirmation?' he wanted to know. 'And when again "confirmed", who is to confirm the confirmer?' Wallace was quite convinced all along that natural selection was not 'the all-powerful, all-sufficient, and only cause of the development of organic forms.' At the end of his 1874 study of Spiritualist phenomena, he reached the following conclusions:

1 Man is a duality, consisting of an organised spiritual form, evolving coincidently with and permeating the physical body, and having corresponding organs and development.

2 Death is the separation of this duality, and effects no change in the spirit, either morally or intellectually.

3 Progressive evolution of the intellectual and moral nature is the destiny of individuals; the knowledge, attainments and experience of earth-life forming the basis of the spirit life.

This is almost straight Kardecism, though Wallace makes no mention of Kardec anywhere in his book. Nor does he mention reincarnation, which suggests that he was inclined to base his conclusions on facts he had witnessed himself (as he repeatedly claimed) rather than on occult theories. However credulous he was to become later, he was well aware in 1874 that communications from the spirit world could be fallible. They must, he said, be 'judged and tested just as we do those of our fellow men'. Spirits, he said, could sometimes provide useful information. He mentioned the fact that Chicago's drinking water supply was apparently discovered by a medium after experts had failed. But the spirits were only a little closer to ultimate reality than we are, merely one step higher on a very long ladder. Wallace's realistic approach is best seen in his sole paragraph on the subject of God: 'Our modern religious teachers', he says, 'maintain that they know a great deal about God. They define minutely and critically his various attributes; they enter into his motives, his feelings, and his opinions; they explain exactly what he has done, and why he has done it; and they declare that after death we shall be with him, and shall see and know him. In the teaching of the "spirits" there is not a word of all this. They tell us that they commune with higher intelligences than ourselves, but of God they really *know* no more than we do.' Wallace points out that this approach runs directly counter to traditional religious beliefs, and that the ultimate or absolute Being (God) 'must necessarily be not only unknown and unknowable, but even *unthinkable* by finite intelligences'. (Italics in original, also small *h* for him, his, referring to God.)

People unfamiliar with Spiritualism or Spiritism are often unaware that practitioners of these beliefs are rather more 'down to earth' than members of most other religions. Theirs are the only religions that anybody has ever even attempted to demonstrate scientifically. They waste little time paying lip-service to established views of the life hereafter and meditating on the mystery of God. Instead, they get out and build orphanages, mental homes, training centres for slum kids; devoting their energies to helping anybody who needs help—material or spiritual—for free. They will know all about God when the time comes, they feel, but meanwhile they get down to the business of improving *this* world rather than worrying about the next one. For them, what you do and think today determines what you are tomorrow. This is not mysticism, but common sense.

The next world, or what I call the psi world, probably bears about as much relation to total and ultimate reality as the moon bears to the cosmos. We were all very excited when Neil Armstrong stepped onto the moon in 1969, but the conquest of our nearest neighbour out there is not very exciting when we think of all the other blobs in the sky, even the relatively few we can actually see. Little attention was given by the general public to the discovery in September 1974, by a group of radio astronomers in Leiden (Holland), of a galaxy two hundred times the size of our own Milky Way, which looks fairly enormous to most of us. We have a long way to go.

I mention Wallace's views at some length to show how an open-minded scientist can arrive at a reasonable set of beliefs on an unpopular subject, solely on the evidence of his own experience and observation and logical deductions therefrom. That was how he arrived at his theory of natural selection, and also how he formulated his theories of the psi world. If he was right about the former (subject to his own reservations) could he not have been essentially right about the latter?

Hernani Guimarães Andrade was born in 1913 (the year Wallace died, incidentally) in a small town in the state of Minas Gerais. He graduated in civil engineering from the University of São Paulo in 1941, and after a seven-year period at Volta Redonda, Brazil's first steel mill, he settled in São Paulo to work for the state water and power authority, where he has remained ever since, being due for retirement in 1976. He became a department director in 1968, and has served on a number of state and federal government commissions. His three sons have all followed him into the engineering profession, and his daughter is married to a doctor.

He has been an active Spiritist since 1930, when he first read Kardec while still attending a Catholic high school run by priests. Kardec's ideas were no revelation to him, however. They merely confirmed what he felt he had always known; that man's soul was immortal and that it returned to earth as often as necessary to achieve total experience. Yet however attractive and logical the ideas of Kardec seemed, Andrade was anxious to see them proved scientifically.

He felt uneasy about the way his fellow Brazilian Kardecists seemed to take every imaginable phenomenon for granted, including many that were obvious fakes. To prove his point, he once put on a performance as a fake medium himself, successfully deceiving a whole room full of people, which left him with an urge to sort out the true from the false, and above all to undertake original research himself.

At about the time Andrade was beginning to explore the psi world, Alexis Carrel published his popular *Man, The Unknown*,[2] where although he admits the reality of many psi phenomena, he states that 'to go beyond one's own field and to dabble in theology or spiritism is dangerous, even for men as illustrious as Isaac Newton, William Crookes or Oliver Lodge'. He goes on to pontificate that 'experimenters trained in clinical medicine . . . are alone qualified to investigate this subject.' This did not prevent Carrel from indulging in a little theology himself, and as one might expect from the holder of such a narrow-minded and intolerant attitude, similar to that of recent Soviet pronouncements about parapsychology being the province of psychologists and nobody else,[3] Carrel became a much-publicised convert to Roman Catholicism.

Andrade, who renounced Catholicism at about the time that Carrel was relapsing into it, had no compunctions about 'dabbling' in Spiritism. He longed to be able to do practical research, but the pressures of his full-time job and the raising of four children left him little time to do more than think and write about the psi world until 1963, when he finally managed to get together a group of like-minded scientists, teachers and students and found the IBPP.

Up to then, Brazilian research into psi phenomena was virtually non-existent, with the sole exception of the work of Eurico de Goes, who made a sincere attempt to record the feats of the medium Carmine Mirabelli. The traditional Brazilian approach to psi research is well summed up in a long and pointless book by the doctor and psychoanalyst Antonio da

Silva Mello, which somehow found its way into an English translation.[4] Typically enough, Mello first heard about Mirabelli in 1928, when Mello was in Paris and Mirabelli had been performing for seventeen years, and his fame had reached Paris although Mello had never even heard of him.

Apparently to oblige his French friends, Mello did later manage to scrape together some second-hand information about Mirabelli, and he devotes sixteen words of his 494-page opus to his own original research. 'When I returned to Brazil, I looked into the case, but could only obtain garbled information.' There began and ended Dr Mello's contribution to psi research. One can almost see him lying in his hammock and making a few vague telephone calls to people who might know something about the man. The idea of actually getting off his backside and going out after the facts simply never occurred to him. When Suzuko Hashizume of the IBPP and I 'looked into' the Mirabelli case in 1973, we put together a bulging file in a few weeks, based mostly on direct testimony from eye-witnesses of his feats, and this twenty years after the man had died.

Andrade's interest in psi phenomena was originally a philosophical one, and he had only observed very few such phenomena when he began to work on his theory of corpuscular psi matter during the 1950s. In the ten years that followed the founding of the IBPP, he amassed several large filing cabinets of original material, and also embarked on a long and costly practical experiment with his Electromagnetic Space Condenser, which I have mentioned elsewhere. He soon discovered what I also found when I came to São Paulo, that there is plenty of evidence lying around if you get out of your hammock and go and look for it.

This is especially true of cases that suggest reincarnation. The IBPP's first file in this category was opened after Ian Stevenson, 5,000 miles away in the University of Virginia, had read about a case in a German newspaper and written to suggest that Andrade might like to look into it. The case involved a family of German descent living about two miles from Andrade's own home, and while IBPP researchers investigated it, they kept their ears open and soon learned of other cases. They have now collected reports of nearly a hundred and examined about thirty in detail.

Andrade's hypothesis as to how reincarnation actually takes place occupies fifty-one pages of his 1958 book. It is prefaced with a statement of the basic facts of biology and genetics, including an account of the (then) new discoveries concerning the DNA molecule which for a time was used in a São Paulo university, being the only up-to-date material in Portuguese available on the subject. It is not easy to summarise, being presented in highly compressed and often highly technical form, but I shall now attempt a full summary of it, together with a short resumé of the parts of his overall psi matter theory that bear on the subject of reincarnation.

We consist of two bodies, the physical body and the psi body. The latter in turn is made up of two components, the astral and the vital. The astral is the repository of the mind, while the vital contains a record of the organic development of our species. These two components are held together by magnetic attraction, forming a field known as the biomagnetic field, or BMF for short. Together, the two components form part of our individual biological organising model (BOM), which is responsible for the growth of the physical body from the cell-division stage to adulthood. All living things have their own BOM, which exists in (at least) five dimensions; four of space and one of time. To be able to function in our physical 3D space, it must lose a space dimension, as we lose one when our shadow is projected onto a wall. But the BOM remains a historical continuum, a record of our evolution to date that has served as a blueprint for our current incarnation.

Under certain rather unpredictable circumstances, we can receive, through our astral component, information from other points in space and time. This is called telepathy, when we send or receive information to or from another mind, living or discarnate. It is called clairvoyance if we actually receive a visual impression of an event past, present or future removed from our point of observation in time or space. If we receive an impression from the future, we call it precognition, though precognitive clairvoyance might be a more precise term. More about this baffling subject in the next chapter.

To the BOM, time is not an ever-rolling stream, but a process of continuous enlargement of its hyperform. To reduce this to three dimensions for present purposes, let us imagine a goods train rolling steadily along a track that encircles the whole earth. We are not sure if it is the train or the track that is moving, but the illusion of movement is produced.

Inside each freight car of the endless train there sits a file clerk with a long card index system in front him. Everything that happens to us is recorded accurately in our individual tray of cards, item by item, and the card tray grows steadily longer and longer as more cards are added, in a time system of its own independent of that of the train being pulled by the locomotive way up front and out of sight.

When an earth life comes to an end, a file is closed. The cards bearing the information about that life are then fed into a machine that records and condenses all this information much as printed pages can be reduced to those microdots that secret agents are so fond of. Our BOM contains the equivalent of one of these microdots for each of our earth lives, in which our total mental and physical experiences are recorded. What exactly happens in between incarnations will probably remain a mystery for some time. Attempts to tell us have not been too successful, perhaps because the state of being we find ourselves in after the formalities of death are over cannot be described in words. We have good evidence for after-death states and for past memories shortly after rebirth, but that interim period must lie beyond our comprehension for the time being.

What seems probable is that at some stage, your BOM feels an instinctive need to return to earth. You (by which I mean your BOM, which contains all your previous yous) may be aware of some form of experience you have lacked in past lives, or you may just feel an urge to enjoy material pleasures again.

If you were an alcoholic in your last life, you will not be cured of the problem just by dying. Death does not solve any problems. In this case, you might want to return to earth for two reasons; to have another drink or to cure yourself and acquire a more constructive habit. It's up to you. You will probably be given all sorts of advice, but nobody will force you to do anything you do not decide to do for yourself. If you raised a large and happy family in your last life, you may want to raise another, or to try a solitary life, even one without love, as so many are, in order to develop your power of resilience as well as your mental processes. If you have led a solitary life, you may want to become a member of a large family.

Your desire to return to earth may not be a conscious one. For many, return is an automatic process, merely a case of attraction by random selection. Just as seeds from a tree are blown wherever the wind takes them, but only take root if they land on soil, so a less-evolved BOM will hover around until it finds an available physical molecule into which to plug itself. Birth is not an accident. The moment of ovulation in a woman has already been shown (by Burr) to produce measurable changes in her life field, and no doubt these changes are also reflected in her biomagnetic field, automatically attracting psi molecules. When her ovum is fertilised by a male sperm, this in turn will attract a complementary psi component. Life begins when the completed cell is ready to divide, and it cannot do this without the orientation of the BOM.

No scientific explanation for the most crucial event in life —the initial division of a living cell—has yet been given. The cell cannot be shown to divide according to known physical laws, yet divide it does. Therefore, there could be a non-physical cause for this effect. I am not suggesting that life literally begins in exactly the way I am describing. This is a hypothesis, not a statement of observed fact. But I do suggest that the search for the real cause behind the phenomenal effect of cell division must take the psi world into account. It is no use just referring to it as an epiphenomenon, an effect resulting from an unidentified cause. We must try and find the cause.

Let us take a closer look at this first self-dividing cell. It has to go through three separate stages before it becomes two identical cells. The first is called prophase (the before-phase), where the initial steps to break in half are taken. The first important step is when the centrosome replicates itself into two, each of which automatically looks for the opposing poles inside the cell. The centrosome is a tiny bit of cytoplasm—that's the stuff that surrounds the nucleus of the cell—and it contains a thing called a centriole, the most rudimentary of our organs. Little star-shaped structures called asters now appear, emerging from each centrosome to form an axis, while the nucleus of the cell breaks up and begins to form delicate filaments that are to develop into the chromosomes.

Now we come to stage two, the metaphase (situated-behind-phase). Here, the chromosomes line themselves up along the equator of the cell and make contact with the filaments of the axis, or spindle, formed by the asters. All is set for the dramatic moment when one cell turns into two cells.

Stage three is called the anaphase (the upward-progresion-phase). The chromosomes divide into two groups and leave the equator of the cell, moving towards its north and south poles. As they do this, the equator starts to contract until . . .

Telophase! (Finality-phase.) The chromosomes seem to lean backwards, as it were, against the outer wall of the cell, in a kind of ropeless tug-of-war. Now the cell elongates into a figure 8 shape, and with a final backward tug the two halves of the eight separate, and suddenly we have two cells instead of one. The chromosomes now leave their positions at the poles and regroup in the centre of the new cells, forming nuclei. We are back where we started, and the whole operation, which is called mitosis, starts all over again. It goes on until something tells it to stop. In this way, human bodies begin to take shape.

Now we see why people like Hans Driesch felt there had to be a 'something else' at work other than normal physical factors in such an astonishingly precise operation as cell mitosis. How does every single component of the cell know exactly what it has to do, when and where? Who tells certain cells to stop dividing by mitosis and do it another way—by meiosis, in which the chromosomes, instead of multiplying themselves do just the opposite, uniting themselves in pairs and dividing their original total by two?

In the 1950s it seemed that science had come up with the answer. The secret of life was summed up in three magic letters; DNA, for deoxyribonucleic acid. This is a substance originating from the cell nucleus that winds itself into the form of a double helix, like two single strings of beads twisted together, along which all the necessary information for the growth of a living being was carried. A total of five Nobel Prizes were handed out to the British and American scientists who first synthesised and later determined the molecular structure of DNA.

It was a great step forward in biochemistry, but it was not the secret of life, as one of the prizewinners was rash enough to claim. What had been discovered was the *mechanism* by which information is carried from cell to cell to its final destination. Not even the ebullient James D. Watson, author of a most enjoyable book on the discovery of the DNA structure[5], has yet told us how the information got there. Moreover, the information carried by the DNA system only refers to the *physical* characteristics of our ancestors. Thanks to DNA, you get your mother's blue eyes, father's black hair, grandpa's ingrown toenails or grandma's loose teeth. You do *not* inherit your ancestors' acquired attributes in this way; your father's love of golf or your mother's skill at the harpsichord. Lamarck thought you did, but he has been proved wrong. As Koestler has pointed out, if he was right, then all Jewish babies should be born circumcised!

Reincarnation is not something that happens suddenly all at once. Andrade uses the verb *plug in* to describe how the psi component actually connects with physical matter, but all he means is that psi and physical component have to fit exactly before they can be connected. It is not like plugging in a toast-making machine. Reincarnation is a long and gradual process. It starts at a very specific moment, when the centrosomes divide in the prophase stage of cell division, and even before that decisive moment preparations have to be made.

Once an egg has been successfully fertilised in a woman's uterus, a baby is on the way, literally. Its BOM has been waiting in the wings for the right moment to plug itself in to that cell. The BOM takes over the job of directing growth from the very start, organising cell division and the formation of organs. Its memory component forces the embryo to recapitulate the entire biological experience of its species. At an early stage it looks as though a human embryo is going to grow a tail and a pair of fish-gills. It grows an appendix, that dead-end turning off the large intestine which serves no apparent purpose except to give you appendicitis, though it is thought to have been needed once for digesting grass. It grows tonsils, the only purpose of which seems to be to give you a week's rest in hospital when you get tonsillitis and have them out.

The BOM is shown in 3D model form like two cones placed base to base, with the time axis running through them from apex to apex. The bottom tip of the lower cone represents our very first experience of life, and in the nine months we spend in the womb we go through it all again. Millions of years go by again in those nine months, as our BOM gradually plugs itself in, molecule by molecule, stepping itself down from four to three dimensions of space, though still retaining a link with its psi habitat in hyperspace.

A baby is not fully conscious for some time after birth, until it has absorbed enough of its BOM to form an active mind of its own. The BOM remains in control of our bodies throughout our lives, though its growth-organising job ceases when we stop growing. After then, it serves to handle minor repairs, or in some cases perhaps even major ones.

Babies are born dead distressingly often, even in countries where health standards are high. Sometimes there is no obvious reason for this, though one possible explanation, admittedly based on evidence from rather dubious sources, could be that reincarnating entities change their minds at the last moment and simply unplug themselves. This may be due to second thoughts or to a sort of stage fright. We even have evidence, from a very good source this time, that reincarnation can actually take place *after birth*. The case of Jasbir/Sobha Ram is one of the most baffling in the literature, and thanks to Ian Stevenson it has been very thoroughly documented. What happened, apparently, was this:

In 1954, a little boy called Jasbir, age three and a half, died of smallpox in a village in the Indian state of Uttar Pradesh. At least, everybody thought he had died, including Jasbir's father, who set about making arrangements for the funeral. Luckily, he set it up for the following morning, for during the night Jasbir seemed to come back to life. Nothing very unusual about that; people do appear to die, like Dr Wiltse, and come round just as the doctor is reaching for his pen to sign the death certificate.

Jasbir did indeed come back to life, or rather his body did.

It was some weeks before he appeared to be altogether himself again, *except that he wasn't himself*. At least, not according to himself! He was, he said, the son of a man called Shankar in the village of Vehedi, about twenty miles away. (By rural Indian standards, this is a long way, and none of Jasbir's family had ever been to Vehedi or heard of Shankar.) He refused to eat the food he was given, saying that he was a Brahmin, a higher caste than that of Jasbir's family. Luckily, a Brahmin neighbour came in to cook for the new Jasbir *à la* Brahmin, or he might have died again, from malnutrition. This went on for nearly two years, during which time Jasbir's father tried to keep his son's odd behaviour a secret from the neighbours.

Jasbir produced a flood of information about his past life as the son of Shankar, including the accident on a horse-drawn chariot that had fatally wounded him. As it happened, there *was* a man called Shankar living in Vehedi whose son, Sobha Ram, *had* been killed in a chariot accident at about the time Jasbir had been dying of smallpox. This was one of more than thirty 'coincidences' that emerged as a result of Jasbir's memories and behaviour as his new personality. When he was finally taken to Vehedi, he correctly and spontaneously identified several of Sobha Ram's relatives, and led the way from the railway station to three different locations he was asked to find. Even at the age of ten, he showed strong identification with Vehedi, where the original Jasbir had never been before.

As for the original Jasbir, the boy who had been dying of smallpox, he simply disappeared for ever. His body was taken over by the Sobha Ram entity in a kind of permanent possession. Studying the facts as reported by Stevenson with his usual openmindedness to all possible normal explanations, by far the simplest hypothesis is that somehow the psi body of Sobha Ram had simply grabbed the dying physical body of Jasbir and stayed there. This raises some interesting points.

It suggests that reincarnation can take place quite quickly. The Jasbir-body did not recover immediately from smallpox, but as soon as it did, it began to behave like Sobha Ram and it *never* behaved like the old Jasbir again. What might have happened is that Jasbir did die, medically speaking, but at the exact moment of the departure of his psi component, that of Sobha Ram, who must have died at exactly the same time (which is possible, though Stevenson could not establish this crucial fact) shot into the vacant body from twenty miles away, like a skilful musical chairs player. It cannot have been a conscious decision on Sobha Ram's part, merely a sort of reflex action resulting from attraction. Either that, or we have to assume the intervention of a third party; a discarnate one, of course. Jasbir himself claimed when he was older that after dying as Sobha Ram he had been told by a holy man to 'hide' in Jasbir's body.

Other cases of this kind of thing have been recorded. It reminds us of the famous Watseka Wonder case of 1878, which involved a fourteen-year-old girl named Lurancy Vennum who suddenly became 'possessed' by the spirit of Mary Roff, a neighbour's daughter who had died twelve years earlier in a lunatic asylum. Mary Roff stayed in Lurancy's vacated body for fourteen weeks, after which Lurancy became her normal self again, growing up, marrying and living happily ever after.

We are lucky this kind of thing does not happen more often. It would be very confusing if we kept waking up to find that some marauding entity from hyperspace had grabbed our bodies while we were asleep and happily dreaming on the astral plane. Instead of 'How are you today?' it would be a case of 'Who are you today?'

To conclude, here is a summary of what I assume to be the esesntial facts regarding reincarnation.

1   We all do it. Everybody now alive has lived before, though not necessarily as a human being. The psi atoms that make up our psi bodies are the same as those that make up the psi bodies of all living things. A human psi body is a highly evolved unit, but its actual components are common to psi bodies of animals, vegetables or protozoa. This is not to suggest that you were a bird or a rhinocerous in your last life. But your psi body may be made up of elements that recently formed the psi bodies of an animal, insect or piece of seaweed. (Though probably not if you are intelligent enough to be reading this book.) If this idea seems hard to swallow, remember that your precious physical body is made up of the same cheap chemicals as most other bodies, organic or inorganic. The main difference between you and a lump of concrete is that your body has been shaped, organised and animated by your personal BOM, which contains a record of your entire physical and mental history.

2   The process of reincarnation is something like that of tying a ship to the quayside. First, a sailor throws a rope at somebody on shore, who catches it, perhaps not the first time, and ties his end to a bollard. The ship then gradually slides alongside until comfortably secured to dry land. If some mischievous fellow cuts the rope, the ship might drift out to sea and get lost.

Our biological organising models 'throw out the rope' when a living cell has been formed. The rope grabs hold of a centrosome, and the information passing along the rope tells the centrosome to divide and fan out to north and south poles of the cell-universe. Then it tells the asters to set up their axis, and to create the tension that makes the cell squeeze inwards around its equator and burst apart into two equal cells. The division of the centrosome is the crucial moment, when a cell becomes a future entity rather than a simple piece of unoriented psi matter.

The rest is straightforward textbook biology, except that it is always the BOM that tells the embryo what to do. The embryo's father and mother provide the raw material, the genes and chromosomes which the DNA carries around on its underground railway system, until the BOM tells them where to get off and start building an eye, a tooth, an aesophagus, or whatever.

It takes time for a BOM to plug itself in to a physical body, just as it does for a big ship to dock in a busy port. The whole operation goes on until the physical body is fully adult. Once we are fully grown, or fully reincarnated, our BOM stays in place to run the mechanism of the body and sees to minor repairs. For most of our lives, it stays out of our conscious minds except in times of crisis or serious illness.

3 At death, our BOM separates from our now useless physical body and reforms in hyperspace, where it exists in a world where time and space have no meaning that we can understand. It continues to feel the urge to evolve towards a final goal that it knows to exist but cannot fully identify. Once it has decided what it lacks, it sets about the business of returning to earth in three dimensions, to go round the course again and accumulate more experience or make up for shortcomings of earlier incarnations.

4 We choose our own reincarnations as a rule, either consciously or subconsciously, though there may be cases when these are selected for us, subject to our approval. Less evolved BOMs may reincarnate by an automatic process of attraction, rather in the way a young man from a simple rural community will marry the first girl who comes along and seems to meet minimum requirements.

5 Sometimes, children retain fragments of memory of their previous lives, and start to behave like somebody else. These cases should not be confused, as they usually are, with those

of imaginary personalities that our ever-inventive subconscious minds create for us when stimulated by hypnosis. It is extremely rare for children to present any information or behaviour suggesting reincarnation, but it is from evidence of such rare cases that we are able to make the reincarnation hypothesis a feasible one. Much more research is needed in this area, about which we still know very little, and have definitively proved virtually nothing. This is one field of research in which any layman can take part. All you need is some children and a tape recorder.

6 Whether the theory of reincarnation is true or not, we shall all find out sooner or later. Those of us who believe it are likely to lead more useful lives and find ourselves in better shape when we come to the end of our present ones. Those of us who believe that death is the end of everything may be in for a nasty shock, from which it may take them a long time to recover.

7 It is possible to live a useful life without worrying in the least about reincarnation, or anything else mentioned in this book. Provided we have a well-balanced subconscious mind, our conscious mind needs do little more than obey the instructions it receives from down below, without of course knowing that it is doing so. Just as all paths lead to Rome, as they say (wrongly, I once got thoroughly lost trying to get there by road!), all mental paths must lead to the same ultimate reality, of which there can only be one. So it does not matter if your personal guide is Kardec, Aurobindo, Edgar Cayce, Gurdjieff, St. Paul, Marx or the Pope. Some of these guides may lead you further towards our collective final destination quicker than others, but what matters most is to decide that you are going to move further forwards, upwards or outwards from where you are now.

In the following chapter we come to the problem of precognition, which must be faced sooner or later. This must be related in some way to the phenomena of telepathy and clairvoyance, but it is much harder to accept and, as yet, quite impossible to solve.

Shakespeare, in one of his very few brushes with the psi world, tells us how Macbeth felt after the three Witches had finished describing his future, or as we would now say, giving him a reading:

> Stay, you imperfect speakers, tell me more.
> . . . Say from whence
> You owe this strange intelligence, or why
> Upon this blasted heath you stop our way
> With such prophetic greeting? Speak, I charge you.

But instead of speaking, the Witches promptly vanish, as psi phenomena tend to just when researchers think they are going to get their hands on them at last. Banquo is led to wonder:

> Were such things here as we do speak about?
> Or have we eaten on the insane root
> That takes the reason prisoner?

This is how Richet must have felt after watching Eusapia Palladino levitate his furniture. It is exactly how I felt after each of my encounters with psychic surgeons and poltergeists. 'Would they had stay'd!' Macbeth complains. Would indeed that we had more and better contacts with sources of this strange intelligence that can provide us with information at a distance in either space or time. But we must make do with what we have, and thanks to a handful of modern seers we do have a certain amount of evidence as to how the psi barrier can be broken. Let the seers themselves describe how they do it.

Chapter 11

BREAKING THE PSI BARRIER

How nothing time is! MRS WILLETT

First of all I see a mist. That mist, like on printing paper, consists of little dots, and if I have good contact with a case I'm involved with, and there's an association between (myself and) the background, then the print will form two lines. These lines are the first dimension. It happens quite often that I see lines and nothing else. That is a sign that I am not sufficiently interested in the case.

If the contact is very good with a case, the print and background, then the lines will cross, and the crosses will start to form figures. This is the second dimension—that will be the flat picture. And as soon as these pictures which are two-dimensional become three-dimensional, then this picture in my mind becomes alive. Then I see rather like we see a movie. I will see movement, I will see colours, rather like I see you sitting there now . . .

THIS is how the Dutch medium extraordinary Gerard Croiset describes how he breaks the psi barrier.[1] His words make an interesting comparison with those of Andrew Jackson Davis quoted at the beginning of Chapter Four. Davis described how his 'sphere of vision' seemed to widen, enabling him to see first through the walls of his house, then of the house next door, and so on until he was looking *inside* the bodies and brains of animals he felt to be thousands of miles away.

Edgar Cayce, the most intrepid time-space traveller of them all, made a few observations during his long series of trance communications that give tantalising glimpses of how he managed to reach over the boundaries of the dimensions. His trance personality ('Psi Cayce') was always rather coy about stating who he was, and when challenged directly he would usually reply 'Look within self!' But now and then he would throw out a few clues as to how he produced information that cannot be explained as due to either chance or fraud.

Psi Cayce would say he was reading the 'soul memory' or picking up recordings from the 'skein of time-space'. He became rather more specific in two trance messages given in 1929 and 1934,* in the first of which we have a rare instance of an identifiable discarnate personality claiming to communicate through the entranced medium; the former Cayce family physician, Dr S. Gay. Psi Cayce always took great trouble to say exactly what he meant, even if this involved syntax of a complexity equalled only by William Faulkner. Here is the entity claiming to be the late Dr Gay on the subject of how information is conveyed through Cayce in trance:

> When the consciousness is laid aside, there is that as takes place much in the same manner as the spring to an automatic curtain roller. This then is able to be pulled down or raised up with the release of the spring. Some call this going into the unknown. Some call this spiritual, or spirit communication. Some call it the ability to gain the force of the activities of the fourth dimension—*which is nearer correct than any explanation that may be given*—the plane that is of the inner-between, or that of the borderland. All individuals occupy this plane through that period or such a time that there is the joining together of such forces as may again bring that individual entity into the realm of physical experience or being. (My italics.)

The voice went on to say that every individual records his experience in a 'total record of himself as an entity functioning in many planes of consciousness'.

Another reference to an immortal psi component existing in a multi-dimensional hyperspace was made in the 1934 reading. 'For the soul lives on,' said Psi Cayce, 'and is released from a house of clay. The activities in the world of matter are only

* Cayceologists can find these under file refs. 538–28 and 5756–14.

changed in their *relationships* to that which produces them and that which the physical body sees in material or three-dimensional form.' (Stenographer's italics.) Later in the same session, Psi Cayce (referring to Cayce in the third person, as he often did) elaborated on this idea of interdimensional communication, ending with one of those humorous observations that make him a constant delight to read:

> How (some would ask) did the body, Edgar Cayce, or soul, attune itself at that particular period and yet not remember in his physical consciousness? This is because *the soul passes from the body* into those realms where information may be obtained . . . This realm from which such information is obtainable is either from those that have passed into the realm of subconscious activity or from the subconscious and superconscious activity of the one through whom information is being sought. This particular body, Edgar Cayce, was able to attune self to the varied realms of activity by laying aside the physical consciousness. If the body, from its material and mental development, were to be wholly conscious of that through which it passes in its soul's activity in such realms, the strain would be too great. Material activity could be unbalanced and the body become demented. And he is thought crazy enough anyway! (Italics in original transcript.)[2]

The statements of Davis (1857), Cayce (1934) and Croiset (1974) are remarkably similar. Is this yet another case of like causes producing like effects? If so, what causes? Nobody is perfect. Neither Davis, Cayce nor Croiset are infallible sources of all knowledge. Davis often got hopelessly tangled up with his own subconscious, Croiset has described how he often fails to receive any impressions when he is working on a case that does not interest him, and Cayce seemed to be at his most fallible whenever attempts to study him were made by such authorities as Gardner Murphy or J. B. Rhine. Croiset, fortunately, has been studied for much of his life by the distinguished Dutch parapsychologist Willem H. C. Tenhaeff, far too little of whose work is available in English.

Each of these unusual men, in his own way, has tried to tell us how he breaks the psi barrier and goes beyond the normal limit of our five known senses. Stuart Edward White's invisible psi friends also had a good deal to say about this psi barrier, which they described as 'the farthest point of exploration possible for humans to reach', adding however that it was 'not a definite boundary'. This suggests that the position of a frontier of consciousness can vary from person to person.

The means of sending or receiving information through channels that seem paranormal is usually known as extrasensory perception, or ESP; a contradiction in terms if ever there was one. How can we perceive anything except through our senses, whether these are recognised as existing or not? 'To anyone who has perceived something psychically the word "extrasensory" is nonsense,' Jocelyn Playfair has written. 'In my experience there was always a feeling of physical effort, however slight, that was far from extrasensory. A word that meant extra to the known five senses would be quite useful, but one which implies extra to all senses is misleading. If more were known about the pineal gland I think it might be clearly recognised that "extrasensory" perception is nothing of the sort.'[3]

The most common forms of paranormal communication, as I mentioned in the previous chapter, are telepathy, clairvoyance and precognition. The first two of these are now widely accepted, and even hostile critics of psi will cheerfully use them to explain away other more complex phenomena. But precognition . . . For many, this is still the hardest of all psi nuts to crack, just as it was for Macbeth.

The idea that the future might be predetermined as well as precognisable raises the uncomfortable question of whether we have any free will or not. Many theories have been put forward to deal with the precognition problem, involving two-dimensional time, particles bearing information travelling backwards, and many other nightmare inspirations of physicists. I once had the chilling idea that what we call free will may not really be free will at all. The implications of this were so depressing that I stopped thinking about it. It is essential to feel that at least we have the illusion of free will.

Ridiculous as the idea of precognition seems, the plain fact is that it happens. I took this for granted at a very early age, because my mother had so many precognitive dreams, that later came true, that they became something of a family joke. (Several have been published.[3]) A more recent instance of precognitive clairvoyance involved my friend Celia, the lady from Pompeii, mentioned in Chapter Two.

Celia was in bed one night waiting for her husband to come home from his regular weekly meeting. She is not the worrying type, so at about 1 a.m. she turned off her bedside lamp and decided to go to sleep. Soon afterwards, still awake, she had a suddenly clear vision of Leo's car parked at a 45-degree angle to a brick wall, with the driver's door wide open and the front of the car damaged quite badly. There was no sign of Leo, nor of anyone else. Convinced that her husband had been involved in an accident (São Paulo traffic is world-famous for its barbarity), Celia got up and dressed, ready to start calling police and hospitals. However, at this point Leo arrived home safe and sound, with his car intact, and all was well. False alarm, they decided.

Four months later, Leo *did* have an accident late at night. Celia was asleep at the moment it happened, and went on sleeping. No dreams, no visions, no warning at all. She only woke up when Leo came home in a taxi, slightly injured and a little shaken. The following morning, he stayed in bed and asked Celia to go and see to the car, which he had left at a garage near the scene of the crash.

Celia went to the garage, one she had never used before, to find the *exact* scene she had been shown four months previously. There was Leo's car, parked at a 45-degree angle to a plain brick wall. The front end of the car was damaged in just the way she had seen. And the driver's door was wide open. She learned that a mechanic had been working on the car until just before she had arrived. He had been inside the car and had gone into the office, leaving the car door open.

For all her psychic gifts, Celia felt nothing at the time of the crash, which was not a serious one. The whole episode seems illogical to the point of absurdity. Where are Celia's extraordinary precognitive faculties when she really needs them? Yet I have good reason to believe that the events I have described took place as reported by Celia, whom I have found to be very meticulous in these matters. Some may feel that stories like this one would be easier to accept, though not to explain, if tests for precognition had been carried out successfully under strict control conditions; and not with those wretched Zener cards, but with real live people!

Well, this has been done.

On January 6th 1969, in Utrecht (Holland), Gerard Croiset made two separate sets of statements, containing twelve and twenty-one items respectively, about two different people. Who were these people? Croiset had no idea. Nor had anybody else. The two in question, a man and a woman, were to be sitting in certain seats chosen by lot from the audience at a public meeting to be held on January 23rd in Denver, Colorado. Seventeen days and 4,500 miles away, in fact.

Croiset's statements were tape recorded, and he was filmed as he made them. Professor Tenhaeff, who supervised the Dutch end of the experiment, sent detailed instructions to his American colleague Jule Eisenbud about the seating arrangements for the Denver meeting. These had been worked out by Croiset himself, unfortunately. (We shall see why in a minute.)

The arrangements were very complicated, and seemed designed to guarantee that nobody could possibly know who was to sit on the two seats in question until they were actually sitting on them. Even then, the number of the seat where the person described was sitting was only to be selected, again by complicated randomising methods, after everybody was in place.

It seemed a sure enough way of testing Croiset's legendary powers of precognitive clairvoyance. But Croiset made an extraordinary mistake in his instructions, which passed unnoticed by Professor Tenhaeff, Dr Eisenbud and the five other supervisors of the test in Denver, three of whom were doctors and the other two university professors. Croiset's instructions had included the phrase 'twenty-four white cards numbered from ten to thirty-four', which anyone can see is impossible, since you need twenty-*five* cards to be able to number them in this way. The most paranormal aspect of the whole affair is that nobody noticed this until it was too late.

All was not lost, however. The test was held, wrong numbers and all, and some very peculiar coincidences took place. The first target number (drawn from twenty-five cards instead of twenty-four) was that of the seat occupied by a thirteen-year-old boy, to whom almost none of the statements seemed to apply. The second number fell to a lady, Mrs E. O., on seat number twenty, to whom some statements definitely did apply. Then the card numbering mistake was discovered, and the examiners did two more shufflings, one using cards numbered ten to thirty-three and another numbering them eleven to thirty-four. The first reshuffle-draw produced seat number twenty-eight, which turned out to be occupied by the father of the thirteen-year-old boy, Mr G. T.

All forty participants in the audience, including those not even sitting on numbered seats, were asked to mark each statement as follows: three points if highly applicable to them, one for possibly applicable, and zero for not applicable. In the first set of Croiset statements, Mrs E. O. scored more than four times as many points as her runner-up, and in the second set, Mr G. T. 'won' by almost as large a margin. There could be little doubt that the majority of the statements Croiset had made in each set applied to these two far more than to anybody else present. And each *was* sitting in a seat drawn by lot, admittedly under some revised rules hastily improvised because of the discovery of the numbering mistake.

Croiset scored well by giving the exact height of both Mrs E. O. and Mr G. T. He described the lady's unusual hairstyle correctly, said she had hurt her nose pressing it against a window (true), connected her with a man whose right sideburn had been shorter than the left one on a certain occasion (true) and made eight other statements of which only two seemed totally inapplicable. (Perhaps they have not happened yet?)

Croiset's statements proved almost entirely applicable to Mr G. T. on fifteen items, doubtful on three and wrong on three. He got the colouring and the styling of his hair, mentioned a pair of green socks with a hole in the heel of one sock, a lens falling out of a pair of spectacles, a mark on the man's big toe, an incident about a broken table-top, a coat stained with a green chemical, and a loud record player. All applicable. Some of the incidents described were not 100 per cent correct, but near enough under the circumstances, when you consider the odds against *any* fifteen statements being applicable to anybody, unless the statements were such that almost all of us would qualify, like 'He has two ears'.

It is very frustrating to wonder what would have happened if Croiset's instructions for this test had not contained a built-in impossibility: the numbering of twenty-four cards from ten to thirty-four. It begins to look as though Croiset brought off a display of mass hypnosis at a distance. Yet however disappointing the test was as a whole, it produced results that are not easy to account for by chance or fraud. Which seems to leave precognition.

In fairness to Croiset, I should point out that this test, which has been published in all its bewildering complexity,[4] is nothing like as impressive as others for which control conditions were rather less confusing. In a well-documented book on Croiset,[5] Jack H. Pollack mentions several other successful 'chair tests' and quotes the psychiatrist Dr Berthold Eric Schwarz as saying that the chair test 'smashes time-space barriers' and 'poses difficult questions' for scientists willing to study the evidence without condemning it beforehand.

It is not easy to draw the line between precognition and coincidence. Three examples from my recent personal experience may help illustrate this; the first I regard as pure coincidence, the second might have been, but the third had me really baffled at the time.

After completing this book, I had planned to spend a couple of weeks in a small house in Portimão, on the Portuguese coast, one of the remotest spots in Europe. I saw myself wandering along beaches, eating fresh cod and drinking wine in total peace. The book was delayed, so I never went, but at the exact time I meant to go there, the Portuguese took over the town of Portimão for talks with African nationalists. The whole place was sealed off, troops invaded the peaceful resort, warships patrolled the coast and helicopters hovered overhead! Some holiday that would have been.

On December 16th 1974 I decided to tune my harpsichord, which takes time (there being 189 strings), and which I had not done since March. It was an odd decision, since I was suffering from cramp in the fingers at the time and could not play it. When I lived in Rio de Janeiro, I always used to tune it when the power failed, which happened at least once a week; tuning being easier in the dark and silence. Since I had moved to São Paulo early in 1973 there had not been a single power cut, and I had only given the harpsichord two or three complete tunings. Anyway, half an hour after I finished tuning on that day, out went the lights.

On January 27th 1975 I took a shower at about 2 p.m. It was not a particularly hot day, though it was near midsummer in São Paulo, and I could not recall taking a shower at that hour ever before. I just found myself with nothing to do and decided to have one. Two hours later, the water supply failed for the first time since March 1973 and nobody in the apartment block took a shower for the next thirty-six hours.

Science fiction author James Blish has suggested, in a story called *Beep*, that there is no such thing as motive. All events are fixed, and 'motives' are merely 'rationalisations by the helpless observing consciousness' which, unable to avoid an event it knows to be coming, 'cooks up reasons for wanting it to happen'. I hope he is wrong.

When people like Cayce and Croiset break the psi barrier, it seems they can be everywhere at once, or wherever they want to be. Psi Cayce would go where he was sent, to a certain patient at a certain address, often in a distant town where the waking Cayce had never set foot. There, he would seem to enter the consciousness of the patient, describe the condition of his body in minute detail, throw in some observations about his past, present and future for good measure, and dictate some of the longest and oddest prescriptions in paramedical history.

Croiset, when working on a missing-person case, will hold a piece of the person's clothing and wait for this to trigger him off on a journey through the dimensions, from one psi field to another. Sometimes he gets lost on his journey and sometimes he returns without any useful information. On many occasions, however, he has reportedly been successful in his search, and a Dutch police officer has publicly credited him (on TV) with having found the body of a missing person. By switching into hyperspace, it seems Croiset is sometimes able to pick up the psi field of a specific person, following its trail like a psychic bloodhound. Other people who have been reported as being able to do this sort of thing include Croiset's fellow Dutchman Peter Hurkos and Olof Jonsson from Sweden. According to Charles Panati, there are well-documented cases of psychometry in the files of the New York City, Baltimore, Chicago and Los Angeles police.[6] Here is one field of activity in which psi gifted persons can be of great service to society. It would be hard for a present-day T. H. Huxley to declare 'supposing these phenomena to be genuine—they do not interest me' if the phenomena in question included the bringing to justice of a child-killer or the location of a wandering teenager.

As Gardner Murphy puts it, we are all encapsulated entities. Our sense organs are just as useful for keeping impressions out as they are for bringing them in. A super-medium able to tune in to all psi fields in the universe at once would go insane in a matter of seconds. It looks as though we can only break the psi barrier either when there is a good enough reason, one approved by an unidentifiable censor, or else simply by accident.

Could not some foundation or university spare the cash needed to set up a training centre for working psychics? There is evidence to suggest that it is possible to develop one's innate or acquired abilities as a medium; the London College of Psychic Studies has a long and impressive record of success in training such people as Eileen Garrett and Bertha Harris. This fine institution is primarily concerned with spiritual development; I am sure it would not wish to achieve fame as a training centre for psychic detectives. What we need is a place where promising psychics are taught the business and put to work for the good of society, much as violinists or nuclear physicists are. They could be as useful as either of these.

One practical result of any such large-scale training programme might be a better understanding of the mysterious phenomenon of time.

It seems that the world beyond the psi barrier is not subject to the laws of time as we understand them. 'How *nothing* time is!' Mrs Willett once exclaimed in one of her trances. Difficult as it is to think of time as anything other than what is registered on our wrist watches, we have to try to imagine the possibility of a dimension in which time is not something that goes tick-tock and marks every hour with a bong or a cuckoo.

Although time is measured nowadays by hyper-accurate atomic clocks and standardised the world over, each of us really exists in our own personal time system. Time can fly or drag according to circumstances. It is no more than an illusion set up mainly by our metabolic rate, the rate at which our bodies go through the physical and chemical processes needed to keep us alive. These rates vary enormously; when we are young our metabolism works quickly and time seems to pass slowly. When we are very old, just the opposite happens. To a schoolboy, a period of three weeks until the end of term is one of appalling duration, but to his aged grandparent a whole lifetime may seem to have gone by far too quickly. If we are locked in a totally dark room for long enough, we lose all sense of the passing of time. If we spend an hour in hypnotic trance we can be made to believe only five minutes have elapsed since we altered our state of awareness. Time is what we think it is.

Thoughts, life, and time must all have a stop, according to Shakespeare's Hotspur, who dropped dead a few lines after making this statement. (Perhaps expecting to prove his hypothesis, and perhaps wrong.) But in the psi world time probably never even had a start. There, the past and the present must exist on the same plane, like the rings on the surface of a pond into which a stone has just been dropped. And if past coexists with present, why not the future as well?

The late Adrian Dobbs, one of Britain's leading mathematicians, propounded a theory as to how precognition could be accounted for in the light of new concepts of time. It involved the use of what he called *psitrons*, or particles of imaginary mass that can interact with particles of real mass and also travel faster than light. Psitrons, he said, can absorb information and then whizz backwards in time into some receptive brain, which thus learns of an event yet to happen. At least, I think that is what he said, though not that clearly. This may make mathematical sense to mathematicians, but it has not made much sense of any kind to anyone else as yet. However, precognition does happen, and if there were simpler hypotheses we would have had them by now.[7]

The nearest thing to such a simple hypothesis I can offer is to suggest that time has two dimensions; our measured earth-time and that of the 'timeless' psi world, where everything that has already happened in our time exists in some recorded form (sometimes known as the Akashic records) and models for everything that *could* happen on our plane already exist or are being spontaneously created (by our thoughts and actions) all the time.

Precognitions do not have to come true, which may be a comforting thought to some. There is a famous case vouched for by Myers of a lady who precognised her coachman falling off his seat on the carriage, landing on his head on the road; an incident that began to happen the following day as foreseen but in which the lady was able to intervene, thus preventing serious injury to the coachman.[8]

Precognition should not be confused with prediction, which is foretelling based on known or assumed data. If we look out of a high window at two cars approaching the same blind corner at the same speed, we can safely predict a collision because we have information the two drivers do not have. Our biological organising models may be in a similar position. What we call precognition may only be a matter of prediction or extrapolation to them. From the hyperspatial dimension in which they originate, they may be able to record information before it is available to our conscious senses. Andrade sees the BOM as something that is always pulling us towards a goal rather than pushing us from behind. This implies that the BOM, or somebody, knows where it is going. We, who are being pulled, have no idea where we are going, though we often get indications in the form of hunches, premonitions or glimpses of desirable future situations which we then unconsciously strive to make come true.

If, as Andrade and others insist, our minds are not abstract conceptions, but real substantial things that can be projected into the future, then there has to be a future of some sort for them to project into. I am not prepared to accept one future only, or that this is predetermined. There must be an infinity of them; some partially predetermined perhaps, sketched in outline and waiting for us to fill in the details. Insofar as we can affect aspects of futures that concern or involve ourselves, I see no reason why we should not have instinctive foreknowledge of the probable results of our present actions. Our subconscious might construct a vision of a particular desire or fear, and in either case a relevant event could happen basically because we hoped or feared it would.

Part of our minds is often in the future. When writing a news story, a journalist gets used to writing 'yesterday' instead of 'today', because to the reader of tomorrow's paper the incident he is describing will have taken place yesterday, not on the day the paper came out. Long-range planners in industry often become so immersed in the years ahead that their minds hardly seem to operate in the present. 'Next year was a pretty good one,' an economist once told me. At the time, I thought he was joking.

Scientists assure us that when space travellers are able to go at speeds close to that of light, they will come back to earth to find that their sons are older than they are. If it is possible to interfere with time mathematically, it may be possible in other ways as well. There is a theory that we are all precognising all the time, as if looking through a peephole in a screen, with our conscious minds some way back from the hole seeing only what is directly in front of it on the other side, while our subconscious minds were right at the peephole, seeing a wider angle that includes a certain amount of past and future. In a study of 349 cases of apparent precognition published in 1934, H. F. Saltmarsh speculated that our subliminal minds were able to receive advance knowledge which was somehow transmitted through the threshold to the conscious mind.

It was once thought that telepathic exchange of information was done by waves, like those used in radio or, in the case of clairvoyance, in television. This theory has been fairly well squashed, since while radio waves will not penetrate a Faraday cage (a system of grounded metal screens), it has been shown over and over again that telepathy can penetrate not only a Faraday cage but anything else as well, over any distance. Telepathy does not obey the physical laws that govern the weakening of a wave.

The field interaction theory seems the most promising. Andrade made this clear in his 1958 book, though he was then unaware of the earlier work of Gardner Murphy and the almost simultaneous ideas of W. G. Roll. More recently, British researcher John L. Randall has formulated a theory which closely resembles that of Andrade (of whom he had never heard until after his paper was published) except that it does not take hyperspace into account.

'There exists in the Universe an entity, distinct from matter but capable of interacting with it, which (to avoid emotive phrases) I will call the *psi factor*,' Randall writes, suggesting that *psi interaction* or intervention by the psi factor has taken place throughout the history of evolution, ever since it first got to work on the molecules in the prehistoric seas of newly-formed Earth.

'There appears to be,' he goes on, 'some sort of overall plan for the development of species (and probably of individuals also), so that minor deviations from the main line of development are corrected. Unhelpful mutations may be removed or compensated for before they are able to express themselves in bodily form. . .' Wallace, the Spiritualist co-author of the theory of natural selection, would surely agree. 'Psi interaction may occur,' Randall continues, 'when a structure is required which is so improbable as to be unlikely to occur by chance.' (The psi factor as missing link?)

Randall, like Andrade, hits on the idea of field interaction to explain how the psi factor could influence physical matter. 'When an ordinary piece of iron is placed in a magnetic field, it becomes itself magnetised and thus increases the strength of the field in its own vicinity. In a similar way, we can imagine that the universal psi-factor ("psi-at-large") which I have supposed to be responsible for the origin and development of life also operates more strongly in the vicinity of its own creations. Thus we would expect a highly complex organism such as man to be associated with a 'psi field' capable of imparting information to biological or biochemical systems in its neighbourhood.'

There is already evidence to support this view. Randall mentions the work of Dr Bernard Grad and Sister Justa Smith, each of whom has used people with claimed healing powers in lab experiments; Grad in Montreal to attempt to heal skin wounds in mice, and Sister Smith in Buffalo, N.Y., to accelerate enzyme action. These were two cases of the mind apparently affecting living matter in controlled laboratory conditions. The invasion of biology by psi has already begun, Randall announces, 'and neither biology nor parapsychology can ever be the same again.'[9]

Sir Alister Hardy was probably the first biologist of note to suggest that a psi factor (telepathy) could play a part in the process of evolution. He originally made the suggestion in 1949, expanding on it in his 1963-5 Gifford lectures.[10] Now that biologists (Hardy, Sinnott and the Rhines), theoretical physicists (Jordan), medical researchers (Grad, Smith) and a host of other individuals have not only acknowledged the possible existence of the psi world but also set up experiments to study psi factors at work, it seems that we may be approaching the end of the search for that elusive 'something else' that started Hans Driesch speculating on that basic mystery.

Gallant last-ditch attempts are still being made to deny the existence of the psi world, psi factors, or psi anything. Dr George Price, a Minnesota medical researcher, once publicly suggested that laboratory evidence for psi must be based on fraud, though he was honest enough to retract this suggestion after doing something critics of psi do not always do—study the evidence. A professor of psychology (behaviourist, one assumes) named C. E. M. Hansel has managed to hold out longer than most anti-psi spokesmen, and even in 1974 he was implying in a BBC broadcast that telepathy, clairvoyance and all the rest 'simply did not exist'.

Certainly there have been cases of fraud, deception and simple error in the turbulent history of psi research, as in the history of most other branches of research. Harry Price, the lone wolf of psi research in Britain in the first half of this century, won himself a very dubious reputation after a promising start as an investigator of physical mediums. The famous Borley Rectory, the 'most haunted house in England' was one case of his that was blown almost to pieces by the methodical work of Dr E. J. Dingwall, Mrs K. M. Goldney and Trevor H. Hall, although in my opinion a few portions of the case remain unexploded.

At the end of Chapter 2 I mentioned the case of the researcher who was caught cheating at Dr Rhine's FRNM laboratory in Durham, NC, and promptly given the boot. This must have been a bitter blow to Rhine, who was almost eighty at the time and had striven all his life to make psi research respectable, surviving all sorts of vicious slanders such as having his picture printed in *Time* (March 4th 1974) under the heading *A Long History of Hoaxes*.

The sacred cows of psi research do not always stand up to close examination. One of the most sacred of all is the case of the two English ladies who claimed to have done a time-switch while on a trip to Versailles and found themselves back in the days of Marie Antoinette. Their book, *An Adventure*, has become a classic, and many pages of speculation have been written about it. However, in a book about a playboy contemporary of Proust named Montesquiou, there are descriptions of fancy-dress orgies held clandestinely in the Petit Trianon at about the time the English ladies had their 'adventure', and their description of one of the apparitions they saw exactly fits that of Montesquiou's secretary. As for Marie Antoinette (what, again?), she was probably a homosexual in drag, which would explain why 'she' kept running away when the ladies approached.[11]

Another sacred psi cow is the Pyramid of Cheops. Pyramid power has hit the headlines recently, claims being made that razor blades will sharpen themselves inside model pyramids, provided you get your proportions right. I have tried this, and it seems to work. I have also found that some types of blade will self-sharpen inside an old (oblong) shoe box. They will in fact do this anywhere; the magic vibrations of the pyramid having nothing to do with it, and I am relieved to see that this has been demonstrated by scientists.[12] It reminds me of the days when swords were treated by plunging them, red hot, into bodies of hapless slaves. The method might still work today, but it is more practical to nitrify the steel, which is more or less what the ancients were doing without knowing it.

I mention these cases to assure readers that I do not swallow everything claimed by members of the psi fringe. Nor do I expect readers to swallow everything I feed them. Nothing becomes true just because I or anyone else says it might be, and some of the more unconventional ideas put forward in this book may well be proved wrong one day. I shall be delighted if they are, and equally delighted if they are proved correct. One of the main purposes of this book is to stimulate researchers more qualified than myself, of which there must be millions, to follow up some of the leads I am attempting to present in a readable manner. As Stan Freberg would say, I am just throwing ideas on the floor to see if the cat will lick them up.

It would be remarkable if there had never been any fraud or human error in psi research. There has been plenty of both in most areas of scientific research that I know of, especially in archaeology, biology, and astronomy, not to mention literature. Remember Piltdown Man? The canals on Mars? Kammerer's Midwife Toad? Yet the above-mentioned sciences have survived. Soviet genetics may even have survived Trofim Lysenko, whose career outshone that of any fraudulent Spiritualist medium in history for sheer sustained humbug. Psi research has survived for some 120 years, and is not going to be shaken to pieces by isolated misdeeds in the Rhine laboratory, or the ravings of eccentric psychologists, Jesuit priests or *Time* magazine.

We have seen, I hope, that there is something we can reasonably call the psi world, and that a few of us can make contact with it, even if like Cayce and Croiset they are not quite sure how they do it. The next question is: what happens there? And what use can it be to us anyway? If it exists, we shall all find ourselves there one day, and that will be the right time, some may think, to start worrying about it. Stewart Edward White summed up what I hope to be the attitude of serious Spiritualists when he said of the teachings of his Invisibles: 'They are also continually warning us that only by a hearty mingling in all worldly matters, a complete sharing of physical life, a whole-souled attention to our own business and our relations to people, will we, or anybody else, ever get anywhere.'[13]

Certainly life is here to be lived, and it can be enjoyed without the least understanding of it. You do not have to be an aeronautical engineer to enjoy a flight in a jumbo jet. Indeed, a friend of mine, who is one, cannot get off the ground without several brandies inside him; he is always computing fatigue and stress factors in his head and deciding that the plane will fall to pieces in mid-Atlantic.

And yet. . . Man is an inquisitive animal, and if something is there he has to go chasing after it, whether it is the moon, Mount Everest, a subatomic particle or a girl with nice legs. People who chase after one of these things do not always understand people who choose to chase one of the others. We do things because we want to, which seems to be part of our evolutionary programme. We may get along without the psi world today, but the time may come when we will wonder how we ever managed without it. People like Homer, Shakespeare and Bach somehow survived and created without television, penicillin, cars or the thoughts of Chairman Mao. The psi world is there, even if it is less visible than Mount Everest. So some of us try and explore it.

Nobody should think of the psi world as paradise, utopia or heaven. Initial glimpses of it may suggest paradise to some, but there is no reason to suppose it is any more 'heavenly' than this one. Roman Catholics may still believe that after death they are taken straight to God, patted on the head and given a medal for being good little boys. Some Spiritualists may believe that they are wafted into a land of milk and honey where, by some mysterious form of *apartheid*, you are surrounded only by those of your own race and social class. Everything is free, and you can have it just by thinking of it. Nice old men keep you busy with lectures on the evolution of the soul, and when you have nothing else to do you descend to the dimension of dense matter and say a few kind words at séances, levitating a table or two to prove that you have survived death. One sometimes wonders why the early Spiritualists did not commit suicide *en masse*, like Tristan and Iseult, just to get to paradise ahead of time.

If we are going to explore this lost psi world, we must expect it to have its evil aspects as well as its good ones. We have two sources of information about it; occult revelations, and accounts from people who really think they have been there. The former are sometimes hard to take seriously, but they should be borne in mind when they seem to coincide with the latter. And one point on which practically every source agrees is that the incident of death does not change personalities very much. The good remain good and the evil remain evil.

This brings us to the question of black magic. There is probably no subject about which more sensationalist fiction, mystification and general nonsense has ever been written, spoken or filmed. It is time to try and get some of the facts straight.

Fortunately, some fine books have been written on the subject; Courlander's *The Drum and the Hoe* being a valuable account of the religious background against which black magic practices take place in Haiti.[14] Much of what he writes can be taken as applicable to Brazil, bearing in mind the difference in size and ethnic mix of the two countries.

Afro-Brazilian religious cult meetings have become tourist attractions in Rio de Janeiro and Salvador, and versions of them have even toured Europe and the U.S. They are colourful shows, with exotically dressed men and women playing drums, gyrating, puffing cigars and drinking gulps of *cachaça* rum as they appear to receive spirits of the departed. The annual ceremony in honour of the sea goddess Yemanjá on the beaches of Rio de Janeiro is one of the most extraordinary spectacles of mass witchcraft in the world. It is not a form of black magic, but a religious festival sponsored by the *Umbanda* cult, one of the strongest of the Afro-Brazilian cults. It is wrong to think of such cults as inherently evil, as is the case with witches, who are no more evil than company directors or politicians, though their powers can be used for good or evil, like anybody else's.

Umbanda is on the whole a highly respectable practice. Though founded on a blend of African rites preserved by descendants of slaves with those of the Roman Catholic church, its millions of members today include men and women of all races and social classes. It stands for all the traditional Christian virtues of love, charity and tolerance, and its members do not like seeing themselves described as pagans by *Time* magazine. (Which a group of them once planned to sue, but gave up after reflecting that nobody they respected would be likely to believe anything they read in it.)

But degenerate forms of *Umbanda* exist, usually known incorrectly as *macumba*, the correct term being *quimbanda*. This is oriented towards the practice of evil, and is as abhorrent to any orthodox *umbandista* as it is to anyone else. Much confusion arises from the fact that there may be no apparent difference in the rituals of an *Umbanda* or a *quimbanda* ceremony. They may use similar candles, bottles, cigars, drums, flowers and dances, and the people involved could be mistaken for each other until you find out what they are up to.

It is not possible to live long in Brazil without becoming aware of these cults, or noticing that they seem to have sprung up spontaneously there as in many other parts of the world with which Brazil has no cultural links. Many a tourist has visited a friendly *Umbanda* ceremony, joining in the colourful spectacle, enjoying the often magnificent singing and drumming, and having his private consultation with an entranced mother-in-sainthood (*mãe de santo*), some of whom surprise him with accurate comments on his problems and give him useful advice.

Everybody in Brazil knows somebody who has found a black magic *despacho* (literally, a despatch) outside his door one morning, in the form of a frog with its mouth sewn up, a dead chicken, or a small leather bag with a live cockroach inside it. When you are landed with one of these things, you head for the nearest *Umbanda* group to have the *trabalho* (work) undone, or *desmanchado*.

David St Clair, whom I knew quite well in our Rio de Janeiro journalism days, has given a lively and alarming account of the *despacho* he found on his doorstep one day, and how he managed to get rid of the *trabalho* it represented after it had threatened to ruin him professionally, financially and emotionally. David kept very quiet at the time about his troubles, though they became a source of concern to his friends, who only learned the full story when his book appeared.[15] Ironically, while the forces of the evil sector of the psi world were doing their best to wreck his life, David was working as a writer for the local *Time* office, where his colleagues included Pedro McGregor, the Spiritist medium and international investment banker (not an unusual combination for a Brazilian!) who has written the definitive study of the various forms of Spiritism in Brazil;[16] and also, for a period, myself.

Stories of black magic effects abound in Brazil, but they are very difficult to investigate, being usually based on hearsay. Most people, understandably, do not want to talk about their own experiences in this field. Few Brazilians of any class will admit that they believe in black magic, but most will hasten to add that it exists all the same. 'Why, only the other day,' they will tell you, 'my cook was telling us about her neighbour's mother-in-law, whose second cousin . . .'

'Is there really such a thing as black magic?' I asked Hernani Guimarães Andrade one day as we sat in his office on São Paulo's noisy Avenida Paulista.

He opened a drawer and handed me a file. 'You might like to look into this case,' he replied. 'Then you can decide for yourself.'

I looked into the case, to be described in the following chapter, and decided for myself.

There is.

Chapter 12

THE PSI UNDERWORLD

The simplest things may become appalling when their cause is not understood. KARDEC

D ECEMBER 1965.

In this month, a respectable Catholic family in the small town of Jabuticabal, 220 miles from the city of São Paulo but within the borders of the state of that name, was first visited by one of the most persistently malevolent poltergeists in history. First, pieces of brick began to fall inside the house, apparently from nowhere, although there was a pile of similar bricks out in the back yard. The family decided that someone was playing tricks with them. But nobody could suggest who, or how, and the phenomena went on for several days, until it became clear that if anybody *was* throwing the bits of brick, it wasn't anybody visible. So the good Catholic family sent for the local priest, who duly came and went through his traditional ritual of exorcism, with much arm-waving and prayer-intoning. The phenomena immediately became much worse.

'The gravity of any formal exorcism only excites their merriment, and they treat it as of no account,' says Allan Kardec, referring to what he calls disorderly spirits, or what we would now call poltergeists. 'The majority of them', he goes on in his usual didactic and precise style, 'seem to have no other object than that of amusing themselves, and to be rather reckless than wicked; they laugh at the alarm they occasion, and at the useless searchings that are made to find out the cause of the tumult.'[1]

Though the family had not read Kardec, they did have a neighbour, a dentist named João Volpe, who knew his Kardec very well, for he had been trained and oriented by Cairbar Schutel, one of the pioneers of the Kardecist-Spiritist movement in Brazil. The Catholic family turned to a Spiritist as a last resort. They always do. Volpe came over to his neigbour's house on December 21st. He soon decided that a quiet and pretty eleven-year-old named Maria José Ferreira who was living in the house with the servants, was a natural medium and was unknowingly enabling the phenomena to take place. He immediately offered to take the girl into his own home, keep her under observation, and do what he could to treat the problem. For a few days all was quiet, but then stones began to fly around the Volpe house whenever Maria José was around. The bombardment became so intense that Volpe was finally able to count a total of 312 stones of all shapes and sizes, one weighing no less than 3·7 kilos.

Then the disorderly spirits began to throw eggs around. They became so fond of this that before long it was impossible to keep an egg intact in the house. One day, a dozen eggs were placed on the egg rack inside the refrigerator. Out in the yard, Volpe's granddaughter was feeding the chickens, when she suddenly noticed three eggs underneath one of them. This would be quite normal, except that it was a cock and not a hen, as were all the others she was feeding at the time. Back in the kitchen, it was found that there were only nine eggs in the fridge, although nobody had opened the door.

Stones kept on falling at all hours. One Sunday the Volpes went to lunch with their next-door neighbours. During the meal, a stone descended from the ceiling and split into two about four feet from the ground, the two parts proceeding in different directions as they fell to the floor. One of the women present immediately picked up the two pieces of stone and noticed that they fitted together like pieces of a three-dimensional jigsaw puzzle. Moreover, they seemed to snap together as if magnetically attracted to each other. The stone was passed around the table, and everybody noticed the strange magnetic effect, which soon weakened and disappeared.

Next door, at the Volpes' home, little Maria José was getting quite accustomed to the behaviour of her unseen playmates. She found that she only had to ask them for a flower, a piece of candy or some other small object, and hey presto, it would appear at her feet! (Kardec assures us that poltergeists are not always evil; they can be merely playing games or just trying to attract attention.) On one occasion, a stone appeared out of the air, tapped three people gently on their heads, and fell to the floor. All three people concerned stated that it was as if they had been struck by a 'ball of compressed air' rather than a stone.

This is an interesting observation. Stones thrown by poltergeists rarely hit people directly. (On cases where physical harm has been reported, I would like to make sure the blow was not a result of a stone rebounding off a wall or other surface.) Some think that the human biomagnetic field acts as a sort of defence barrier against missiles from hyperspace, while others assume that the poltergeist doesn't really want to hurt anybody, but just to attract attention the way bad-tempered children do—by flinging anything within reach as far as possible. The latter hypothesis was popular in Kardec's time, but I prefer the former.

When a poltergeist really loses its temper—watch out!

For a few days, nothing serious happened to or around Maria José. João Volpe gave her special treatment in his private study, where on two occasions stones appeared in the presence of Volpe and a doctor colleague. One landed with considerable force on a writing desk, shattering its glass cover. Phenomena also took place in the open air; on one occasion as Volpe and a friend were walking along the street with Maria José, the girl suddenly mentioned that she would like a little brooch for herself, whereupon one fell at her feet. Shortly afterwards, Maria José was pelted with sugarapple fruits while she was out in the yard. The fruit had been inside a bag in the house. Then stones would fall onto her plate while she was trying to eat her meals. The spirits still retained a certain sense of humour; Maria José was trying to pick a guava from a tree in the garden, but found she could not reach it. So she asked Mrs Volpe to pick it for her, and as the lady stretched out her hand, the guava simply vanished.

Then one day all hell was let loose, and for almost three weeks a succession of plates, glasses and even heavy flower vases was flung about the house in all directions, until the Volpes had no unbroken crockery left at all. Invisible hands began to slap Maria José on the face or the bottom, leaving clearly visible bruises. The spirits began to bite her all over her body. They threw chairs at her, and even a large sofa. A gas cylinder was wrenched away from the wall and hurled in her direction. Pictures jumped off walls and flew from one room to another. On one occasion, two witnesses actually saw a glass dish from the kitchen and a mirror from the bedroom cross in mid air before heading for bedroom and kitchen respectively.

Attempts were made to suffocate Maria José by forcing cups or glasses over her mouth and nose while she was asleep. There are indications that they also tried to violate her, though the poor eleven-year-old's descriptions of such attempts were none too precise. Next, about forty days after the initial outburst of brick-throwing, they began to attack her with needles.

It was always her left heel. Needles would simply appear thrust deep into the girl's tender flesh, even while she slept with her shoes and socks on, and sometimes even while she was out walking. On one occasion, fifty-five needles had to be extracted at the same time. When her heel was bandaged, the bandages would be wrenched off without the knots being untied.

On March 14 1966 Maria José caught fire. She was eating her lunch at school when her clothing suddenly began to smoulder from a round burn that had appeared as if from a cigar-butt. The same afternoon, the Volpes' bedroom burst into spontaneous combustion, and while João Volpe was ripping the bedclothes off the burning mattress, he burned his hand quite badly on the pillow, which had caught fire *inside* without his noticing.

Maria José stayed with the long-suffering Volpes for about a year. The phenomena eased off somewhat, but never stopped altogether for long. Finally, Volpe took her to Chico Xavier's

Spiritist centre in Uberaba, which serves as a kind of final court of appeal for really tough cases involving spirit possession. In front of Chico, Brazil's most respected and trustworthy medium, the obsessor came through and announced:

'She was a witch. A lot of people suffered and I died because of her. Now we are making her suffer too...'

The Volpe's home circle gave the little girl all the intensive treatment they could, with special prayers and appeals for help from their spirit guides in addition to repeated magnetic passes over her body. They managed to do away with the really serious attacks, such as those with needles, but the spirits refused to stop throwing things around, especially fruit and vegetables. They had come to stay.

Maria José's life came to an unexpected and tragic end. When she was thirteen, she went back to live with her mother, and one day in 1970 she was found dead. She had apparently committed suicide by taking formicide mixed with a soft drink, dying almost at once. The psi underworld had finally claimed her.

I took the file back to the IBPP office, where I found research director Suzuko Hashizume and secretary Virginia Bressan at work putting a new file together in their usual neat and thorough way, with transcripts of taped interviews, press clippings, background material and investigator's field reports. Once these two girls get their hands on a case, the file seems to grow by itself.

Hernani Guimarães Andrade was drafting a letter to his French colleague Emile Tizané, a retired police officer who has spent much of his life investigating poltergeist phenomena in France.

'Well,' he asked me, 'what did you think of the Jabuticabal case?'

'Very interesting,' I replied. 'But why do these things only seem to happen to uneducated teenagers in remote rural areas? Haven't we got any good black magic going on here in São Paulo?'

Hernani opened a drawer of his file cabinet. 'Here,' he said, 'take a look at this one. It's still being investigated—and the person concerned lives just around the corner.'

Now, from the researcher's point of view, who would be the ideal witness for a case of black magic? A Roman Catholic would be preferable to a Spiritist, since the latter would be predisposed to believe in it. A trained psychologist would be even better, for he or she ought to be able to find rational explanations for the phenomena, or at least would try and find them.

I read through the file and decided it was too good to be true. Then I made arrangements to meet the person involved, and after some additional questioning and checking I decided it could be true.

The girl, whom I will call Marcia F., struck me as a sensible and well-balanced person. With her Catholic upbringing and master's degree in psychology, she did not seem a likely candidate for a black magic curse. However . . .

At the end of May 1973, when she was twenty-eight, Marcia went for an outing with her aunt Elma, who brought along her little daughter. The three of them drove out of São Paulo in the early morning, reaching the Atlantic coast an hour or so later. At about eleven o'clock they went for a stroll along one of the many beaches that make up the 'Brazilian Riviera' either side of the port-city of Santos.

As they walked along the edge of the calm ocean, Marcia caught sight of something lying in the sand, just beyond the reach of the waves. It was a small plaster statue of a woman, about six inches high, and most of its paint had been washed off by the waves that must have lapped around it at high tide. Marcia thought it would make a nice ornament for the apartment in São Paulo she shared with another single girl. She stooped to pick it up.

'Better leave that where it is,' Elma warned. She recognised it as a statue of the sea goddess Yemanjá. It was a long time from August 15th or New Year's Eve, Yemanjá's two traditional feast days, but somebody had evidently been making a private offering to her out of season. The statue was her property, like the white flowers that would have been thrown into the sea along with a request of some kind.

Catholic psychology teachers have no time for superstition. 'How can a statue do any harm?' Marcia said, as she picked it up. Elma said nothing. She was not a Spiritist or an *umbandista*, but she had heard about people who interfered with those ceremonies . . .

Marcia took the statue of Yemanjá back to her apartment. Although the sea had washed most of the paint off, it still had one blue eye, a skin-coloured area around the lower right jawbone and neck area, and smaller patches on each arm and on the back at about the level of the right lung. It made an attractive ornament. She propped it on the mantelpiece and promptly forgot about it.

A few days later she was violently sick with food poisoning after eating a piece of chocolate. This had never happened before, although chocolate was a normal part of her diet. Hardly had she recovered from the initial effects of the poisoning, when she began to lose weight rapidly and feel generally run down. She became pale, her skin taking on a greenish-yellow tinge. She began to lose her memory and to find difficulty in relating to her work, surroundings, and friends. Her colleagues at the faculty where she taught asked what was wrong, but Marcia said it was just the after-effects of food poisoning and would soon pass.

Then she had a hemoptysis; spitting blood from the lungs or bronchial tubes in everyday language. She went to a local clinic for X-rays and a thorough check-up. The first X-ray, taken on July 4th 1973, showed a patch in the right lung that could mean tuberculosis. She was given a Mantoux test (for allergic reaction to the TB bacillus) and a sputum test which came out positive, meaning that she did indeed have a form of TB. Nothing paranormal about that, but what was rather unusual was that within five weeks she was pronounced free of the disease, which usually takes a year to treat and often longer. It can often be fatal.

The doctor told her to have a good rest, and Marcia went to stay with her parents in the small town 300 miles from São Paulo of which her father had once been mayor. The little statue of Yemanjá stayed on the mantelpiece of her apartment.

A few days after her return from a two-month stay in her peaceful home town, Marcia's pressure cooker blew up in her face, showering her with boiling beans and water. She suffered second-degree burns on both arms and on the right side of her face and neck. She was rushed to a first-aid post for treatment, and spent the next few days resting at home.

Then the oven exploded. There were three people in the kitchen at the time, when a sheet of flame shot out of the lower part of the stove, which was unlit, directly towards Marcia, as if it were trying to reach her. Marcia immediately fetched a gas-fitter who took the stove apart and could find no explanation for the incident, in which the door of the oven had been blown open suddenly, although the spring-hinge was new and strong. Marcia decided to trade the stove in for a new one, just in case . . .

A few days later, a friend visiting São Paulo from her home town told her that at the very moment her pressure cooker had exploded, her photograph had jumped off the wall of her parents' home. There had been no wind, the string had not broken, and the nail had not fallen out of the wall. The photograph had simply jumped to the floor.

Every good psychologist knows that coincidences will happen, but to Marcia there were getting to be too many of them. A friend mentioned that her statue of Yemanjá might have something to do with them.

'Nonsense,' she replied. 'How can a statue do anything?' She gave her friend a lecture on the principles of behaviourist psychology, in which she had been trained and taken her master's degree, and which she now taught at a university faculty in São Paulo.

'Behaviour is something that depends on external forces,' she explained. 'I can only evaluate what I can really see. Any

250 THE INDEFINITE BOUNDARY

interior, or non-observable event is not relevant. There cannot be any relation between a statue and a burn or a dose of TB . . .' The textbook phrases came tumbling out.

Behaviourism, the school of psychology founded by J. B. Watson, reduces man to an object situated between a stimulus and a response. It explains such crucial life situations as whether or not a girl accepts an invitation to lunch, but it does not explain the appearance of a Michelangelo. Arthur Koestler, in *The Ghost and the Machine*, calls it 'flat-earth psychology'. The contemporary behaviourist B. F. Skinner has made the earth-shattering discovery that the mind does not exist and suggests that so-called mental events should be ignored or rejected.

Still on her best behaviourism, Marcia decided that her TB had been brought on by her lack of resistance after the period of food poisoning. The pressure cooker explosion was bad luck, the oven incident was just another incident. These things happen.

Then, while Marcia and her room-mate were crossing the busy street outside their apartment building, the girl in front dropped the car keys in the middle of the road. As Marcia bent to pick them up, the lights changed and the nearest car did his best to imitate Emerson Fittipaldi chasing another world Formula 1 championship, as most São Paulo drivers always do, missing Marcia by inches. As she crouched on the road with cars roaring past her on both sides, she had a sudden impulse to commit suicide by flinging herself in front of a car. She fought the impulse off, and eventually reached the safety of the island in the middle of the road.

Some time later, as she was opening the window of her 15th-floor apartment, she again felt an impulse to kill herself. 'It was like a voice inside me saying "go on, throw yourself out",' she told me. Again, she was able to fight the impulse; one wonders whether some cases of suicide are the results of such impulses felt by people without the self-control to ward them off.

Marcia eventually did what all Brazilians do in the situation she was in. Casting aside her Catholic upbringing and her behaviourist education, she headed for the nearest *Umbanda* centre. As it happened, her room-mate knew a good one. What finally made up her mind to take this drastic step were the strange experiences she began to have at night. She had never had sleeping problems before; her busy schedule and the racket of São Paulo, one of the world's noisiest cities, usually made her drop off as soon as her head hit the pillow. But now it was different. She would feel strange sensations around her that kept her awake all night. Her bedroom would be full of— the only word she could find was *presences*. She felt herself being touched all over the body, and one night came the ultimate horror, the phenomenon known to occultists as *incubus*.

The dictionary says this is an evil spirit that descends on sleeping women and has sexual intercourse with them. The dictionary may be right.

Perhaps understandably, it took some time and much tact to get the details, which Marcia only gave when we had convinced her that the IBPP never reveals the true identities of its patients without their consent.

To a suggestible and frustrated single woman, an ordinary erotic dream could easily be mistaken for an incubus. Marcia, however, is neither suggestible nor frustrated, and old enough to know the difference between an erotic dream and something else. It is slightly unusual for an attractive and intelligent girl in her late twenties to remain unmarried in Brazil, but Marcia is one of the new generation of *brasileiras* who are reacting against centuries of male domination and making careers for themselves in many professions.

Marcia gave us the facts. She had, she said, felt the sensation of complete coitus. She had felt the weight of a body on top of hers, and the 'presence of a male organ', in her own words, inside her. She had never been able to identify the face of this entity, but could clearly recall her efforts to push him away. The experience had taken place for several nights in succession, and had only ceased after she had been treated by a Spiritist from her home town who had unexpectedly turned up one day when she was staying with her parents and told her she needed help.

The director of the *Umbanda* centre in São Paulo listened to Marcia's story and immediately told her that hers was a straightforward case of a *trabalho* being put to work on her, in revenge for her unlawful removal of the statue. (At the insistence of her room-mate, Marcia had mentioned the statue episode and brought it along to the centre).

It was only at that point that Marcia realised that she had been afflicted in some way or other on parts of her body that corresponded to the remaining patches of paint on the image of Yemanjá. The burn marks on her arms, face and neck matched closely; the patch on the back was just about where her first X-ray (which I examined and showed to a radiologist who knew nothing of her case) revealed a lesion in her right lung. True, the statue still had a piercing blue eye, and Marcia would rather not think about what that might have led to . . .

The *Umbanda* medium told her to take the statue back at once to the spot on the beach where she had found it. This she did at the first possible opportunity, and after two months of treatment at the centre her problems went away and her life returned to normal. Recalling her three months of torment almost a year later, she took a very matter-of-fact approach to the whole business. Previously, she told me, she would not have been able to accept the fact that observable events could be caused by the mere presence of a small plaster statue. Now, she was prepared to admit that they could. It was as simple as that. Marcia is no longer the behaviourist psychology teacher she was, though it must be said that her rational attitude while the phenomena were taking place may have saved her from a worse fate, possibly even death.

Moral: don't pick up things you find on Brazilian beaches.

A *Scientific Explanation for Black Magic* is the title of a master's thesis I hope some anthropologist will write one day. Black magic exists or has existed in almost all countries and cultures, and has taken many forms, often becoming an accepted part of the local folklore. The term itself is derived, as mentioned in Chapter Two, from *necromancy*, or *nigromancie*; divination by the dead. Some may feel the subject is like that of flying saucers, which have also been reported all over the world—a case of people's imaginations being stimulated by previous reports.

Yet there is an important difference. Flying saucers have only become widely popular since after World War II, and press reports of them have made the subject familiar to anybody who can read. With our heads full of reports of sightings of these things, it is easy to think we are seeing one every time a weather satellite orbits the earth just after sunset. I have seen one of these, and they can look very convincing.

Black magic, however, has existed since long before the days of instant communication and mass suggestion. It has come into existence spontaneously among cultures that knew nothing of other cultures, and among people that cannot read newspapers or books. Just as the 19th-century Spiritualists in the U.S. knew nothing of the Roman theurgists, neither do the *macumbeiros* of Brazil know anything about Dr Faustus, or the *kahunas* of Hawaii. They have discovered black magic for themselves, and they practise it because it works.

So-called magic phenomena, black or white, are provoked by means of long-established practices, involving rituals, symbols, objects and elements that vary little in the various cultures that go in for them. In general, they seem to be based on an exchange of favours between incarnate and discarnate, or man and spirit. Incarnate man wants a favour done; he wants a better job, to marry a certain girl, to win the state lottery, to stop somebody running after his daughter, to prevent an enemy from winning an election, or to wreak vengeance on an employer who has fired him. Discarnate spirits, for their part, want to enjoy the pleasures of the flesh once more; a good square meal, a drink of the best *cachaça* rum, a fine cigar and perhaps even sexual relations with an incarnate being.

The spirit has the upper hand in all this. He calls the shots. He wants his meal left in a certain place at a certain time, and the rum and cigar had better be of good quality. Incarnate man is ready to oblige, and it is remarkable how members of Brazil's poorest classes, who are about as poor as anyone can be, will somehow manage to lay out a magnificent banquet for a spirit who has agreed to work some magic for them, when they cannot afford to feed their own children properly.

Who are these spirits? Orthodox Kardecists and Umbandistas see them as inferior discarnates living in a low astral plane, who are close to the physical world, not having evolved since physical death, and feel attracted to the pleasures we have to offer. In Umbanda they are known as exus, spirits who seem to have no morals at all and are equally prepared to work for or against people. Like Mafia gunmen, they do what the boss says without asking questions.

The exu reminds us of the traditional spirits of the four elements; the gnomes of earth, the mermaids of water, the sylphs of air and the salamanders of fire. These creatures are traditionally thought of as part human and part 'elemental', integral forces of nature that can act upon human beings subject to certain conditions. There is an enormous number of different exus, each with his own speciality. To catch one and persuade him to work for you, it is necessary to bribe him outright with food, drink and general flattery. An exu is a vain and temperamental entity, and despite his total lack of morals he is very fussy about observing the rituals properly.

Just how complicated and prolonged 'magic' rituals can be is described by Carlos Castaneda in one of his books about the teachings of the old Yaqui Indian he calls Don Juan.[2] You cannot help admiring Castaneda's patience as he spends hours rolling around the floor looking for 'his spot', or years mastering the ritual of preparing the various plants through the 'magic' powers of which he finally achieves nothing more than the good old-fashioned OOBE (out-of-body experience). Don Juan's life is one long ritual, as obscure as it is complex. He cannot just go out and pick a peck of peyote and eat it. He must spend days and nights wandering around remote valleys until the plant decides to pick him. It all rather reminds me of Mad magazine's do-it-yourself coffee table, which takes at least a year to complete. (After making the table in a few hours you plant a coffee bean outside, making the pot and cups while you wait for the bean to grow).

Anthropologists explain this kind of nutty behaviour by claiming that ritual is a psychological necessity for backward peoples who have to invent their own reality and impose it on the 'real' reality (i.e., the university-trained anthropologist's), which primitives are too dumb to understand. The value of Castaneda's books is that they show this supposedly invented reality to be rather more real than earlier anthropologists chose to believe.

Don Juan insists that his roots, herbs and mushrooms are real entities. The peyote-person is called Mescalito, and if he likes you he can do all sorts of things for you, although all 'he' really seems to do is separate the psi body from the physical after months of elaborate preparation. (Edgar Cayce used to do the same thing twice a day just by lying down and closing his eyes.)

Another of Don Juan's plants, the datura or devil's weed, works its magic with the help of two lizards, of which you have to sew up the eyelids of one and the mouth of the other. In Brazil, toads are often used to further black magic curses; the macumbeiro (sorcerer) will get hold of a piece of the victim's clothing or hair and stuff it inside the toad's mouth, which he then sews up. After suitable incantations and further ritual, the toad's sufferings will somehow be transferred to the physical body of the victim, presumably by means of the fields surrounding their respective psi bodies.

Something like this seems to have happened to Marcia, the girl who picked up the statue of Yemanjá. Nobody was putting a curse on her on purpose, but in her case she literally stumbled upon an object that must have contained an evil force-field with which she interacted unawares. If Marcia had claimed that somebody was out to get her for a specific reason, I would have grounds for supposing some of her experiences to have been due to nervousness arising from suggestibility. But the fact that they happened without her having any suspicion that the statue could be responsible makes her case more interesting. It suggests that an innocent party is able to get involved with somebody else's black magic and suffer accordingly. This happened to a school teacher friend of mine in Rio de Janeiro once. Fresh from England, he had no time for black magic, and one day he was strolling along the beach with some Brazilian friends when they came across some candles and bottles left from a ceremony probably held the night before. The Brazilians carefully avoided them, but my friend kicked some sand over the bottles and candles with a disrespectful gesture. For the following seven days he had an agonising pain in his leg, which went away as suddenly as it had come. Seven weeks later, it came back for one day only, and seven months later it returned with such a force that he had to go into hospital for two days. Later, I learned that he had then gone to an *Umbanda* medium in desperation, and been told that the pain would also return in seven years. Apparently, this did not happen, perhaps because my friend changed his attitude towards the psi underworld.

The case of Maria José, the little girl who was apparently done to death by black magic methods, comes more properly under the heading of what we call poltergeist activity, or RSPK, (recurrent spontaneous psychokinesis), which can be just as dangerous. There is a current school of thought which claims that RSPK is no more than a materialization of the thought-forms of a repressed teenage epicentre. I find it more probable that a poltergeist is exactly what Kardec said it was more than a hundred years ago—an undeveloped spirit playing naughty games and occasionally becoming really violent.

Brazil, especially the city of São Paulo, seems to get more than its fair share of RSPK activity, though it may be that the IBPP has worked harder than other research institutes to track down its poltergeists. It has gathered evidence for about thirty cases, twenty of which I have studied in some detail. On three of these cases, phenomena took place in the presence of investigators, and I have been poltered, if that is the right word, twice myself. No two cases ever seem to be identical and there seem to be exceptions to any rules we try to make concerning RSPK, but six general categories of poltergeist activity can be broadly defined:

1 *Stone Throwing.* This is often the first stage. When it occurs at all on a case, it tends to occur before any other kind of phenomenon. Stones or bricks bombard the roof of the victim's house, sometimes appearing inside the house even when doors and windows are closed—as they tend to be when this sort of thing starts to happen! Once, a carload of people was pelted with stones while driving in the bleak countryside near Brasilia, on their way from a wedding ceremony. This case was written up the day after it happened by one of the victims, a well-known Brazilian surgeon, and was summarised in my previous book, as was my own first encounter with a poltergeist.

My second took place on September 24th 1974, in a rural slum area near the town of Carapicuiba, half an hour by train from São Paulo. I arrived at the site at 2.30 p.m. to follow up reports of stone-throwing that had appeared in a local paper and been confirmed for me by a police officer who had been sent for by the frightened residents involved. ('This case sounds like your job rather than ours,' the policeman told me, when I explained what our institute was.)

I had difficulty in finding the house, since I only had the street name and not the house number, but posing as a roof-repairer I made some enquiries and found that nobody had heard anything about a roof being damaged; even, as it turned out, the people living nearest to the houses affected. Finally I came to a group of six small houses, all of which showed clear signs of having been pelted with stones and bits of brick. Several thick roof tiles were broken, some were missing, and some clean new ones had obviously been fitted recently as replacements.

The house nearest the road (which was completely deserted except for a dog or two) had a large concrete block on the roof, which had shattered three tiles. As I arrived, and before I had even had time to introduce myself, a woman washing clothes in the yard pointed to the block and told me it had fallen at that moment, or certainly less than five minutes previously. There was a pile of similar concrete blocks near the road, and the only position anybody human could have thrown it from was on the road along which I had been walking for more than five minutes, meeting nobody on it at all. It was a sparsely-populated area on the side of a hill, end you could see for several hundred yards in all directions. The older children were all in school a mile away, and after we had recovered the block I asked the largest child around to see how far she could throw it. She couldn't even lift it. I calculated that to throw it from the pile by the road, some thirty feet, would have needed great strength, not to mention a motive. Nobody except small boys or madmen throw stones at their neighbours in rural Brazilian communities, and I was soon assured there were neither within, as you might say, a stone's throw.

The bombardment had been going on almost daily for more than three weeks. The six families involved agreed that nobody visible could have kept it up that long without being caught, especially as the police had been out and searched the area and the residents themselves had mounted a kind of makeshift home-guard system, keeping watch in all directions.

Less than ten minutes after my arrival, as I was standing talking to two of the women on the open ground between two of the houses, a hail of stones or pieces of brick fell out of a cloudless blue sky, rebounding off the roof of one house onto another at a lower level. I cannot say how many stones there were; I clearly saw a small puff of tile dust as a projectile struck the roof directly in my line of vision about ten feet from where I was standing, and a small piece of broken tile landed at the feet of the woman I was talking to. I picked it up at once; it showed signs of having been recently broken. We scanned the area, and decided that the nearest house in the line the bombard-ment appeared to have come from was too far away to be a normal source.

All six housewives were thoroughly bewildered and frightened by the bombardments. Nobody had been hit directly, which was interesting, for there were tiny children all over the place.

Perhaps our auras really can ward off attacks from hyperspace. One woman had been hit on the leg by a stone that had rebounded off the ground, and one couple had been inside their house by the open door when a stone had whizzed past their noses as they faced each other a few feet apart.

One house, I discovered, seemed to have been attacked more than any of the other five. There were still more than twenty pieces of broken brick and tile on the roof. Would there, I asked, be a teenage girl living there? Sure enough, there would, and she was fetched out to say hullo to me. She was a plump and amiable girl, belonging to a family of Protestants who had no time for the spirits, and there seemed to be no reason why anybody would want to attack her.

It is a cherished tradition in psi research that there is always an epicentre around in the form of a teenage boy or girl. I am sorry to say that this tradition is not respected by the Brazilian poltergeist. Of the twenty cases I have examined, teenage epicentres could only be identified on six of them, five more offering possible epicentres aged twenty-three to forty-three, and at least one on which there were no signs of a single epicentre at all, the area affected measuring about 300 by 400 by 450 yards. There is a good chance that there will be a teenage girl or boy around when unusually persistent RSPK phenomena take place, but it is definitely *not* an essential condition, in my opinion. If this is so, it makes rather a hash of the repressed-teenager-materialising-her-frustrations theory, which never appealed to me much in the first place. Some of our best epicentres, indeed, have been far from repressed.

So much for bombardments, which seem mainly intended to draw the attention rather than to cause severe damage to people or property. Next in order in the usual sequence of events, we have:

2 *Raps.* The citizens of the psi world chose this method back in 1848 to introduce themselves to the world of the incarnate and usher in the era of modern Spiritualism in the U.S. (There are reports of raps in what later became the Fox family home in Hydesville, N.Y. from as early as 1843, but it

was on March 31st 1848 that they became public knowledge. They also announced, incidentally, that there was a body buried in the cellar, which indeed there was). Like stone-throwing, rapping and thumping on the floor seems to be a way poltergeists try to draw attention. This they certainly succeed in doing in my experience, but I have not yet found a way of discovering what it is that the attention is supposed to be attracted to. On the Ipiranga case (referred to as PK-15 in my previous book), we had limited apparent success with letter-cards spread on the kitchen table. Some of these were turned over or rearranged, though we could not rule out normal explanations for this. We never got any coherent messages, but I recommend trying this method on future cases.

The raps Suzuko Hashizume and I tape-recorded (independently) on the Ipiranga case were extremely loud and clear, and on two successive nights they took place at the exact moment one of us was dropping off to sleep. When we later made normal raps with an assortment of broom handles and our own heels, we noticed that several sympathetic vibrations were set up as vases and small ornaments began to buzz and shake, an effect we had not noticed at the time of the supposed psi raps.

3 *Displacement of objects.* This is by far the most common phenomenon among our twenty Brazilian RSPK cases, there being evidence for it on thirteen of them. Having attracted the attention by bombardments and rappings, the poltergeist then starts rearranging the furniture. In addition to the phenomena on the Ipiranga case I have already described, we witnessed a number of other such phenomena. Suzuko's raincoat was transported from the back of a chair to the inside of a kitchen cupboard, and her open umbrella from the bathroom to the yard. A pillow was whipped off a bed while she was in it. A piece of soapstone landed in the hallway early one morning (when the origin of a displaced object is not known, as in this episode, we call it an apport) and my own umbrella was moved from a rail in the bathroom to a corner of the shower cabinet.

On the Sorocaba case, a heavy wooden shelf crashed to the

floor in a room that was empty except for a sleeping poodle, while everybody in the house was under observation by an IBPP researcher. Suzuko had her recorder on at the time and recorded the noise clearly, also the yelp of the poodle as it was rudely awakened.

Every researcher dreams of actually seeing an object *start* to move paranormally. I have not yet done this, though a most reliable investigator, W. G. Roll, has done so on three of the many cases he has covered so thoroughly.[3]

4 *Fire*. This has broken out inexplicably on seven of our cases. Items burned include clothing, bed linen, furniture and also a parrot, the inside of a handbag, a pair of pyjamas (with a man asleep in them) and a dog's backside. On one case, a small baby was almost burned to death. On the Ipiranga case, both girls involved had almost all their clothes ruined by repeated small outbreaks of fire, even when clothes were inside a plastic bag, which did not burn.

The IBPP has five qualified engineers among its members, and they know all there is to know about normal spontaneous combustion. This can take place, for instance, if you leave rags soaked in linseed oil lying about in summer. Damp grass and certain foodstuffs can also catch fire on their own under certain conditions. A ball of steel wool once combusted during a hot and humid night in my Rio de Janeiro apartment, which was alarming, but quite normal.

On the 1970 Suzano case (recently published in full), the IBPP was given absolutely unshakeable testimony from three police officers, and twelve other people, for paranormal spontaneous combustion. In February 1975 I went to Suzano to check their testimony. 'If I live to be 100,' one told me, 'I'll swear that the calendar hanging on the wall in front of my nose caught fire by itself. I even put my finger in the flame, to make sure it was real, and I burned my finger.' This was only one of several such incidents.

5 *Miscellaneous*. Almost every RSPK case has some unusual feature. During the Ipiranga one, clothing and even a whole bedroom floor would suddenly become soaked with water,

which would dry out as mysteriously as it appeared. On other cases, strange voices have been heard and materialised parts of bodies seen, but these phenomena are too similar to ordinary hallucinations, auditory or visual, to amount to useful evidence.

One case that turned up just down the road from where I was living in São Paulo in 1974 involved a very respectable and apparently happy Catholic family with two lively teenage boys. One of the boys was walking upstairs one evening when he saw an arm disappear into a bedroom. He was alarmed, thinking it must be a burglar, and even more alarmed when the whole house had been searched and everybody realised it could not have been anybody incarnate. The boy stuck to his story after prolonged interrogation both from his parents and from myself. (I was in one of my real Scotland Yard moods that day; there is nothing I enjoy more than seeing a Catholic groping for a normal explanation of phenomena that point to the existence of spirits!) In the same house, a mirror had fallen from a wall, a light bulb had left its socket and fallen to the floor at an angle of about 45 degrees, a stiff tap had turned itself on within earshot of the whole family, a heavy door had opened just before somebody reached for the handle, and a table lamp had had a sudden fit of the shivers in a draughtless room. But on the whole this was rather a half-hearted poltergeist, and I managed to find possible normal explanations for all these incidents except that of the boy's vision of a human arm. This had seriously upset him for a week, and nothing could shake his story.

6 *Black Magic.* This is a feature of poltergeist cases that has not received the attention I think it deserves, and a study of it might lead to clues as to the cause behind general RSPK phenomena. We need all the clues we can get in this bewildering and often alarming field of research. It may be felt that I am being over-imaginative in linking black magic to the poltergeist, but no imagination is needed to recognise the fact that both exist, or that the evidence that turns up on cases of the latter often points to the former. Not always, by any means, but we have clear evidence of black magic at work on six of

our twenty Brazilian cases, which makes a respectable percentage.*

I have already described some of the physical phenomena of the Ipiranga case. This one also provided me with a first-hand view of black magic at work, so I shall now go into the background of it in more detail. The family involved consisted of the mother, her daughter, her youngest son, and his wife. The poltergeist, which was active for about six years, drove them out of three homes in succession and only ceased activity when Iracy, the daughter, got married in January 1974 and the mother went to live with relatives elsewhere.

Iracy, our main source of information about the case, was also the family's main breadwinner. Attractive and intelligent, she had a well-paid job with a multinational company in São Paulo, and she struck me as a girl of strong character with a realistic approach to life, including the phenomena that had been part of her own life for nearly a quarter of it. Her mother was a calm and amiable lady of Portuguese stock who had separated from her husband long before the phenomena began. Her two brothers were the black sheep of the family; one was in jail and the other was thought to be involved in drug dealing. We only met him once as he seemed to spend most of his time travelling, and he struck us as a very sinister individual. His wife Nora looked at first like the perfect epicentre for a poltergeist case. Quiet and friendly, she was also in a clearly advanced state of neurosis, perhaps due to the fact that she had no children in six years of marriage and seemed unable to hold a regular job.

The first incident in the Ipiranga case, which took place in 1968, was one of pure black magic. A *despacho* of bottles, candles and cigars appeared one day in the garden of their original house, indicating that somebody was doing a *trabalho*

* D. Scott Rogo has suggested that 'poltergeist and possession-poltergeist, although resembling each other, may well be two different phenomena'. This is a very useful line of inquiry, but when Rogo goes on to say that 'the Roman Catholic viewpoint of evil infestation does fit the fact(s) better than any other explanation', I am led to wonder if he has ever heard of Kardec.[6]

against the family, though nobody could imagine who, or why. Then another candle appeared inside the house and set fire to a curtain, which was a little harder to ascribe to a living person, though still quite possible. Next, Nora became violently obsessed, spending days and nights in bed muttering in a strange voice and finally trying to jump out of a top-floor window. She was taken to hospital, but escaped and found her way home—she was never able to explain how and could remember nothing of the incident later.

Iracy's and Nora's clothes began to catch fire in the second house, and objects began to disappear and reappear with such regularity that it almost became a family joke. Iracy's prized collection of woolly animals was especially popular with her unseen enemy. One appeared on the roof of the building, another was projected into the middle of a busy street inter-section outside the house, and when Iracy managed to recover it, with some difficulty and at the risk of being run over, she got home to find another animal missing. Looking out of the window, she saw it in the middle of the same street intersection. This sort of thing happened so often that Iracy finally dumped her entire collection of animals in a river. She suspected that some sort of evil was at work, and rivers are thought to be the best place to dispose of objects affected by black magic practices.

In the third house, where the family spent only one month in 1971, loud knocks on the front door were heard, which could not have been caused by anybody incarnate, Nora's husband's pyjamas caught fire while he was asleep in them, and finally the house, which was brand new, caught fire while there was nobody at home. Mother and Nora came back from shopping to find the house full of smoke; the fire had started in a bedroom and destroyed two cupboards and an entire bed—mattress, frame, sheets and all.

An interesting feature of paranormal spontaneous combustion (PSC) is that it comes in two forms. Sometimes it will be no more than a brief outbreak, like my ball of steel wool, and will put itself out without doing serious damage. At other times it will completely destroy the object in question. The interesting feature of the former variety, which in my view points to a paranormal explanation, is that often objects that are highly inflammable will *not* burn themselves out. If somebody was playing tricks and furtively applying lighted matches to pieces of nylon or cotton clothing, these would either go up in flames at once or, in the case of certain fabrics, crinkle up and melt. Every schoolboy knows how to start a fire with the aid of the sun and a magnifying glass. By holding the glass still, the sun will be focused onto a point on, say, a piece of paper, which will gradually darken and burst into normal flames. It often looks as though poltergeists are able to do something similar. PSC burn marks are almost always small round holes, as if made by a cigar butt, and more often than not, they remain small, as if insufficient energy were available to enable them to spread and destroy the object attacked completely.

Outbreaks of fire, and just about everything else, became far worse in the fourth home to be attacked by the Ipiranga poltergeist. Having ruined Iracy's entire collection of clothing, it began to work its way through the replacements she kept having to buy. One morning, when she was in the bathroom, her handbag caught fire inside, totally destroying her paper money and documents. Almost every day, somebody lost something or other and had to search the house for it. The kitchen knives turned up neatly arranged in a flower vase. Clothes and shoes would move from bedroom to living room or staircase. Small objects would hide themselves under beds. Iracy's fiancé's identity card vanished and turned up inside a drawer under the kitchen sink that was extremely hard to open. One day, the bedclothes tied themselves in knots. Normal life became impossible, and Iracy began to feel the strain. The whole family suffered from the poltergeist, but she seemed to be the main target.

One day she received a phone call in her office, just after her extension had been changed, telling her that her married sister in Rio de Janeiro was seriously ill. A friend offered to drive her there at once, but had a major accident (his first) while on the way to pick her up. Iracy and her mother finally got to Rio by bus, only to find the sister alive and well, wondering what all the fuss was about. Two or three similar incidents involving telephone false alarms took place, and Iracy even hired a private detective to track down the mysterious caller, without success.

Worst of all, however, were the *despachos*, which kept coming in a variety of forms. One day, four passport-sized photos of Iracy appeared on the living-room floor, folded and sewn up with threads. Each photo had been taken in a different year, and Iracy could not recall where they had been kept. Then the *patuás* began to turn up. A *patuá* is a small leather pouch closed by pulling a thread round the top edge, popular with Brazilians for keeping coins or buttons in. These began to appear all over the place, even out of doors. One turned up in Iracy's bed, containing a live cockroach. Another fell out of Nora's dress in full view of her aunt (one of the many relatives and friends who gave us supporting testimony on this case). When they did not contain live insects, the *patuás* would be found to have disfigured photographs of Nora's husband or brief messages telling him that Nora was running around with another man. This she vehemently denied, and there was no evidence that she was.

Altogether, it was fairly obvious that somebody was trying to drive the family out of its mind altogether. There were two possible discarnate suspects: a former boy-friend of Iracy's who had committed suicide, and an elderly aunt who had died somewhat neglected by the rest of the family, who might have borne a grudge against them for abandoning her. There were also some possible suspects from the land of the living. Iracy, we learned, had had a brief affair with a man who was already married, unknown to her. His wife might well have learned of the affair, gone to a *quimbanda* centre and ordered a *trabalho*. Then there was the possibility that the Ipiranga case was one of a *trabalho* rebounding on the person who had originally ordered it. David St Clair reports such an instance in his book already referred to, in which his maid became very ill soon after he had managed to have her spell broken by a 'white magic' medium. We never got to the bottom of the Ipiranga case, which ended after Iracy got married and settled into a bright new home of her own with her unusually sympathetic husband, who had stuck by her through the worst of the phenomena.

While Suzuko Hashizume and I were investigating the Ipiranga case, Mr Andrade and Carmen Marinho were documenting another in the nearby town of Osasco. Here, there was clear evidence that a black magic curse was being carried out with the help of standard RSPK phenomena. Two neighbouring families had been having a long dispute about the boundary line separating their properties, and one family was found to have ordered a *trabalho* against the other. This took effect in the usual ways—stones pounding onto the roof, rappings at all hours, clothes catching fire inside drawers and closets, plus a bizarre detail in the form of a large cigar being found inside a closed saucepan while a meal was being cooked in it.

Can we explain the poltergeist? This is in fact the title of a recent book,[4] and the fact that the title takes the form of a question suggests that the answer is no, at least by normal explanations. This brings us to the subject of Occam's Razor.

William of Occam (or Ockham) lived from about 1284 to 1349 or 50. He was a pioneer in many areas, including separation of church from state (for which Pope John XXII excommunicated him). He is best remembered for the remark *'pluralitas non est ponenda sine necessitate'*, which nowadays is taken to mean 'don't fall back on a paranormal hypothesis until you have exhausted all the normal ones'. (The actual words mean 'plurality is not to be posited without necessity'). This is known as Occam's Razor, perhaps because it was meant to cut off some of the dead wood that encumbered Catholic thinking even in his time.

Explanations, Occam insisted, should be as simple as possible. However, in the case of the poltergeist, we do not have any simple explanations. In fact we have none at all. Occam's Razor is an admirable weapon, but it should not be used to put forward 'normal' explanations that are more far-fetched than a simple paranormal one, as it often is. Parapsychologists determined to ignore any sort of spiritistic hypothesis have suggested that RSPK is some sort of translation into action of a repressed desire on the part of the epicentre. This strikes me as complete nonsense, especially as there have been poltergeist cases where there has been no human epicentre at all. Also, who or what is supposed to be losing all that energy expended by whatever it is that throws furniture around?

The simplest hypothetical explanation for the poltergeist yet put forward is also one of the earliest; the one contained in Kardec's *Mediums' Book*, mentioned at the beginning of this chapter. This book was first published in 1861 and has been widely ignored by psi researchers ever since. Kardec was one of the first to collect and publish reports of poltergeist activity, many of which appeared in his *Revue Spirite* from 1858 onwards. 'Facts of this nature,' he says, 'often have the character of unmistakable persecution.' One of his cases involved a family of six sisters who had their clothing torn, cut or scattered around the house every day for several years!

Poltergeists (which he calls disorderly spirits) do their tricks, Kardec says, because they want to drive people out of 'their' homes, or because they have a grudge against a certain person, or simply because they have nothing better to do. They need a medium (epicentre) of some kind in order to be able to make noises and throw things around. This is often a girl at the age of puberty, though not always. Such girls seem to be the best source of the vital energy the spirit has to steal, though by no means the only one; such energy can also be extracted from other people or from nature.

Teenage girls, as I have shown, seem to turn up on poltergeist cases more often than any other identifiable group. Why could this be?

In Chapter 7, I quoted some of the views of spirit author André Luiz on the subject of the pineal gland, the full functions of which remain a mystery today. According to André, this is the gland that only awakens fully around the age of fourteen, after serving up to then as a 'brake on sexual manifestations'. At puberty, the pineal gland secretes 'psychic hormones' or 'units of force that act in a positive manner in the generative energies'. It serves to recapitulate sexual experience of the past and awaken new desires. Small wonder that the age of puberty is a trying one, both for child and parent. The child suddenly acquires a strong new force, and it may be that when this force is not channelled into violent activity, like sports or equally violent courting, it will be readily available in abundance for marauding entities to steal and put to their own purposes.

This may prove to be an important clue in the hunt for an explanation for RSPK. The unspent energies generated by teenagers' pineal glands may not be *essential* for the production of poltergeist phenomena; but they may make them easier to produce and consequently more violent. Perhaps if Brazilian girls played hockey or lacrosse there would be fewer poltergeists in São Paulo.

I doubt very much if Max Freedom Long had ever heard of Kardec, but his first-hand field research gives much support to the latter's views on the behaviour of disorderly spirits. Long investigated the native magicians of Hawaii—the *kahunas*, or keepers of the secret—with a fresh and open mind some fifty years ago, knowing at first very little about previous psi research of any kind.

In his books, Long offers simple explanations for almost every known psi phenomenon, basing his theories on what he learned himself from the few *kahunas* to have survived after the arrival in Hawaii of Christian missionaries, those traditional destroyers of native cultures. According to *kahuna* lore, man has no less than three spirit bodies (*kino aka*, or 'shadowy' bodies), one each for the subconscious, conscious and superconscious, or what Long calls the low, middle and high selves.

The beliefs of the isolated *kahunas* show an astonishing

similarity to many of the ideas I have mentioned in this book.* Even more remarkable is their resemblance to age-old beliefs of a Berber tribe in the Atlas Mountain area of Northwest Africa investigated early in this century by an English journalist, W. R. Stewart. The Berbers, whose folklore dates back to the times of the Great Pyramid (which they claim they helped build), even used some of the same words as the Hawaiians, such as *quahuna* and *atua* (god), which are near enough to *kahuna* and *akua* to suggest a common origin, though modern Berbers speak no dialect in any way related to Polynesian.

The poltergeist, says Long, is no more than a low spirit or 'low self' that steals 'vital force' from the living, with which it can solidify its 'shadowy body' enough to enable it to move solid objects, though it does not become visible itself in the process. 'Because the entire stolen charge of vital force can be used or expended in one action,' he says, 'they can perform feats of amazing strength.' It is also the low self, he adds, that causes such a lot of confusion at Spiritualist séances, answering questions put to it either by guessing or reading sitters' minds, since it is unable to think properly for itself.[5]

Back to Allan Kardec for the final word on low spirits. Just as we employ servants to do rough work for us, he says, so do superior spirits hire inferior ones to attract the attention of the incarnate with their bangs and crashes; which may not be intended to frighten people, but merely to attract their attention!

Kardec himself once heard four solid hours of knocking going on around him, but instead of panicking or rushing off to a priest to be exorcised, he sent for a medium he trusted who told him that a friendly spirit just wanted to give him some advice on his work!

'When soldiers are on parade,' Kardec observes with his

---

* Most astonishing of all is the *kahuna* belief that the shadowy body of the subconscious interpenetrated the physical and was a *mould* of each cell and tissue of it. A biological organising model, in fact!

usual solemnity, 'the drum is no longer beaten to awaken them.'

Kardec has nothing to say on the subject of outright black magic, either because he never observed any or because he was reluctant to touch on such a disagreeable subject in his books, which were meant to help people lead more positively-oriented lives. Yet if we take Occam's Razor principle and regard Kardec's as the simplest explanation for poltergeist activity yet put forward, backed up by Long's independent studies of *kahuna* practice, we should have no difficulty in extrapolating a provisional general theory of black magic.

I will not do so here, because there is enough trouble in the world already and I have no wish to add to it with everybody putting curses on their neighbours. (Anybody who does this must bear in mind that an enlightened victim can reverse the process, so that you end up being clobbered by your own weapon!)

To many, black magic means Aleister Crowley, weird old men muttering in African huts, or W. P. Blatty's *The Exorcist*. (The film version of the latter was rightly regarded as a rather poorly made comedy by Brazilians, and I joined a São Paulo audience in roaring with laughter all through it.)

To others, including myself, it can mean ordinary people like Marcia, Iracy or little Maria José having their lives systematically ruined and even ended by a very real force. It is a subject that must be taken seriously, even if it never happens to you. . .

EPILOGUE

If I were to find myself a year hence holding precisely the views
I hold today, I should consider I had wasted the intervening
period.—WHATELY CARINGTON

To be taught is nothing; everything is in man, waiting to be
awakened.—PARACELSUS

W HAT does it all mean?
If there is any truth in the ideas I have tried to present
in this book, why has it not already become generally accepted?
If we really are immortal souls associating with physical matter
as often as we have to in order to achieve a state of total
experience and win the right to move on elsewhere, why is
everybody not already aware of this fact?

On the other hand, if the whole Spiritist philosophy is a
load of rubbish, why has nobody managed to come up with a
more feasible explanation for the origin and purpose of life?
Most extraordinary of all: why do intelligent and rationally-
minded people persist in believing that we *are* immortal souls,
etc., and that the basic tenets of Spiritism have been demonstrated over and over again by fully qualified men in almost
every field of science? We have more than enough of what
would be called proof in any other field of study; what we do
not have is general acceptance of the proof.

Colin Wilson puts it very neatly.

'It seems to me that the reality of life after death has been
established beyond all reasonable doubt. I sympathise with
the philosophers and scientists who regard it as emotional
nonsense, because I am temperamentally on their side; but I
think they are closing their eyes to evidence that would con-

vince them if it concerned the mating habits of albino rats
or the behaviour of alpha particles.'[1a]

To those who disagree, let me put essentially the same question that Lodge once put to his (then) materialist friend Richet.
'When you die and find that you have survived death after all,
and feel like telling the world of this great truth, what exactly
are you going to do about it?

'Locate a good medium and convey a written or spoken
message offering information about yourself unknown to anybody living? Give a vivid description of how it feels to die?
Make a few predictions that come true? Tell somebody where
their lost wallet is? Don't bother; it has all been done, and it
didn't work.'

I remember once attending a press conference in Rio de
Janeiro given by a British traffic control expert who was
on a study visit there. He had spent half an hour walking
around the city centre, and the experience had left him rather
dazed.

'Why don't you have more accidents?' he asked. It so happened that in his half-hour survey he had not actually seen
one take place in front of him.

'We do,' I replied. 'Stick around a bit longer and you'll see
some.' Brazil then enjoyed second place in world road-slaughter
figures, and still does. The expert did not stick around, but went
back to London's orderly streets in total bewilderment.

The point of this story is that people tend to base opinions
on what they actually see for themselves. This is quite natural
and commendable. What is less commendable is that people
do not, as a rule, accept the opinions of others if they happen
to go against their own. And as for paranormal phenomena
that point to the existence of a psi world, people do not
generally believe in them unless they come across one, or unless
one comes across them. It is like flying saucers; if you see one,
you believe in them. If, like me, you never have seen one, you
do not, however much you respect the integrity of people who

tell you they have seen one and support their claim with good evidence.

Earlier in this book I mentioned the need for emotional as well as intellectual conviction. In the case of Rio traffic accidents I have both; after living ten years in London without seeing a single fatal accident, I saw seven people lying dead in the middle of various Rio roads in the first week I spent there. In the case of survival of death, most of us have to be satisfied with intellectual conviction only, based (I hope) on the mass of evidence available. For emotional conviction, we will have to wait.

'The day of the Lord so cometh as a thief in the night', wrote St Paul (I *Thessalonians* V:2), and the same point was made to St John the Divine; 'Behold I come as a thief' (*Revelation* XVI:15).

So do psi phenomena—they catch you with your pants down, and like thieves they cannot penetrate your natural defences unless you leave them unlocked now and then. If you keep your capsule well sealed, nothing paranormal will ever happen to you. If by chance it does, you will be able to laugh it off and pretend it didn't.

Colin Wilson again:

'The main trouble with human beings is their tendency to become trapped in the "triviality of everydayness" (to borrow Heidegger's phrase), in the suffocating world of their personal preoccupations. And every time they do this, they forget the immense world of broader significance that stretches around them. And since man needs a sense of meaning to release his hidden energies, this forgetfulness pushes him deeper into depression and boredom, the sense that nothing is worth the effort.'[1b]

Wilson quotes a passage from Ouspensky describing how the latter, as a young journalist who had not yet discovered his *guru* Gurdjieff, would sit in the office of the Moscow paper where he worked, trying to rouse enough enthusiasm to write a piece on the Hague Conference. 'It is all so tedious,' Ouspensky laments. 'Diplomats and all kinds of statesmen will gather together and talk, papers will approve or disapprove, sympathise or not sympathise. Then everything will be as it was, or worse.' In despair, he opens a drawer of his desk which is full of books on life after death, magic, the occult and Atlantis. To hell with the Hague Conference, he thinks, as he immerses himself in what really matters.[1c] I know that feeling only too well.

Up to 1971 I had no experiences you could possibly call paranormal. My mother kept having precognitive dreams, but they were regarded as quite normal by the family, perhaps because we are half Scottish by descent, and the Scots are seldom impressed by their relatives' (or their own) achievements to the point of actually discussing them. I was certainly interested in psychical research, but was far more interested in several other things, such as music, motor racing, architecture, chasing after girls, and agitating for family planning. My modest library consisted of all available paperbacks by Joseph Conrad and Raymond Chandler, which I read practically non-stop, and still do. I had no interest in Spiritism and very little in any kind of religion, apart from certain sentiments regarding Roman Catholicism which could probably be explained by the fact that the other half of our family is of direct Huguenot descent. (Fourteen ancestors burned at the stake, no less.)

But in 1971 the position changed somewhat. In describing here how this came about, I hope I will be able to show that, in my case, paths into the psi world were all around me if I cared to explore them, or even notice them; and that the same probably applies to a great many other people.

For four years, 1967 to 1971, I worked in an atmosphere of 'trivial everydayness' as a writer in the press section of the U.S. Agency for International Development (AID) in Rio de Janeiro, which occupied the top twelve floors of a modern and comfortable building in the centre of town. From my window on the 19th floor, I could see the local airport and the docks nearby. Ships and planes came and went all the time, on their 'urgent voluntary errands', as Auden puts it, reminding me that there was another world beyond the Bay of Guanabara.

The job had its trivial aspects—some of my colleagues spent half their lives worrying about their pensions or complaining about the quality of the coffee in the AID cafeteria—but I was kept busy. From eight to five I pounded out press releases on the Alliance for Progress, summaries of the day's news that might interest AID officials, or drafts of speeches to be made at the opening of hydroelectric dams. I was lucky in being able to travel around the three million square miles of Brazil and get an overall view of the country denied to most foreigners. AID projects were often located in the country's poorer and remoter regions, and my work was full of contrast. After a day tramping through a slum area of Salvador, Recife or Manaus, I might have to go to an official reception in a luxury hotel to interview a state governor or cabinet minister. On such occasions, as everybody guzzled imported Scotch and shrimp mayonnaise, it would usually be announced that thanks to some vast new loan the slum I had just visited was about to disappear overnight.

Back in the Rio office, there was always plenty to do, usually at very short notice. Unlike Ouspensky, I had no time to read books on the occult under the desk. As it happened, my office colleague, who handled the Portuguese-language press material, was a Spiritist, and in all the years we worked side by side we scarcely discussed the subject. On one occasion, Julio happened to remark that he believed in life after death, to which I added that I did too, and that was that. We went back to our typewriters and our stories on the Punta del Este conference.

After hours, life was as full as in the office. American diplomats and government officials, unlike others (especially British), become ordinary human beings away from their desks, and there were parties all the time, usually very enjoyable ones. I found time to keep up my musical activities, playing trombone in the Municipal Theatre youth orchestra and arranging medieval and renaissance pieces for Roberto de Regina's superb early music group. I built myself a harpsichord from a kit and took lessons from Roberto, in my opinion the finest living harpsichordist. Whenever possible, I would grab my trombone and head for the nearest jam session, playing with people like Booker Pittman, a neglected pioneer of jazz from Kansas City who emigrated to Brazil and died there, and once even with a talented young pianist named Sergio Mendes, who soon left for the U.S. and gave pop music a new sound. I would sit up until 2 a.m. listening to fine musicians like the sax virtuoso Victor Assis Brasil and local U.S. resident trumpeter Bill Vogel. Back home, I would barely be able to get through a chapter of Chandler or Conrad before dropping off to sleep.

Then, in 1971, my life took a right-angle turn. The U.S. foreign aid programme was slashed, and my job along with over a hundred others at AID ceased to exist almost overnight. We were offered generous golden handshakes to get out, and acting on the advice of a veteran American journalist friend, I took the money and ran. I moved into a beautiful old house high in the hills overlooking the Bay of Botafogo and began to write a novel. It seemed the only thing to do.

U.S. Ambassador C. Burke Elbrick had been kidnapped while I was working at his embassy (of which the AID mission was a part), sparking off a period of savage repression of anything that could be considered political thinking to the left of that of Genghis Khan. I had plenty of inside information about the episode, and after failing to interest any publisher in a non-fiction account of it, I decided to do it as a novel. (I abandoned the project when I learned that Graham Greene was writing one on a similar theme. Perhaps I shouldn't have.)

Life was relaxed and comfortable, and no longer full of everyday trivia. I had a big garden, plenty of friendly British and American neighbours, and more free time than I had ever had before, plus enough money to live on. I did things I had never had time to do—I wrote a small book on the landscape architect Burle Marx and arranged a Bach organ sonata for a local baroque quartet. When I needed money, I did translation work for a Brazilian publishing firm, and when I didn't, I spent all the time I could in my garden pruning trees and designing the world's largest compost heap.

My defences were down, in fact, and one day the psi world broke in and got me.

The man responsible was an old friend, Larry Carr, an American actor who had come to Rio to do a film and stayed on for eight years, becoming a member of a Spiritist centre and an expert on the local paranormal scene. One day, Larry stopped by for lunch as he often did, for my maid was the only person in the world who could make brown rice eatable. As we ate, I asked Larry if he had heard of a fellow called Lourival de Freitas, who had been making a name for himself in Europe as a 'psychic surgeon'. A friend in England had written me for details.

'Sure, I know Lourival,' he replied. 'I've watched him operate several times.' This gave us something new to talk about for the rest of the meal, and I learned to my astonishment that one of Lourival's regular 'operating theatres' was in a house just up my road!

I had known Larry on and off for about six years, and though I knew he was interested in Spritism I had no idea how far he had got himself into it. He, in turn, had never suspected I had any interest at all in the subject, and like a good Spiritist had never raised it himself. We talked all afternoon, with Larry telling me things I would not have believed had he not been the most honest and truthful person I knew.

He told me about how Lourival de Freitas would drink a whole litre of pure alcohol before carving somebody open with an ordinary pair of scissors, or extracting diseased tissue by rubbing a drinking glass over the skin and waiting for it to pop out. He told me about another psychic surgeon named Edivaldo Oliveira Silva who performed operations with his bare hands, as described fully in my previous book. He told me about the time he had spent as a member of an *Umbanda* centre, and the day he had walked over broken glass in the company of the head medium. A well-known plastic surgeon had actually seen him do this, as he later confirmed to me. He had, he told me, been ready to call an ambulance and could not explain how Larry's feet were unscratched after the feat.

(Controversy rages over the glass-walking stunt. D. Scott Rogo, an energetic and well-informed psi researcher, appears to have done it in front of a camera and claims the trick is easily mastered,* being merely a question of even weight distribution and bringing the feet directly downwards. Maybe he is right, but shortly after reading his article I brought a bare heel directly down onto a splinter of glass buried in my bedroom carpet and had to go to a doctor to have it extracted. It hurt like hell. Larry had never learned the 'trick' but had simply done it one day, walking normally.)

Larry told me about other things, but what impressed me most of all was the way he described the change that had taken place in his own life after he had begun attending Spiritist meetings. For all his honesty, I thought, he could have been deceived by skilful trickery on the part of the mediums he had witnessed in action, though I have no evidence to suggest that he was. But he could hardly have been under the impression that his personal problems had been solved if they had not been.

I decided that this Spiritism business might be worth looking into. Larry was off to a meeting that evening at a centre run by Pedro McGregor, with whom I had a nodding acquaintance from the days when we both did part-time work for *Time* magazine in Rio. I knew that Pedro was a Spiritist medium in addition to a writer and a successful economist, also that he had run for election as a state deputy, which tended to make me suspicious of him, Brazilian politicians being what they are. (With notable exceptions; in the 1974 elections a well known and active Spiritist, Dr José Freitas Nobre, came second out

* At least, he has been photographed *standing* on bits of broken glass and *lying* on them with a girl standing on his abdomen and thorax. This is not the same as *walking* over glass, and probably a lot easier. See *Psychic*, December 1973, pp. 50–1.

of about fifty candidates for São Paulo federal deputy. I cannot prove that all his votes came from Spiritists, but none of his voters could have failed to be aware of his close involvement with the movement.)

At our first meeting inside Pedro's centre, I soon found out why he was one of Rio's most respected mediums. He took one brief look at me (or my aura) and proceeded to give me an uncomfortably accurate overall description of my past and present life. I was impressed enough to come back for more, and became a regular member of his centre, where subsequently he gave me much information about my future which has proved correct.

When I got to know Pedro better I found that despite his taciturn nature and occasional vagueness, even incoherence, when discussing psychical matters, he was an extremely practical person with a tremendous concern both for individual human beings and the future of the human race. He had made a lot of money and given most of it away through his centre's extensive social welfare programme, saving the rest to bring up his three children.

One day, as we sat in his house discussing the paranormal in general, he casually mentioned the name of Hernani Guimarães Andrade, an engineer who lived in São Paulo and took a scientific interest in psi phenomena. Pedro thought I ought to try and meet him, but could not remember where he lived. Neither his name nor the institute he ran were listed in the São Paulo phone book.

I had no idea how to start looking for a man with a common surname in a city of seven million people. Then one day I picked up a book in a bookshop and saw his name on the back cover as 'editorial consultant'. This was a clue, so one day in November 1972 I took a bus to São Paulo, where I knew nobody except an English friend who ran a private language school.

I had visited São Paulo many times on writing assignments, but had never even faintly considered going to live there. The food and climate were better than those of Rio de Janeiro, but everything else was a lot worse. It would be about as logical to move there as for an American to leave Miami Beach for central Manhattan. Yet at some point during the 250-mile bus journey along the highway AID helped finance, the idea slipped into my head that this was exactly what I was going to do.

Arriving in São Paulo early one Monday morning, I headed at once for the publishing house, where I saw rows of books on Spiritism, by authors whose names were vaguely familiar, such as Allan Kardec and Chico Xavier. An obliging secretary immediately put a phone call through to Mr Andrade's office, and told him that a British writer from Rio would like to meet him.

Half an hour later I was in his office, and an hour later I left with the feeling that we were old friends. Mr Andrade said I would be welcome to work with his institute, the IBPP, whenever I liked. He could not offer me any money, since he financed the whole thing largely out of his modest salary as a civil servant, but I was welcome to write about anything I might find in the IBPP files.

This was the kind of offer psi researchers are seldom given. But I still had to earn a living somehow. Leaving Mr Andrade's office with the assurance that I would be back, I dropped in on a translating agency a friend in Rio had mentioned to me. The owner was glad to see me and promised me all the work I could handle, at far higher rates than I had been getting in Rio.

I went to lunch with my English schoolmaster friend, who offered to put me up in a spare room in his school. That afternoon, I did some exam invigilating for him, during which time I got to know a very attractive blonde; a psychologist as interested in the paranormal as I was.

So, in one incredible day I had been offered a job, a place to stay, a chance to do research with the IBPP, and the prospects of a beautiful friendship with the blonde. What more could I ask? To add to all these coincidences, who should turn up the very next day in São Paulo but Hugh Lynn Cayce, the son of the medium Edgar Cayce, whom I much admired. Would I mind coming along and interpreting for Mr Cayce's press conference, Mr Andrade asked me? I did so, had lunch with him and went along in the evening to the lecture he gave on his father's life and work. Then I went back to Rio, staying long enough to pack and say good-bye to my neighbours, and early in 1973, after a quick trip to Europe, I installed myself in São Paulo. I had the distinct impression that somebody or something was giving my life a firm push in a new direction. To this day I have never been back to Rio. Why would I? I sometimes think I shall feel the same way about this world after I die. Why bother to go backwards in evolution?

One day it occurred to me that the few people who had really helped me when I had needed help were either Spiritists or else closely involved with Spiritism. My very first paid writing assignment in Rio had been the result of a recommendation from David St Clair, who has written a book on the more exotic aspects on Spiritism in Brazil (*Drum and Candle*). During my years with AID, life had been made more enjoyable by the presence of my kind and witty Spiritist colleague Julio de Queiroz, who always found time to help me on an assignment when I ran into difficulties. I had been eased into the psi world by Larry Carr and Pedro McGregor, and finally I had found myself welcomed by an all-Spiritist, research institute. None of these people had ever tried to 'sell' their beliefs to me. Their attitude was a welcome contrast to that of members of other faiths; I was once driven to put a card on the gate of my Rio house saying NO MORMONS TODAY, PLEASE!

'It is right that a person should learn of the secrets of Nature only so much as corresponds to his own degree of development', said the Austrian philosopher Rudolph Steiner. Spiritists feel the same way; they do not stuff their faith down your throat, but wait for you to ask your own questions in your own time. They are convinced that the master will appear when the student is ready, and not before. We all have to educate ourselves; the very word *educate* really means to lead out, to bring something out that is already there. What we usually call education is really no more than *induction*, to cram unwanted knowledge into an unwilling receptacle. True education should enable us to form our minds much in the way that matter is formed. Just as matter needs a nucleus and an orbiting layer of electrons, so to do the mental electrons (the bions of Andrade's psi atom model) need a nucleus to orbit around. They cannot form a unit of knowledge in their free state any more than free electrons can form a unit of matter. The ideal education system would be no more than the provision of nuclei of information which our bions bind into molecules of knowledge.

I am not trying to suggest that Spiritists are the only ones who have seen the light. Nor are they, at least none that I have met. 'Spiritualism', said Conan Doyle, 'is a religion for those that find themselves outside all religions'. On the other hand, he added, 'it greatly strengthens the faith of those who already possess religious beliefs.' I might add that it also places the responsibility for man's evolution firmly on his own shoulders, and I think it is time man assumed this responsibility. Mumbling at a priest encapsulated in a confessional cage may give temporary satisfaction to some, but it is about as logical, in the long view, as clearing up the mess made by a leaking water pipe without bothering to mend the leak.

The automatic writings of Stainton Moses, whom I mentioned briefly in Chapter 4, offer us a fascinating sample of the conflict between an orthodox clergyman and the new set of beliefs that he found himself having thrust upon him much against his will at first. While his hand was writing communications from a number of purported spirits, Moses remained fully conscious and carried on a lively dialogue with them. What they had to tell him, he says in his *Spirit Teachings*, 'seemed to me to strike at the root of much that I had previously accepted as *de fide*'. At one point, he accuses his communicators of vagueness, to which they retort:

> We are they who preach a definite, intelligible, clear system of reward and punishment, but in doing so we do not feign a

fabled heaven, a brutal hell and a human God. You are they who relegate to a far-off speck the day of retribution and encourage the vilest to believe that he may enter into the very presence of the Most High sometime, somewhere, somehow, if he will only assent to statements which he does not understand, which he does not believe, and in the truth of which he feels no sort of real interest.

'It is our task', Moses was told on another occasion, 'to do for Christianity what Jesus did for Judaism. We would take the old forms and spiritualise their meaning, and infuse them with new life. Resurrection rather than abolition is what we desire.' Moses's faith in his church was given a severe battering: 'Christendom's divisions, the incoherent fragments into which the Church of Christ is rent, the frenzied bitterness with which each assails other for the pure love of God; these are the best answers to the foolish pretension that Christianity possesses a monopoly of Divine Truth.'

Moses' unseen instructor was even more outspoken than André Luiz when the subject of theology was raised.

In the ponderous volumes which contain the records of man's ignorance about his God, may be found the bitterest invective, the most unchristian bitterness, the most unblushing misrepresentation. Theology! It has been the excuse for quenching every holiest instinct, for turning the hand of foeman against kindred and friends, for burning and torturing and rending the bodies of the saintliest of mankind, for exiling and ostracising those whom the world should have delighted to honour, for subverting man's best instincts and quenching his most natural affections . . . To such base ends has man degraded the science which should teach him of his God.

Stainton Moses kept asking his spirit friends for some sort of proof of their identity. 'All this is caviare to the world,' he complained, referring to the long-winded moral advice he was being given. 'They think more of a good thump on the head, or a floating chair, than of all your information, which, by-the-by, is hard enough to get.'

'Friend,' they replied, 'you cannot have the mathematical proof that you crave. Nor can we give you proof exactly when you wish for it. Nor would it be good for you if we were able. All is arranged wisely and well.' The real proof of their authenticity, they said, lay in the contents of their teaching. However, they did oblige with some very strong cases of spirit identity, some of which Moses was later able to check. (How many music lovers, for instance, could name the birth date, school and teacher of the composer T. A. Arne, also nine of his works and the original source of his popular tune *Rule Britannia*?)

'We labour for something higher than to show curious minds that we can do badly under certain conditions what man can do better under other conditions.' (Presumably, this was an excuse for not making Moses's furniture float around or giving him 'a good thump on the head'.) 'Nor do we rest content even with showing man that beings external to himself can interfere in the order of his world. If that were all, he might be so much the worse for knowing it.' The master, in fact, will not appear until the pupil is ready.

For all his initial doubts, Stainton Moses was soon converted to Spiritualism by the evidence of his own hand. He in turn was largely responsible for convincing his friend Frederic Myers of the reality of a spirit world. And Myers, of course, has opened more doors into the psi world than anybody else before or since. The roundabout methods of Moses's spirit guides seem to have produced the results they sought.

I mention the experience of Stainton Moses to show that the psi world seems to be all around us, but will reveal itself to us in its own time, not ours. The spirits are not going to thump us on the head just because we ask them for a sign. That is not the way they do things, and there is not much we can do about it. We will not be given the signs until whoever gives them thinks we are ready to interpret them correctly.

This book has contained some fairly startling theories, stories and claims. I do not expect or want anybody to believe any of them just because I say they are true. This is why I have included some episodes from the psi research history of the past 125 years or so, to help people realise that it is now possible for a rational man to base his belief in such things as survival of death, communication with spirits, and so on, on *actual evidence* rather than his personal desires or religious conditioning.

Evidence at second hand is not enough. It may lead to intellectual, but not emotional conviction. For total conviction, one has to have direct experience of the psi world oneself. I have no magic recipe to offer as to how to have such an experience, but I would suggest that an encapsulated man trapped in his 'trivial everydayness', devoting most of his energy to worrying about his pension, trade unions, the school reports of his children, or the next economic crisis, is never going to have one.

The widespread use of such substances as marihuana and LSD-25 acid in recent years suggests that many people today feel a subconscious need to break out of their capsules and the trivia of their everyday lives. I have never tried either of these, and have no wish to, for a great many reasons; mainly that the latter is unquestionably very dangerous while the former reduces normally intelligent people to giggling vegetables in a matter of minutes, and I prefer my brain, for all its defects, the way it is. The works of Carlos Castaneda should convince anybody that drug-induced paranormal experience might possibly lead, in four or five years, to the level of consciousness that a well-adjusted 'psychic' can achieve in a few minutes. And I have yet to hear of any worthwhile discovery being made by a drug-affected mind that was not already well known by owners of minds nourished with reading and thought rather than acid or pot. There are many ways of opening the doors of perception. Not all of them enable you to control what comes through the open doors, or to get them shut again.

We live in the age of the panacea; the remedy for all diseases, evils or problems. We can achieve instant *nirvana*, we are assured, by means of alpha rhythms, biofeedback, apple cider vinegar, transcendental meditation, carrot juice, scientology or yogurt. At a price, of course. Let us see what at least one country has been able to achieve in the way of correct living without any of these things. Here are some extracts from a recent account by a traveller in a land new to him:

> . . . they did not believe in God, nor did they believe that there is survival of the soul after death. Yet their practice of moral ethics was very high, higher than what we observed in the U.S., European countries, Muslim countries, or other places such as (four countries named). People were acting towards each other very politely. They were kind, gentle. No noise on the street . . . No trash on the streets or trains. No fights or arguments in busy places. No beggars. No poverty on the streets. No prostitution . . . No stealing things . . .
>
> When we said we are very grateful for what you are teaching us, they said no, we are just exchanging ideas . . . We are not teaching you anything. Make your suggestions, tell us our mistakes so that we can be more helpful to humanity. They said tell us your experiences so we can learn.

Where is this amazing country? Here is how the traveller, Dr Gültekin Caymaz, MD, a Muslim from Turkey, concludes his report:

> At present in People's Republic of China people are practising religious rules very strictly as was suggested by Christ or other prophets while officially they profess that they don't believe in God, soul or life after death.[2]

Dr Caymaz makes it clear that he is not an advocate of Communism as practised in China. Nor am I. Nor do I advocate Catholicism as practised in Latin America. Indeed, I am not advocating anything at all except that members of countries that have been professing Christianity and other religions for 2,000 years and more might try practising what they preach and seeing where it gets them. The basic beliefs of Spiritism grafted onto a country that already practises the kind of behaviour advocated by most religions, and seldom practised by any of them, might make something like Utopia.

To conclude, with due acknowledgment to Allan Kardec, André Luiz, Hernani Guimarães Andrade and the authors of the Book of Common Prayer, here is a creed for the last quarter of the second millenium, AD—a psi creed, if you like:

I believe in a Supreme Intelligence, First Cause of all things, originator and animator of matter visible and invisible; an entity as yet indefinable and incomprehensible which for the sake of convenience may be designated with the code name God.

I believe that the cosmos, of which we are only aware of a barely significant fraction, was created and is still being created by this entity, a quantum of which is contained within every living being. I believe this for the simple reason that an intelligent, harmonious and incomprehensible effect such as the Universe must have a source with similar qualities, and since we cannot even measure the extent of the effect, we cannot think about how to describe the cause.

I believe in matter; in atoms, elements and molecules and their psi equivalents, all of which are directed by 'God' with limited help from the living beings inhabiting various parts of the cosmos. I regard our planet Earth as one of countless millions of points in space where efforts are being made, with varying degrees of success, to develop the quantum of creativity that is the natural birthright of every living being. I very much doubt that Earthman is the most advanced of living beings, or the most backward. He is somewhere in the middle of the scale, with much achieved and much more to achieve.

I consider all human beings to be immortal, or rather to possess an immortal component, with what we call birth and death as mere points on the graph of our personal evolution. I regard the physical body as representation in three dimensions of a hyperform which has a permanent existence outside our physical space. We call this hyperform by the code name BOM (biological organising model). The BOM is in a constant state of evolution, and the purpose of physical-body life is to help it evolve.

I take the question of reincarnation for granted, and assume that it takes place when the BOM connects itself, after going through a process of reduction both in size and number of dimensions, to the first cell of the future human embryo, which it then guides through the whole history of evolution of the species, recapitulating not only the development of physical form but also that of the mind. This goes on long after birth; and we are only fully reincarnated around the age of seven, and the pineal body continues to act as a brake on the libido until we are equipped to realise our carnal desires to the full. When we have stopped growing our BOM remains in position, interwoven with every cell in our physical bodies, to serve as the mould of our ideal temporary selves. At death, the BOM dissociates itself from the discarded flesh (which should be burned, since it no longer serves any useful purpose whatsoever; its elements should be used to fertilise the soil rather than to clutter up useful land with cemeteries), and reforms itself in its original hyperspatial habitat. It then instinctively seeks a further reincarnation, often as a member of its former family, in order to pay off old debts or to win new credits for its balance sheet. This process goes on until the BOM has no more need of Earth incarnations. What happens after that is so far in the future for most of us that we need not worry about it yet.

I believe that certain individual human beings have been re-incarnated to serve as mediums of the Supreme Intelligence, for the purpose of correcting the course of humanity. Their joint efforts do not seem to have been very successful, yet I believe that such overall evolution as the human race may achieve will be largely due to their teachings and examples. Such men include (most dates being approximate, and the minus sign denoting BC):

Vishnu, Brahma and Shiva	? — ?
Hermes Trismegistus (Thoth)	? — ?
Akhenaton (Amenhotep IV)	—1375 — —1358
Moses	—1350 — —1250
Lao-Tze	—604 — —531
Siddhartha Gautama (The Buddha)	—563 — —483
Confucius	—551 — —479
Jesus of Nazareth (The Christ)	—4 — 29
Mohammed	570 — 632

It would appear that since the last of these, there has been no further attempt to correct our course, though I sometimes wonder if the Supreme Intelligence made a final desperate effort in the mid-19th century, only to give up in despair after its efforts had been dismissed as fraud on the part of 'mediums'. Perhaps we are now regarded as mature enough to control our own courses. We must assume the S.I. knows what it is doing.

I would have to agree that we have erred and strayed from the course of logical evolution like lost sheep; that we have done things we ought not to have done, and left undone a great deal we ought to have done. I can hardly agree that the remembrance of our manifold sins and wickednesses is grievous, though, or that the burden of them is intolerable. If they were, would we go on sinning?

What else is there to believe in? Ah yes, the communion of saints (or beings who have evolved past the need to reincarnate), the forgiveness of sins, the resurrection of the (psi) body, and the life everlasting, Amen.

Finally, I insist that we are in charge. We are both the cause and the effect of our own selves. Our world was, is, and always will be what we made, make, or will make of it.

GLOSSARY

Many terms used in psychical research do not as yet have generally accepted meanings. This list indicates meanings of some such terms as used in this book. (P) means that the subject in question is a postulate, i.e. that it has been assumed or suggested but not yet proved.

BIOLOGICAL ORGANISING MODEL (BOM)—'An energetic structure, situated beyond our physical space, formed of psi matter. The origin of the qualities and properties of living beings, it serves as a biological mould or model for them. In the case of man, it connects itself to the fertile egg and orients its epigenetic evolution.' (Andrade) (P).

BIOMAGNETIC FIELD (BMF)—The magnetic field generated by the bion (see below), this is the means by which the biological organising model exercises its holomorphic ('whole-forming') organising action upon living beings. (P).

BION—The particle of the psi atom corresponding to the electron; the quantum of vitality. Negatively charged. (P). (Not to be confused with Reich's postulated bion—a basic unit of living matter wholly situated in 3D space).

CLAIRVOYANCE—The ability to perceive something that isn't there, but is somewhere else. Not to be confused with hallucination, which is seeing something that isn't there or anywhere else either.

DISCARNATE—As an adjective, it means disembodied or not in the flesh, opposite of incarnate. It doesn't sound quite right as a verb, though *desencarnar* in Portuguese means to leave the physical body. English-speaking Spiritualists use rather coy verbs like 'pass on' instead of 'die', though I see no harm in using the words 'die' and 'death' in their usually accepted sense, without implying that death is any more than a transitory episode, and not the end of everything.

FOURTH DIMENSION—Einstein means three of space plus one of time. Here, the meaning varies according to context, but usually I mean the next dimension of space, which is almost certainly not the last.

HYPERSPACE—A space of more dimensions than the three we are aware of. Never mind how many for the time being.

IBPP—Instituto Brasileiro de Pesquisas Psicobiofísicas (Brazilian Institute for Psychobiophysical Research). Founded in São Paulo, 1963, by H. G. Andrade to invesigate paranormal phenomena from a scientific point of view.

INTELECTON—The quantum of intelligence of the psi atom. Positively charged, corresponding to the proton. (P).

MATERIALISM—The belief that everything in the universe can be explained by physical laws, and that there is no reality but that of physical matter. Since nobody is too sure nowadays what physical matter is, I do not see how one can claim to be a materialist any longer.

OOBE—Out of body experience. The feeling that some part of you has detached itself from the physical body while retaining some degree of consciousness. Some Americans call it OBE, which also means Order of the British Empire. Brazilians call it *desdobramento* ('undoubling'), and they also have the verb *desdobrar* (to 'undouble'—why not?).

PARANORMAL—Something that cannot be classified as coming within the range of normal experience, or that cannot yet be scientifically explained. Like many words, it depends on how it is interpreted. Telepathy, for instance, happens far more often than the appearance of a supernova in our galaxy, so we should regard it as normal, however rare and unpredictable.

PARAPSYCHOLOGY—The study of paranormal (as defined above) phenomena. Another misleading word, since such phenomena have as much to do with biology and physics as with psychology. A word to be avoided in Brazil unless you want to be mistaken for a Jesuit.

PARAPYROGENESIS—Paranormal spontaneous combustion, a rare but important feature of poltergeist cases. Two well-documented cases from Russia (Liptsy, 1853 and Iletski, 1870) are to be found in Proc.SPR, Vol. 12, pp. 319–29. In my experience, its presence almost always indicates black magic practices at work.

PERCEPTON—The quantum of perception-memory of the psi atom. Neutrally charged, corresponding to the neutron. (P).

PERISPIRIT—From the Greek *peri-* (roundabout) and the Latin *spiritus* (breath, spirit). 'The semi-material envelope of the soul. During incarnation, it serves as the link or intermediary between the incarnated spirit and the matter of his fleshly body; during erraticity, it constitutes the spirit's fluidic body, inseparable from the personality of the spirit.' (Kardec) (P).

PRECOGNITION—The acquiring of knowledge about an event before it can be said to have happened in our usually accepted sense of time.

PSI—The twenty-third letter of the Greek alphabet. Widely used in both physics and parapsychology to denote something postulated, e.g. psi particle. Proposed by Thouless and Wiesner (1947) to apply to paranormal faculties, and fully defined by them in Proc.SPR, Vol. 48, pp. 177–96. Proposed by me here to replace 14-letter words like parapsychology wherever possible to make life easier for both readers and typesetters.

PSI ATOM—The basic unit of psi matter, with a structure analogous to that of physical matter. Postulated in 1958 by Andrade as the *spiritual atom*, a term he later abandoned because of the confusing connotations of the word *spirit* (q.v.). The psi atom originates in hyperspace, and consists basically of a psi nucleus (psion), made up of psi protons (intelectons) and psi neutrons (perceptons), with an orbiting layer of psi electrons, or bions. (P).

PSI MATTER—Postulated by Andrade to denote the *substance* of which objects animate or inanimate are formed in hyperspace. (P).

PSI WORLD—Used here to denote what is misleadingly called 'the next world' or 'the world beyond'. It isn't beyond anything except our senses (usually); it is right here.

PSYCHOBIOPHYSICS—Ugh! An awful mouthful of a word, but it does accurately describe the study of psychology, biology and physics in their paranormal aspects. Should really be 'parapsychoparabioparaphysics', but this practice of word-welding has to stop somewhere.

RIEMANN'S SURFACE—G. F. B. Riemann (1826–66) was a pioneer of non-Euclidean geometry, or one in which there are an infinite number of dimensions. Crookes never followed up his very interesting 1898 reference to it. He implied that he felt instinctively aware of another dimension of space.

SPIRIT—A word with no less than 16 definitions in my *American Heritage* dictionary. I use it reluctantly in a you-know-what-I-mean sense, though I prefer *psi entity* for the human component that survives death, and *psi body* for the thing in which our psi components are housed.

SPIRITISM—A science, philosophy and religion codified by Allan Kardec (1804–69) and defined by him as 'the relation of the material world with spirits, or the beings of the invisible world'. A Spiritist believes in the fact of communication with psi entities, and is of course also a Spiritualist, though the reverse may not be true. The two words are generally almost interchangeable, but by 'Spiritist' here I usually mean a follower of the doctrine codified by Kardec.

SPIRITUALISM—The opposite of theoretical materialism. Says Kardec: 'Whoever believes that there is in the universe something which is not matter is a Spiritualist.' (I assume he meant physical matter.) There are, he said over 100 years ago, Spiritualists who ridicule the Spiritist belief, but they are pretty close together nowadays. If you think you consist of more than bits of carbon and other cheap substances, then you are a Spiritualist whether you like it or not. Welcome to the club.

TELEPATHY—Defined by its inventor, F. W. H. Myers (1882) as 'the transference of ideas and sensations from one mind to another without the agency of the recognised organs of sense'. For his original definition and re-definition, see Proc.SPR,Vol.1 (p. 147) and Vol. 2 (p. 118).

APPENDIX

PSI MATTER

by

Hernani Guimarães Andrade

Adapted from A *Teoria Corpuscular do Espírito* (The Corpuscular Spirit Theory), by Hernani Guimarães Andrade (1958). Copyright retained by the author. This appendix translated from the original Portuguese by G. L. Playfair; copyright retained by the translator.

H. G. Andrade: Bibliography

1 A *Teoria Corpuscular do Espírito*. São Paulo: privately printed, 1958.
2 *Novos Rumos à Experimentação Espiritica*. São Paulo: Livraria Batuira, 1960.
3 *Parapsicologia Experimental*. São Paulo: Edição Calvario, 1967.
4 A *Matéria Psi*. Matão: O Clarim, 1972.
5 *Il Tensionatore Spaziale Elettromagnetico*. Metapsichica, July-Dec. 1972.
6 *Psi Matter*. Journal of Paraphysics, Vol. 7 No. 2, 1973.
7 *The Ruytemberg Rocha Case*. (tr. E. Dubugras). São Paulo: IBPP, 1973.
8 *The Suzano Poltergeist*. (tr. G. L. Playfair). São Paulo: IBPP, 1975.
9 *Ronaldo and Jacyra: A Case Suggestive of Reincarnation*. (in preparation).

It has often been observed that the phenomenon of life seems to disobey the Second Principle of Thermodynamics, which states that energy may only be transferred in one direction (from hot to cold or from an upper to a lower level), and that our physical universe shows a constant tendency towards entropy or disorganisation. It is in effect running down like a clock of which the key has been lost. (This Principle was, of course, never intended to apply to 'open systems' or 'living matter', and is mentioned here only for purposes of analogy).

This universe of ours seems to have begun as a huge agglomeration of particles in a state of intense movement, containing zones of considerable energetic imbalance. Some of these still exist today, for some parts of the universe are much hotter than others. Physical matter has transformed itself by natural laws into ever more stable structures, as it has come into contact with lower temperatures and caused all of our various chemical compounds to come into existence—always by a process of energetic degradation. When we come across organic molecule formations that show a high degree of energy accumulation, we have to assume that there must be an energy source capable of forming them, such as ultra-violet rays or a state of high temperature or pressure.

Yet, in the face of this state of steadily advancing chaos, with all forms of energy doomed to disperse in a downward direction, we have the fact of life. This behaves in just the opposite manner, like a swimmer making good progress against a strong current. Rather than tending towards total entropy, life heads resolutely in the other direction—towards coherence, harmony and evolution. Life is negative entropy indeed.

Purely materialistic attempts to explain the origin of life collapse before the inexorable principle of increasing entropy. Materialists have to face the fact that there is a highly intelligent organising principle at work in the protoplasm of living beings, which they cannot reasonably explain as being due to chance, or to the dialectical evolution of matter. In an influential textbook, The Origin of Life, A. I. Oparin has suggested that the life-principle is merely the product of natural selection at molecular level in the formation of colloidal aggregates, or coacervates. But if this were true, an extremely fortunate form of chance would have to intervene, leading towards an organisation able to replicate itself indefinitely (until 'told' to stop) and set up a harmonious interdependence among its component parts. To ascribe the phenomenon of life to chance plus natural selection seems as unreasonable as to ascribe it to the mysterious properties of solar energy. Both these factors undoubtedly play an important part, but neither provides a full explanation.

The phenomenon of life has been with us for rather less than half the period of time that has elapsed since our Earth took its present shape. How life appeared, organised itself, and overcame all the many obstacles found in its path towards evolution in such a short time, is very hard to explain along purely materialistic lines, especially in our century when serious doubts have arisen as to exactly what 'matter' is in the first place.

It is not so much the high energy constitution and the astonishing dissymmetry to be found in living matter that surprises us, as the perfection of organisation that we can see in it, in which the aim of every separate function can immediately be identified. Living matter has an amazing ability to make use of every resource, every natural law, and every quality of substance, in order to carry out what appears to be a gigantic master plan, of which we are only able to perceive a few isolated details. Everything in the behaviour of living matter suggests the manifestation of *something that seeks and thinks*—in fact something that behaves intelligently, which inorganic matter does not.

Life creates order out of chaos, and there is no satisfactory materialistic explanation as to why this should be so. This fact becomes much less mysterious, however, if we admit the possible existence of an actual non-material component (the *psi component*) that guides living molecules along their predestined path.

Most biological phenomena take place thanks to the specific properties of protoplasm (which literally means 'the first mould'), the substance fundamental to all organised living beings. This is the level at which we find the three basic characteristics of living matter in operation: vitality, perception and intelligence. At this level, we also find these three factors associating themselves into a permanent state of co-existence.

How can we ascribe to physical matter the faculty of suddenly embarking upon a movement towards increasing organisation (in defiance of the Second Principle of Thermodynamics) only *after* reaching an advanced stage of molecular complexity? We know that proteins and nucleic acids form themselves according to natural laws and events. But what known law or event can explain the behaviour of these substances at the point where they reveal rudiments of intelligence, social collectivism, and discernment between what is useful for their growth and what is not?

We can provide a chemical explanation for the way a large organic molecule assimilates a substance that helps it to self-reproduce, and eventually to produce a whole colony of molecules. But the enigma remains: how do these molecules reach a state of association, after a certain number of attempts, that human social organisations are often unable to achieve even after considerable planning, experiment and thought?

We will make no progress towards an understanding of life unless we admit that an *extra-material principle* takes part in the process of forming living substance, a principle endowed with the same faculties that are reflected in the conduct of adult human beings. It is not being suggested that this principle intervenes ostensibly in the operation of the natural laws that govern physical matter, or that it replaces or contradicts such laws. It makes use of them, imposing an orientation and a determinism of its own, under which the laws of chance give way to the action of an intelligent will.

This principle, the *psi factor*, manifests itself as a source of order out of chaos; a plan of action with well-defined aims. We can go even further and suppose (without disappearing altogether into a cloud of metaphysical speculation) that the whole history of life on earth is only part of a long-term plan drawn up with a specific objective in view. What this objective may be, and who or what has it in view, are speculations better left for the time being to philosophers, theologians and mystics.

Two important features of living matter are the large size of its component molecules, and the constant presence in its composition of a high proportion of such low-weight elements as hydrogen, carbon, oxygen and nitrogen. The molecule is a homogenous whole, within which the different energetic levels of its component atoms combine harmoniously, by the process known in chemistry as valence.

The molecule is formed by what may seem to be blind natural forces, but once formed it adopts a distinctly intelligent course. As it moves around in its protoplasmic jelly, looking for the chemicals it needs in order to grow, it is already behaving, in embryonic form, much in the same way its end product will behave. Every reaction of its infinitesimal intelligence is a forerunner of the structural behaviour of the future organised and completed being. The autocatalysis of molecular substance is the first instance of the domination of matter by a living will, the start of a process that is to culminate in the desire to reproduce the species through the act of sexual love.

To explain the phenomenon of interaction between matter and the psi function or component, we must take some liberties with traditional concepts of physics, even those of modern physics with all its ambiguities and uncertainties. In Chapter six of this book, a brief summary is given of the proposed model of the psi atom, postulated along lines analogous to those of the Rutherford-Bohr physical atom model. To recapitulate briefly:

The psi atom, the fundamental constituent of psi matter, consists of three principal particles: the *bion*, *intelecton* and *percepton*. These are (respectively) negatively, positively and neutrally charged as are the electron, proton and neutron of physical matter. Each contains a quantum (respectively) of vitality, intelligence and perception-memory.

The natural habitat of psi matter is a hyperspace of at least five dimensions, four of space and one of time. Psi matter interacts with physical matter on our plane by means of fields;

the electromagnetic properties of physical matter and the *bio-magnetic fields* of psi matter.

Psi matter is molecular in structure. Just as material atoms have affinities among themselves, enabling them to unite and form molecules, so do simple psi-atoms have the ability to originate combinations, or psi molecules. These are organised in a manner analogous to that of physical molecules, and from such organisations emerge the bodies of the psi world, including the *biological organising models*. These originate in the biological process through the interaction of psi molecules with the organic molecules that enter into the composition of living tissue.

A biological organising model (BOM) is formed by a succession of reincarnatory stages in a continuous process of evolution, or enlargement of its hyperform. A biological being is the result of a harmonious conjugation of physical and psi factors; the former contributing the phenomena of autocatalysis, chemical selection and combination, enzymatic action, electrical and other processes governed by physical laws. The latter registers and preserves biological experience in its space-time structure, impressing its individuality on the living being and helping it to evolve by means of a rapid recapitulation of its entire experience.

Psi matter interacts with physical matter by a process of field attraction. Under the influence of a sufficiently intense field, the trajectory of the bions of the psi atom undergoes an alteration, which leads to a partial loss of the four-dimensional form of the bionic layers. In this way, the psi atom acquires a form that is intermediary between three and four dimensions. In the same way, its properties are altered, to assume the qualities of both the psi and the physical atom. This partial loss of one dimension causes the appearance of a field generated by the spins and orbits of the bion. (This is the biomagnetic field, or BMF mentioned above.) Once operating in our three-dimensional space, the psi atom behaves much like a physical one, except that it is never wholly in three dimensions. Its bions and nuclei are only partially deformed, and the field originating from the spins of its bions will vary in proportion to the extent of this partial deformation.

The mutual influence between electro- and biomagnetic fields in the neighbourhood of physical matter will lead to constant deformations in the bionic layers of psi atoms, leading to their frequent magnetic polarisation. The greater or lesser number of bions in the layers around psi elements will determine their greater or lesser susceptibility to magnetic polarisation.

Both bion and electron are energetic charges that can originate a magnetic field. Both are also susceptible to alterations in their kinetic state whenever they are in the presence of a variable magnetic field. In such a situation, an electron will immediately change its orbit and start to move in a direction almost perpendicular to that of the field which has disturbed it. Just as a physical atom sets up a magnetic field of its own when it is submitted to the action of a magnetic field, so does a psi atom, when it is close to physical matter. Its bions suffer the influence of the three-dimensional field, altering their orbits accordingly in order to become partially operative in three-dimensional space.

When a psi atom becomes thus polarised, a biomagnetic field is set up, and the psi atom becomes operative as an intermediary between psi and physical matter, enabling the formation of bodies that show properties common to either type of matter. This is not to suggest that full interaction of physical and psi worlds is always possible. The most likely *plug-in* stage is that of the living molecule, which is a very large object compared to a single atom. This is the point of departure for the process of individual organic growth, so it seems the logical stage for the plugging-in of the psi factor.

The term *plug-in* is used deliberately. The psi-factor does not interpenetrate physical matter, strictly speaking. It merely exercises an influence over it by means of the interaction of the respective fields. Such interaction is not always total. Plug and socket must fit each other, as in the case of household appliances. Let us examine four possible situations:

First, we have the case where a physical molecule is much

smaller than a psi-atom, and gives off a low-intensity magnetic field. In this case, the molecule will exercise a barely perceptible influence on the psi-element, and the physical substance involved can hardly be said to be 'animated'. Molecules of low atomic weight come into this category, such as those of hydrogen and oxygen. Nevertheless, the weak action of the field set up by these molecules will serve to attract a certain number of psi atoms, to form a kind of layer of psi matter superimposed on the physical space occupied by the object in question. This layer is what is known as an aura, possessed by inanimate as well as animate objects.

In the second case, we have molecules of small volume but with a more intense field, such as those of mineral salts, copper, lead, and other minerals of high atomic weight. These molecules, though small in volume, are made up of heavy atoms, and so have larger molecular weight, so the concentration of material mass in a small space will set up a stronger magnetic field. As in the first case above, polarisation of psi atoms by such molecules as these is imperfect and unstable, and consequently there is again no 'animation'.

In the third case, we have molecules that are larger than the psi atom they attract. Here, there will be considerable action on the part of the molecule over the psi atom, but the latter will not be able to respond with equal intensity. Molecules such as those of hemoglobin and hemocyanin probably come under this category. They can be said to be animated up to a point, but their psi component is too small to exercise any detectable influence over them.

Finally, we have the case of a molecule and a psi atom of practically the same volume. Here we will have maximum interaction between the fields attached to each, with the psi component exercising its full influence on the molecule of physical matter, giving rise to an animated being of full autonomy and stability—a *biomolecule*, the basic unit of biological growth and the building block of living creatures.

As soon as the biomolecule comes into existence, it is guided along its evolutionary path by its psi component, the BOM, which carries in its perceptons a miniaturised memory-record of all previous processes of growth and association. The BOM directs the biomolecule into chains of nucleic acids and proteins, in an elementary lesson in social organisation, with the DNA chain carrying the purely physical characteristics of its ancestors (condensed in the genes) along a sort of trans-spatial cable of information. The self-reproduction of the DNA chain and the synthesis of proteins through various catalysts lead to the first experience of cell division and multiplication. Next, the information contained in the particles of the psi atom causes embryonic organisms to develop cells that will eventually grow into organs needed to carry out the essential functions of the living species concerned.

This process takes place over and over again, with physical matter always obeying the same immutable laws, but with the psi factor constantly evolving, as it acquires new experience in its successive associations with physical matter. The history of evolution is the history of the progress of the psi factor. Physical matter does not evolve at all; what evolves is the psi matter that interacts with it and guides it. All forms of inorganic matter, and some rudimentary forms of organic matter, are much the same today as they always have been. Higher species of living beings, including *Homo sapiens*, are not.

The original biomolecules must have been formed at points along the chains of polypeptides that floated around on the waters, colliding with each other to form occasional spirals or skeins. As their joint material mass increased, they were able to attract and hold more and more complex psi elements through their biomagnetic fields, until the time came when a group of psi elements large enough to survive the process known as physical death was evolved. As millions and millions of rudimentary living beings were formed and destroyed on the stage of earthly life, long before recorded history, the psi-elements gradually grew into compound formations that were finally able to animate what we would now recognise as a plant, an animal, or—much later—a human being.

Natural selection and the fight for survival undoubtedly

guided all early forms of life, as they still do to some extent, enabling the psi component to guide them through the early stages of evolution. We have literally had to learn and remember everything from scratch. Prehistoric biological organisations must have originated from combinations of proteins and nucleic acids, thereby forming nucleoproteins similar to our modern bacteriophages and viruses. Later, these learned to form themselves into associations, governed by the laws regarding colloids and coacervates, until they reached the stage of plasmatic organisation of living matter.

Much has been achieved in the history of biological evolution, though there is still much more to be achieved. The time will come when psi matter no longer has any need for association with physical matter in order to evolve, and the human race will be transformed, like chrysalis into butterfly, into something else. Perhaps some human races have already undergone such a process.

Faced with any stimulus, an inanimate object invariably responds with a reaction based on inertia, impeding the action of the force brought to bear on it. This can be demonstrated by striking a brick wall with the bare fist. But a living being reacts otherwise. It uses intelligence in order to avoid a source of aggression, or at least to neutralise its effects.

If we saw an inanimate object behaving like a living being— if, for instance a tennis ball we were trying to serve repeatedly kept jumping out of the way of our racket and refusing to be served, we would have to assume that there was some intelligence attached to the tennis ball.

Tennis balls do not behave this way, though they often seem to, but something similar does happen every time the presence of polarised psi elements causes bits of physical matter to behave intelligently and overcome their natural inertia. Any mechanical stimulus applied to a biomolecule will provoke an immediate reflex in the psi element attached to it, and the latter will register the stimulus and react intelligently. Such a reaction will lead to an alteration of the orbits of the bions around their psi nuclei, which in turn will react by modifying the magnetic moment of rotation that relates them to the movement of the bions. These tiny alterations, added together, lead to rudimentary bionic currents that reveal themselves by almost imperceptible contractile reactions; the foundations of the characteristics of motility and irritability peculiar to protoplasm.

Originally surrounded by liquids, forming colloids and coacervates, and submitted to stimuli and movements of all kinds, biomolecules gradually stop being pushed around by the laws of chance, thanks to the infinitesimal intelligences that animate them. They become organised, contrary to the natural tendency of matter. They accumulate experience in their perception-memory banks, applying their elementary knowledge in their struggle to survive in hostile surroundings. They associate with each other through mutual interest, and progressively impress the physical matter that constitutes them with the characteristics of an organised living being.

Behind all living matter there is a psi component, stimulated and affected by all the various problems that arise from the experience of association with physical matter, known in the case of humans as incarnation. Physical matter itself is inert and passive, eternally subjected to the whims of blind chance, unable to accumulate experience as it is pushed or pulled from one composition to another. It is the psi component that moves steadily forward, unable to stagnate or mark time as it helps build increasingly complex organisations. The inexorable tendency towards total entropy, ultimate symmetry and maximum disorganisation gives way to the organising power of the psi factor, and its irresistible ascending dynamism. Instead of regressing to probable states as determined by the laws of thermodynamics, organic matter moves on to achieve the plasmatic state of living substance.

The psi factor has learned to play with nature's dice. It has taken advantage of the rules of nature's games in order to conquer life through its power of ideoplasty, or the shaping of ideas.

This ideoplastic ability takes two forms; one in the evolution of species and the other in the evolution of an individual human being. In the first case, it works towards the introduction of a systematic tendency towards progress for all living beings considered as a whole. It is the fundamental cause of the apparent purposefulness of evolution, under which living beings seem to be equipped in advance with organs, before they can be expected to know what to do with them, a fact that in itself points to the weakness of natural selection as a theory to account for the *whole* phenomenon of evolution, as one of its original proponents himself admitted. (See Chapter 8—G.L.P.)

In the second case, the psi factor with its ideoplastic action plays the part of an *organising model* for every cell, from the first division to the stage of adulthood of the being concerned. While the genes inside their chromosomes are at work inducing the *physical* characteristics of the future adult being and helping build its body, the psi factor is building up the mind, the component that is always to be in charge of its human complex.

Let us imagine that a man with no knowledge of electronics whatsoever is listening to his radio set one day, when it suddenly stops working for no apparent reason. If he is unable to call for expert assistance, what can the man do? He can start to dismantle the set, perhaps hitting it a few times in the fervent hope that it will start to work again as inexplicably as it stopped. Eventually, faced with a bewildering organisation of valves, condensers, transformers, wires or printed circuits, he will conclude that this apparatus, which normally brings him the voices of the world at the touch of a button, has been planned and put together by somebody who knew what he was doing. He can shake or hit his radio as long as he likes, but it will probably not work again until it has been examined and repaired by somebody who knows how these things are made.

So it is with the human body, the most complicated machine there is. Our eyes are television receivers, our ears are sonic transformers, our brains are computers, our lungs are bellows, our hearts are hydraulic pumps, our nerves are telegraph cables, and so on. Did all this evolve by chance, or was it designed and created as radio sets are?

It is not being suggested here that the traditional sciences of genetics and embryology are in any way at fault; merely that they are not yet complete. Geneticist and embryologist are in the position of a man solving a crossword puzzle unaware of the obvious fact that somebody set the puzzle in the first place, and that the solution already exists. We can enjoy doing crossword puzzles without knowing anything about who set them, but we need to know far more than we do at present about the source of logical will that first set the puzzle of life. Putting the pieces in place is not enough; we need to know how and above all why the puzzle was first set.

It is quite possible that science will soon produce living beings in the laboratory by artificial methods. This will no doubt be hailed as a great achievement, and Nobel prizes will probably be awarded on the strength of it. But it will be worth remembering that this memorable feat was first achieved by nature millions of years ago, without the aid of human intelligences, Nobel prizewinners, research grants, or the availability of any desired equipment and raw material to order. How is nature supposed to have managed this feat, unaided?

It is suggested here that there must be something interacting with all matter that is directly and solely responsible for the whole overall phenomenon of life and evolution. This is something of which we are all unconsciously aware, though we tend either to ignore its existence, or to classify it under the imprecise word *spirit*, the metaphysical and religious connotations of which have led to its rejection by science.

It is further suggested here that this 'something' is not an abstract conception, but a real substance with a composition of its own analogous to that of physical matter.

It is hoped that the psi matter hypothesis, outlined in brief here and referred to in various parts of this book, will enable future researchers in many fields to take a new approach towards the solving of what still remains the greatest mystery in our mysterious universe—life.

LIST OF REFERENCES

JASPR, Proc.ASPR: Journal, Proceedings of the American Society for Psychical. Research.
JSPR, Proc.SPR: Journal, Proceedings of the Society for Psychical Research.
Paraps.: Parapsychology.
Dates in brackets are those of original year of publication.

Introduction

1 PLAYFAIR, G. L. *The Flying Cow*. London: Souvenir Press, 1975.
2 WALD, G. *The Origin of Life*. Scientific American, August 1954 (p. 47).
3 FEILDING, E., BAGGALLY, W. W. and CARRINGTON, H. *Report on a Series of Sittings with Eusapia Palladino*. Proc.SPR, Vol. 23, Part 59, 1909 (p. 569).
4 FEILDING, E. *Can Psychical Research Contribute to Religious Apologetics?* Dublin Review, April–June 1925.

Chapter 1

1 MARGENAU, H. *A Principle of Resonance*. Paraps. Newsletter, May–June 1957 (p. 3).

Chapter 2

1 ANDRADE, H. G. *The Ruytemberg Rocha Case*. (tr. E. Dubugras) São Paulo: IBPP, 1973.
2 Realidade (São Paulo), November 1971 (pp. 73–8).
3 DODDS, E. R. *Supernormal Phenomena in Classical Antiquity*. Proc. SPR, Vol. 55, Part 203, 1971.
4 JAMES, W. The American Magazine, October 1909.
5 PODMORE, F. *The Newer Spiritualism*. London: Unwin, 1910.
6 LANG, A. *Presidential Address*. Proc.SPR., Vol. 25, Part 64, 1911 (p. 367).

Chapter 3

1 HARRISON, V. G. W. Letter in JSPR, March 1972 (pp. 51–2).
2 MEDHURST, R. G. (coll.), GOLDNEY, K. M. (gen. intro.) and BARRING-

TON, M. R. (ed.) *Crookes and the Spirit World*. London: Souvenir Press, 1972 (p. 217).

3 HUXLEY, T. H. *Life and Letters*. (1900) Vol. 1, p. 240.

4 HUXLEY, T. H. *A Liberal Education*. (1868).

5 FEILDING, E. *et al. Op cit*. (Intro. ref. 3) pp. 309–569.

6 FEILDING, E. *et al. Sittings with Eusapia Palladino*. Introduction by E. J. Dingwall. New Hyde Park: University Books, 1963 (p. xx).

7 JAMES, W. *Address by the President*. Proc.SPR, Vol. 12, Part 30, 1896 (pp. 5–6).

8 HODGSON, R. *A Further Record of Observations of Certain Phenomena of Trance*. Proc.SPR, Vol. 13, Part 33, 1898 (pp. 405–6).

9 MEEK, G. W. and HARRIS, B. *From Séance to Science*. London: Regency Press, 1973 (pp. 108–60).

10 RICHET, C. *On the Conditions of Certainty*. Proc.SPR, Vol. 14, Part 35, 1899 (p. 156).

11 LEAF, W. *Rivista di Studi Psichici* (Editorial by G. B. Ermacora and G. Finzi) (review) Proc.SPR, Vol. 11, Part 27, 1895 (p. 172).

12 FIRSOFF, V. A. *Life and Quantum Physics*. Paraps. Review, Vol. 5, No. 6, November–December 1974 (p. 11).

Chapter 4

1 DAVIS, A. J. *The Magic Staff: An Autobiography*. (1857).

2 HARDINGE, E. *Modern American Spiritualism*. London: James Burns, 1870.

3 EVANS, W. H. *Twelve Lectures on the Harmonial Philosophy of A. J. Davis*. Manchester: Spiritualists National Union, 1924.

4 ANON. *The Harmonial Philosophy by Andrew Jackson Davis Edited by a Doctor of Hermetic Science*. London: William Rider, 1917.

5 HARE, R. *Experimental Investigations of the Spirit Manfestations*. New York: Partridge & Brittan, 1855.

6 GASPARIN, A. de *Des tables tournantes, du surnaturel et des Espirits*. Paris: Dentu, 1854.

7 THURY, M. *Des tables tournantes, considérées au point de vue de la question de physique générale qui s'y rattache*. Geneva: Kessmann, 1855.

8 MCGREGOR, P. *The Moon and Two Mountains*. London: Souvenir Press, 1966 (p. 105).

9 KARDEC, A. *The Spirits' Book* (1857), *The Mediums' Book* (1861), *The Gospel as Explained by Spirits* (1864), *Heaven and Hell* (1865), *Genesis* (1867). Short treatises: *What is Spiritism?*, *Spiritism Reduced to its Simplest Expression*. Original publisher: Dentu, Paris. Currently available editions in English: *The Spirits' Book*

(tr. A. Blackwell), São Paulo: Lake, 1972; *The Mediums' Book* (tr. A. Blackwell), London: Psychic Press, 1971.

10 DINGWALL, E. J. *The Critic's Dilemma*. Privately printed, 1966.

11 HALL, T. H. *The Spiritualists*. London: Duckworth, 1962.

12 CROOKES, W. *Researches in the Phenomena of Spiritualism*. (1874) London: Psychic Book Club, 1953. (Expurgated passage is printed on p. 21 of the edition listed above—ref. 2, Ch. 3).

13 MOSES, W. S. *Spirit Teaching*. London: Spiritualist Press, 1949.

14 WILSON, C. *The Occult*. London, Hodder & Stoughton, 1971. (p. 491).

15 MEDHURST, R. G. *et al*. *Op cit*. (Ch. 3, ref. 2) p. 7.

Chapter 5

1 DOYLE, A. C. Letter to James Ryan, September 1913.

2 CARR, J. *How Good a Witness Are You?* Drive, Summer 1974.

3 BARADUC, H. *L'ame humaine, ses mouvements, ses lumières, et l'iconographie de l'invisible fluidique*. Paris: Ollendorff, 1897.

4 NICOL, J. F. *Old Light on 'New' Phenomena*. Psychic, June 1971.

5 PAUL, St. *1 Corinthians 15, verse 44*.

6 DRIESCH, H. *Presidential Address*. Proc.SPR, Vol. 36, Part 99, 1926.

7 LODGE, O. *The Possibility of Survival from the Scientific Point of View*. Proc.SPR, Vol. 34, Part 90, 1924

8 JOLLY, W. P. *Sir Oliver Lodge*. London: Constable, 1974.

9 LODGE, O. *Raymond or Life and Death*. London: Methuen, 1916.

10 CARINGTON, W. *Telepathy*. London: Methuen, 1945.

11 BURR, H. S. *Blueprint for Immortality*. London: Neville Spearman, 1972.

12 BURR, H. S. and NORTHROP, F. S. C. *The Electro-dynamic Theory of Life*. Quarterly Review of Biology (10), 1935 (pp. 322–33).

13 RUSSELL, E. W. *Design for Destiny*. London: Neville Spearman, 1971.

14 SMYTHIES, J. R. *The Extension of Mind*. JASPR 36, 1951 (pp. 415–25).

15 RHINE, L. E. *Mind Over Matter*. New York: Collier-Macmillan, 1970 (p. 372ff.).

16 ROLL, W. G. *The Psi Field*. Proc. Paraps. Asoc. 1, 1957–64.

17 SINNOTT, E. W. *Biology of the Spirit*. New York: Viking, 1955.

18 MURPHY, G. *Field Theory and Survival*. JASPR, Vol. 39, 1945 (p. 181).

19 HARDY, A. C. *The Living Stream*. London: Collins, 1965 (Ch. 9).

20 THOULESS, R. H. and WIESNER, B. P. *The Psi Process in Normal and 'Paranormal' Psychology*. Proc.SPR, Vol. 48, Part 174, 1947.

Chapter 6

1 ZOELLNER, J. K. F. *Transcendental Physics* (tr. C. C. Massey) London: W. H. Harrison, 1880.

2 JORDAN, P. Atomic Physics and Parapsychology. Int. Philosophic Symposium, St Paul de Vence, April 1954. Paraps. Foundation, 1957.
3 NEWMAN, J. R. (ed.) The World of Mathematics. New York: Simon & Schuster, 1956 (pp. 2383–96).
4 WEISS, P. and TAYLOR, A. C. Reconstitution of complete organs from single-cell suspensions of chick embryos in advanced stages of differentiation. Proc. Nat. Academy of Sciences, Vol. 46, No. 9, September 1960 (pp. 1177–85).
5 BERGIER, J. Les mystères de la vie. Paris: Le Centurion, 1957.
6 PAUWELS, L. and BERGIER, J. Impossible Possibilities. St Albans: Mayflower, 1974 (p. 252).
7 TAYLOR, J. Black Holes: The End of the Universe? London: Souvenir Press, 1973.
8 DE LA WARR, G. and DAY, L. New Worlds Beyond the Atom. London: Vincent Stuart, 1956.
9 CORTE, L. P. Letter to the author, January 2nd 1975.

Chapter 7

1 XAVIER, F. C. Letter to the author, March 22nd 1974.
2 STEVENSON, I. Xenoglossy. Proc.ASPR, Vol. 31, 1974.

The Works of 'André Luiz'

The Nosso Lar Series:

1 Nosso Lar (Our Home), 1944.
2 Os Mensageiros (The Messengers), 1944.
3 Missionários da Luz (Missionaries of the Light), 1945.
4 Obreiros da Vida Eterna (Labourers of Eternal Life), 1946.
5 No Mundo Maior (In the Greater World), 1947.
6 Agenda Cristã (Christian Agenda), 1948.
7 Libertação (Deliverance), 1949.
8 Entre a Terra e o Céu (Between Earth and Heaven), 1954
9 Nos Domínios da Mediunidade (In the Domains of Mediumship), 1955.
10 Ação e Reação (Action and Reaction), 1957.
11 Evolução em Dois Mundos (Evolution in Two Worlds), 1959.*
12 Mecanismos da Mediunidade (Mechanisms of Mediumship), 1960.*

Other works by 'André Luiz':

13 Sexo e Destino (Sex and Destiny), 1963.*
14 Conduta Espírita (Spiritist Conduct), 1963.†
15 Desobsessão (Deobsession), 1964.*

16 *Estude e Viva* (Study and Live), 1965.*
17 *E a Vida Continua* . . . (And Life Goes On . . .), 1968.
18 *Sinal Verde* (Green Light), 1971.‡

All the above were automatically written by Francisco Candido Xavier and published by the Federação Espírita Brasileira (FEB), Rio de Janeiro, except:
  * Automatically written jointly by Xavier and Waldo Vieira.
  † Automatically written by Vieira alone.
  ‡ Published by the Comunhão Espírita Cristã (CEC), Uberaba.

Chapter 8

1   WEATHERHEAD, L. D. *Psychology, Religion and Healing.* London: Hodder & Stoughton, 1968.
2   STEVENSON, I. *The Evidence for Survival from Claimed Memories of Former Incarnations.* JASPR, April, July 1960.
3   STEVENSON, I. *Twenty Cases Suggestive of Reincarnation.* Proc.ASPR, September 1966. Revised edition: University of Virginia Press, 1974.
4   Paraps. Review November–December 1972 (p. 14).
5   BANERJEE, H. N. and OURSLER, W. *Lives Unlimited.* Garden City: Doubleday, 1974.
6   MÜLLER, K. *Reincarnation Based on Facts.* London: Psychic Press, 1971.
7   MIKLÓS, J. *A Genetic Hypothesis for Parapsychology; Postulating Psi-Genes.* (Proc. I International Conference on Psychotronic Research). Prague: Z. Rejdak, 1973 (Vol. 2, pp. 167–71).
8   The Observer. August 25th 1974.
9   GRANT, J. and KELSEY, D. *Many Lifetimes.* London: Gollancz, 1970.
10 DICKINSON, G. L. *A Case of Emergence of a Latent Memory Under Hypnosis.* Proc.SPR, Vol. 25, Part 64, 1911.
11 BERNSTEIN, M. *The Search for Bridey Murphy.* New York: Doubleday, 1956.
12 WEATHERHEAD, L. D. *The Case for Reincarnation.* Tadworth: M. C. Peto, 1960.
13 The People, April 19th 1959.
14 PRINCE, W. F. *The Case of Patience Worth.* Boston SPR, 1927.

Chapter 9

1   MULDOON, S. and CARRINGTON, H. *The Projection of the Astral Body.* London: Rider, 1929.
2   MONROE, R. A. *Journeys Out of the Body.* London: Souvenir Press, 1972.
3   MYERS, F. W. H. *Human Personality and its Survival of Bodily*

Death. London: Longmans, Green & Co., 1903. (Condensed edition ed. Susy Smith, New Hyde Park: University Books, 1961.)

4 RICHET, C. *Traité de métapsychique.* Paris: Alcan, 1922.

5 SHERMAN, H. *You Live After Death* (1949). Greenwich: Fawcett, 1972.

6 SHERMAN, H. and WILKINS, H. *Thoughts Through Space* (1951). Greenwich: Fawcett, 1973.

7 WHITE, S. E. *The Betty Book.* New York: E. P. Dutton, 1937.

8 SALTMARSH, H. F. *Evidence of Personal Survival from Cross Correspondences.* London: G. Bell & Sons, 1938.

9 ROLLO, C. *Thomas Bayes and the Bundle of Sticks.* Proc.SPR, Vol. 55, Part 200, 1967.

10 *The Case of the Will of Mr James L. Chaffin.* Proc.SPR, Vol. 36, Part 103, 1927.

11 TYRRELL, G. N. M. *The Personality of Man.* Harmondsworth: Penguin Books, 1947.

12 CUMMINS, G. *The Road to Immortality* (1932). London: Psychic Press, 1967.

13 CUMMINS, G. *Swan on a Black Sea* (ed. S. Toksvig, Foreword by C. D. Broad). London: Routledge & Kegan Paul, 1965.

14 GAULD, A. *A Series of 'Drop-in' Communicators.* Proc.SPR, Vol. 55, Part 204, 1971.

15 STEVENSON, I. Letter to the author, December 31st 1974.

Chapter 10

1 WALLACE, A. R. *Miracles and Modern Spiritualism* (1874). London: Psychic Book Club, 1955.

2 CARREL, A. *Man the Unknown* (1935). London: Burns & Oates, 1961 (p. 205).

3 ZINCHENKO, V. P. et al. *Parapsychology: Fiction or Reality?* Moscow: Questions of Philosophy, October 1973 (Russian).

4 MELLO, A. da S. *Mysteries and Realities of This World and the Next* (tr. M. B. Fierz). London: Weidenfeld & Nicolson, 1950 (p. 384).

5 WATSON, J. D. *The Double Helix.* New York: Atheneum, 1968.

Chapter 11

1 CROISET, G. BBC World Service, August 26th 1974.

2 CAYCE, H. L. *Venture Inward.* New York: Harper & Row, 1972 (p. 114–5).

3 PLAYFAIR, J. N. C. *Religion, Science and Personal Experience.* Tomorrow, Spring 1963 (pp. 135–52).

4   EISENBUD, J. *A Transatlantic Experiment in Precognition with Gerard Croiset.* JASPR, Vol. 67/1, January 1973.

5   POLLACK, J. H. *Croiset the Clairvoyant.* New York: Doubleday, 1964.

6   PANATI, C. *Supersenses.* New York: Quadrangle, 1974.

7   DOBBS, H. A. C. *Time and ESP.* Proc.SPR, Vol. 57, Part 197, 1965.

8   MYERS, F. W. H. *The Subliminal Self.* (Ch. 9) Proc.SPR, Vol. 11, Part 29, December 1895 (p. 497).

9   RANDALL, J. L. *Psi Phenomena and Biological Theory.* JSPR, September 1971.

10 HARDY, A. C. *Op. cit.* Chapter 9. (See Ch. 5, ref. 19.)

11 JULLIAN, P. *Robert de Montesquiou—a Fin-de-Siècle Prince.* London: Secker & Warburg, 1967 (p. 140).

12 New Horizons. (Toronto) Summer 1973.

13 WHITE, S. E. *Op. cit.* (See Ch. 9, ref. 7) Chapter 4.

14 COURLANDER, H. *The Drum and the Hoe.* Berkeley/Los Angeles: University of California Press, 1960.

15 ST CLAIR, D. *Drum and Candle.* Garden City: Doubleday, 1971.

16 MCGREGOR, P. *Op. cit.* (See Ch. 4, ref. 8.)

Chapter 12

1   KARDEC, A. *The Mediums' Book* Part 2, Ch. 5 (See Ch. 4, ref. 9.)

2   CASTANEDA, C. *The Teachings of Don Juan.* Berkeley: University of California Press, 1968.

3   ROLL, W. G. *The Poltergeist.* Garden City: Nelson Doubleday, 1973.

4   OWEN, A. R. G. *Can We Explain the Poltergeist?* New York: Garrett, 1965.

5   LONG, M. F. *The Secret Science Behind Miracles.* Santa Monica: De Vorss, 1954 (pp. 273–4).

6   ROGO, D. S. *Demonic Possession and Parapsychology.* Paraps. Review, Vol. 5, No. 6, November–December 1974 (pp. 18–24).

Epilogue

1   WILSON, C. *Op. cit.* (Ch. 4, ref. 14), pp. (a) 33, (b) 21, (c) 37–8.

2   CAYMAZ, G. *Christianity in China.* A.R.E. Journal, January 1975 (pp. 34–6).

INDEX